Triathlon!

Aurum
Press

Triathlon!

A tribute to the world's greatest triathletes, races and gear

MATTHEW BAIRD

Triat

hlon!

Foreword by
Mark Allen

△ Mark Allen wins 1989's epic showdown with Dave Scott at the Ironman World Championships in Hawaii

Oh my God! This is a book about triathlons that will charge your training batteries with images and stories to keep you going for ten lifetimes! It's a book that introduces you to athletes from all eras of the sport who set new standards in just about every race they entered. You'll identify with every one of them and have enough motivation reading their stories and history to fuel a few decades of solitary indoor bike sessions.

Reading *Triathlon!* will also expand your knowledge about the races that take place in locations that the entire world talks about and will open your eyes to iconic events in less publicized corners of the globe that you may not know a whole lot about. But after experiencing these events through the eyes and words of author Matthew Baird, you will unquestionably realize that you have a completely new bucket list filled with stunning places and totally awe-inspiring races that you absolutely have to experience before you retire your racing flats and hand your favourite bike over to an upstart from a younger generation.

The sport of triathlon is barely four decades old. But depending on when you were bitten by the bug and how diligently you scoured the magazines for reports from around the world since then, there's a lot that you likely missed. I'm guilty of that myself. I raced with as much gusto and commitment as anyone for fifteen years starting in the early 80s and then completing my career with a victory at the Ironman World Championships in Kona in 1995. I know just about every facet of what happened during those precious years.

◁ Allen has a record six men's Ironman World Championship titles, a record he shares with fellow Californian Dave Scott

But that is not the sum total of what this sport is about. There are another twenty years of incredible athletes, performances and races that have happened since then – almost too many for one person to keep track of. But each and every gut-wrenching victory is important and has added to the fabric of our sport's still unfolding history. Every new race has brought something unique, special and extremely challenging and has widened the opportunities for triathletes everywhere to experience triathlons in new and glorious ways. Baird's watchful eye has seen the best of these and is bringing them to you right now in the pages that lie ahead.

You may know the likes of Simon Lessing, Paula Newby-Fraser and Greg Welch. But do you have equal knowledge of Emma Snowsill, Simon Whitfield and Javier Gomez? Matthew will introduce you to our sport's heroes past and present. What about races? Most people know of Challenge Roth in Germany, the Ironman World Championships in Hawaii, maybe even Escape from Alcatraz held in San Francisco, California. But there's more! What about Slateman in the UK? Have you experienced Israman in Israel? How about OtillO in Sweden? These are just a few of the gems you'll get to know more intimately and certainly want to experience first-hand after reading about them.

Matthew doesn't stop at athletes and races though! He finishes with key information about a part of the sport that we triathletes can yap about endlessly with our compatriots and fellow competitors. I'm talking about the equipment, the nutrition, the kit we will wear in the races that count most. Yes, this book will spark new dreams of places yet to conquer. It will give you stories of the greats in the sport that are guaranteed to get you fired up for your training. It will seed new thoughts about the equipment that will be your race day support crew to make it all happen. Enjoy!

Mark Allen
Six-Time Ironman Triathlon World Champion

www.markallencoaching.com
www.fitsoul-fitbody.com
www.art-of-competition.com
www.markallenspeaking.com

Introduction

Triathlon may have a short history compared to its single-discipline components of swim, bike and run, but the sport has already packed a treasure trove of iconic moments, athletes, races and kit into its four-decade lifespan. It reached its fortieth birthday in 2014, and we felt that now was the time to celebrate triathlon in all its gruelling, gritty and grandstanding glory. The fruit of our labour is this attempt to showcase the major athletes, landmark events and ground-breaking gear that have made the sport what it is today.

While some multisport historians point to the 'Les trois sports' events in France during the 1920s as the beginnings of triathlon, our focus is on the modern-day incarnation of the sport, which began at Mission Bay, San Diego, on 25 September 1974. Inspired by the aptly-named Dave Pain's run-swim biathlon, local runners Jack Johnstone and Don Shanahan conceived the idea for a three-discipline race (a 9.7km run followed by an 8km bike and 450m of swimming).

Forty-six competitors raced that day, with Bill Phillips the first winner of a modern-day triathlon. Further events would pepper the Californian sporting calendar throughout the decade and, in 1978, Ironman was born on the island of Hawaii. By the 1980s Julie Moss's televised crawl along the Hawaii finish line would propel the sport into the world's living rooms, and the Big Four of Dave Scott, Scott Tinley, Scott Molina and Mark Allen

dominated the race scene, inspiring legions of would-be triathletes to follow a three-disciplined sporting path.

The pages of this book tell the memorable stories, from those of Scott et al. to the present day's Brownlee brothers and Miranda Carfraes, and cover the achievements of the sport's lesser-known heroes, with world-beaters from San Diego to Sydney, Patagonia to Perosinho, and show just what a global sport triathlon has become.

From the beginner-friendly Hever Castle event in England to 226 of triathlon's toughest kilometres at the Norseman in the Norwegian fjords, the race entries were chosen for a combination of their beauty, accessibility or toughness, atmosphere and/or the hosting of classic battles from the triathlon archives, with each listing also showcasing the sport's greatest photographers. Many of the events have also been selected because of what they offer the age-group athletes who fill the starting lines the world over.

The triathlon gear brands, meanwhile, have been selected for their lasting legacy and innovation, our focus ranging from the early designs of Quintana Roo to today's cutting-edge releases in all-things neoprene, carbon and Lycra.

We hope the athletes, races and shiny bits of gear you see in these pages inspire you on your own multisport journey. We'll see you on the start line of the Norseman in 2018!

▷ A lone cyclist on the course at Celtman, Scotland

Glossary

Age-grouper
The name for non-professional athletes participating in triathlon.

Aquathlon
Like duathlon (see below), aquathlon is part of the multisport family. Lacking a cycle leg, the standard distances are 2.5km run/1km swim/2.5km run.

Big Four
A group of athletes – Dave Scott, Scott Tinley, Scott Molina and Mark Allen – who dominated triathlon in the 1980s.

Blue carpet
The finishing straights of the world's triathlon courses (often in ITU racing) are often lined with a blue matting.

▽ Athletes exit the swim stage at Valencia, 2013

Bonk
A bonk happens when an athlete is struck by a sudden bout of fatigue and loss of energy (usually due to depletion of glycogen in the muscles and liver) and metaphorically hits a brick wall. The most famous example involves Julie Moss crawling along the finish line at Ironman Hawaii in 1982.

Challenge
Based in Germany, a major race organizer of middle- and long-distance triathlons worldwide.

Distances
Distances can vary from course to course, but the four distances below are universally regarded as triathlon's key quartet of race lengths. Anything above long-distance/Ironman is defined as an Ultra.

Sprint:
750m swim/20km bike/5km run

Standard/Olympic:
1.5km swim/40km bike/10km run

Middle/Ironman 70.3:
1.9km swim/90km bike/21.1km run

Long/Ironman:
3.8km swim/180km bike/42.2km run.

DNF/DNS
DNF (did not finish) records that an athlete failed to complete a race. DNS means they did not start.

Domestique

An athlete chosen to assist their team leader(s) throughout the event by chasing down breakaways and controlling the bike pace, thus sacrificing their own race. Canada's Simon Whitfield famously secured a Beijing Olympic Games silver medal using this tactic, with Colin Jenkins his domestique.

Drafting

The process by which one athlete follows directly behind another athlete. The following athlete gains an advantage by doing less work, but still travels at the same speed as the lead athlete. In most triathlons drafting is illegal on the bike, but it's never illegal during the swim. In all Olympic-distance ITU elite events (including the Olympics) drafting is legal.

Drag

Refers to negative aerodynamic forces that inhibit the motion of an object. Aerobars and wheels are just some objects that triathletes use to minimise drag.

Duathlon

Triathlon's run/bike/run sibling. Generally thought to have begun in the mid-eighties in New York State. The most famous such event is Powerman Zofingen in Switzerland.

ETU

The European Triathlon Union, a federation that oversees the European Championships and many races throughout Europe.

Hit the wall (see *bonk*)

Ironman

Now owned by the World Triathlon Corporation, Ironman organizes the world's most famous long-distance series of races, the culmination of which is the Ironman World Championships in Hawaii every October. Also known as M-Dot and IM. The other major long-distance race organizer is the Challenge Family.

△ Cyclists during Ironman South Africa

ITU

The International Triathlon Union (ITU) is the worldwide governing body for the multisport disciplines of triathlon, duathlon and aquathlon. It organizes both the ITU World Triathlon Series and ITU World Cup Series at Olympic-distance level.

M-Dot (see *Ironman*)

Point-to-point-course

A point-to-point course starts and ends at different locations. Examples include the Celtman and the Strongman.

Split

The time it takes to complete one of the race disciplines. For example, Alistair Brownlee won the Olympic Games in 2012 with a 17:04min swim split, a 59:08min bike split and a 29:07min run in a total time of 1:46:25.

Starting waves

To prevent congestion on the race course, athletes are started in various waves following each other, often determined by age or athletic prowess.

T1 and T2

Transition 1 (T1) is the changing area between the swim and the bike course sections; Transition 2 (T2) is the bike-to-run changing area.

Wheel dimensions

The two wheel sizes generally used are the 650c and 700c. A 650c has a diameter of 571mm, whereas a 700c wheel has a diameter of 620mm.

The Triathletes

Mark Allen

Highlights

- Ironman World Champion, 1989, 1990, 1991, 1992, 1993, 1995
- ITU World Champion, 1989
- Powerman Zofingen Champion, 1993
- Ten-time Nice Triathlon winner

As epochal years in triathlon go, 1989 arguably edges 1978 (the birth of Ironman) and 2000 (the sport's Olympic Games debut) as the most seismic of the sport's history. The year saw the first ITU World Championships in August before the greatest race in the history of triathlon unfolded two months later. Standing above the contenders in these watershed events was Mark Allen, the Californian who blew away the field at the inaugural ITU worlds in Avignon, France, and finally escaped the immense shadow of Dave Scott to break his Ironman World Championship hoodoo at the seventh time of asking.

Born on 12 January 1958 in Glendale, California, Allen showed glimpses of athletic promise in the pool and on the running trails in his youth, but it wasn't until he witnessed a 90-minute ABC highlights package of Ironman Hawaii that the triathlon bug bit hard. It was February 1982 and the year when the leading woman – college student Julie Moss – collapsed 400m from glory and proceeded in a famous crawl to the finish line, being passed by Kathleen McCartney on the way. The event brought tears to Allen's eyes back in San Diego, and he signed up for the next edition of the race in October 1982.

Allen failed to finish that first venture on the lava fields of Hawaii, but later in the year he took the first of his 10 victories at the Nice Triathlon in France. A lucrative deal with Nike followed, as did his romance with the woman who planted the triathlon seed in his mind, Julie Moss. Allen (now known as Grip, a nickname coined by future fellow Big Four member Scott Tinley) also began

to make inroads in Hawaii, finishing fifth in 1984 and taking second in 1986. The winner each time? Fellow Californian Dave Scott.

The rivalry came to a head in 1987 with some pre-race sparring in the media that continued throughout the race, with Allen tapping Scott's heels on the swim. After 26 kilometres of the marathon, Allen had created a 4:30min lead before hitting the wall, succumbing to walking pace by kilometre 35, when Scott passed him on the other side of a TV truck. Allen finished second and would require medical treatment post-race after internally bleeding during the run. The 1988 Kona was one to forget for Allen (two punctures) and Scott (knee injury), with final Big Four member Scott Molina taking the title. The stage was set for a titanic battle in 1989.

Allen was in formidable form in 1989, crossing the line 1:18mins ahead of Britain's Glenn Cook to become the first-ever ITU world champion in Avignon. 'It was such an honour to be crowned the champion at a distance that I was much less famous for being able to race,' Allen said in 2014. 'Today you're either a short-distance or a long-distance triathlete. When I competed you were expected to not only race both extremes but to be world class at both.' Allen would win eight other races before Hawaii in 1989, with Scott warming up by breaking the Ironman record in Japan. The 13th edition of Ironman Hawaii took place on 14 October, and, as in 1987, the pair were pretty much inseparable for the duration.

As a man who trusts the intangibles more than most, Allen cites an unusual source of inspiration

△ The Californian star adopts the aero tuck on the tri-bars in the eighties

behind his late victory. 'At the half marathon point, I was ready to just give up. I'd been there six times before and never won, and now it was looking like Dave would continue his string of victories. But then I recalled the image of a 110-year-old Huichol Indian shaman, Don José Matsuwa. He had a peaceful but powerful look that said, "I'm happy just to be alive.". And suddenly, I was just happy to be racing side-by-side with the best guy in the world!' At kilometre 37 of the run Allen made his move to produce a 2:40hr marathon to smash Scott's Kona record by 20mins.

Competitor magazine's Bob Babbitt soon christened the race Iron War; entire books were devoted to the showdown and the duo are routinely being asked about it over 25 years later. Allen would go on to match Scott's record of six Ironman World Championship titles, establishing another Kona record with his 8:07hr finish time in 1993 and taking his final Hawaii title in 1995 in another epic showdown, this time with the German Thomas Hellriegel.

Since hanging up the two-piece suit, Allen (who separated from Moss in 2002) has moved into coaching, public speaking and is a globe-trotting fitness consultant. Like Scott, he's always generous with his time and remains a passionate advocate for the sport of triathlon. And like Scott, he'll forever be a six-time men's Ironman World Champion. A feat we doubt will ever be bettered.

Simon Lessing

▽ Lessing makes it a trio of Olympic-distance world titles with victory in Cleveland over Luc Van Lierde in an unbelievable 1:39:50 time

△ Lessing pulls away from Aussie star Brad Beven halfway through the run at the 1995 ITU Worlds in Cancun to take his second ITU world title

🏅 Highlights

- ITU World Champion, 1992, 1995, 1996, 1998

- ITU Long Distance Champion, 1995

- ETU European Champion, 1991, 1993, 1994

- Escape from Alcatraz winner, 1996, 2003 and 2004

Along with his rival and fellow Brit Spencer Smith, Simon Lessing dominated ITU racing in the 1990s, taking a record four ITU world championship titles between 1992 and 1998, three European championships and the ITU long-distance world championships.

Although he was a classic all-rounder, it was Lessing's devastating, long-loping run that spread fear throughout the ITU circuit and left a legion of the world's best racers – including Brad Beven, Luc Van Lierde, Hamish Carter and Spencer Smith – in his wake. As Smith remarked ruefully, 'It was game over if you left the bike together.'

Born on 12 February 1971 in Cape Town, South Africa, the nephew of Nobel literature laureate Doris Lessing grew up under apartheid, the country's system of racial segregation that led to widespread sporting boycotts and the International Olympic Committee's refusal to recognize South Africa. Signs of the single-mindedness he would become famous for were evident early on – he reportedly removed duplicate books from his school library and gave them to a local black school – and he excelled in swimming, duathlon, sailing, track and cross-country. Under the watchful eye of his mother, a swimming coach, and David McCarney, one of South Africa's top triathletes, his burgeoning multisport talents were prodigious. His first triathlon was in 1986, and by 1988 he was the South African Triathlon Champion. Lessing was then due to spend two years doing National Service but, being a supporter of the End Conscription Campaign, he decided to leave

South Africa and, thanks to his English mother, began racing under the British flag. He arrived penniless, sourcing food and lodgings at a youth hostel in Kensington, and sleeping in his bike bag at races. Within three years, however, he'd clinched his first European championship title, in Geneva in

September 1991. A month later he came sixth at the ITU World Championships – the last time he missed an ITU podium until August 1999. His next 16 ITU races saw him net 13 wins, including one long-distance ITU World Championship, two more European championships and four ITU World Championships: the most memorable being an amazing 1:39:50 triumph in Cleveland, Ohio in 1996 and his gritty final Worlds victory in 1998 in Lausanne. He also took a trio of Escape from Alcatraz Triathlon titles throughout the decade.

Two decades on it remains impossible to talk about Lessing without mentioning Spencer Smith, the West London-born racer who beat Lessing at the 1993 ITU Worlds in Manchester – a classic event played out in torrential rain. When Smith was threatened with disqualification after discarding his helmet in Salford, Lessing refused to become World Champion on a technicality as he believed Smith had won fairly.

Yet, like Seb Coe and Steve Ovett, there was a needle between Smith and Lessing. 'I hated getting beaten by Simon, and I'm damn sure that was the case with him,' says Smith. 'Simon definitely got me up in the morning. If I wasn't training, I knew he was. That was a big motivator for me.' The animosity came to a head at the 1995 Bath Triathlon, when Lessing was penalized for drafting. 'Simon cleverly used the traffic to get back up to me,' says Smith. 'My dad, Bill, was not impressed, hence an on-air discussion on the BBC. It looked like something from Jerry Springer!'

The 2000 Olympics in Sydney were predicted to be the crowning moment of Lessing's career, coming soon after his MBE from the Queen, and in the lead-up to the games the British sports media perceived him as nigh-on invincible. But Lessing finished a disappointing ninth, by most accounts enduring a thoroughly miserable stint in Australia. Two weeks later, however, Lessing's Olympic disappointment was followed by the birth of his first daughter.

After his fourth-place at the Manchester Commonwealth Games in 2002, Lessing moved to Colorado to focus on Ironman. Like Smith, Lessing's long-distance venture had highs (a win at Lake Placid in 2004) but failed to match

△ Strong at all three disciplines, Simon Lessing was the dominant force of Olympic-distance tri in the nineties, taking a record four ITU world titles

his short-course career. Lessing dropped out during the bike leg at the 2004 Ironman World Championships in Kona, with fierce winds and back problems cited. Wins at Ironman 70.3s in Florida in 2004 and 2005, Wildflower in 2005 and Vineman 70.3 in 2006 followed, but a chronic spinal disc herniation and 'hamstrings as stiff as steel rods' ensured he couldn't race frequently against competitors 15 years younger.

A final flourish at Boulder Peak in 2008 hinted at more in reserve, but Lessing's focus is now on coaching athletes and hosting CEO Challenges; he made fourth place at the Austin 70.3 in October 2008, the final race of his pro career and the last time the triathlon world would see his unmistakable stride on the circuit.

Looking back in 2014, Lessing is proud of what he and the Bevens, Carters and Welchs of the sport achieved.

'I don't think a whole generation of athletes – including Greg Welch and Hamish Carter – are given enough credit for what they achieved. The sport is where it is today because of our hard-core style of racing and the precedents we set. So I don't think today's athletes are any better. We could hold our own, for sure.'

The Triathletes
Greg Welch

△ Welch is one of triathlon's most popular performers and is still a compere of Ironman races

'The bottom line is that the doctors tell me that I'm done as a competitive athlete or I may be dead.' As exits from the race scene go, Greg Welch's retirement press conference in January 2000 is one of the most emotional witnessed in triathlon. Three months earlier a post-race analysis had recorded that Welch had suffered 18 heart attacks while racing at Ironman Hawaii. The attacks started in the water and continued on the run, with his heart rate rising to 300bpm. Believing it to be an asthma attack, Welch's famous determination saw the Aussie icon still finish 11th.

Only Welch's supreme physical condition saw him survive (*60 Minutes* had previously awarded him its 'World's Fittest Human' title), but his dream to enter the Olympics on his Sydney doorstep lay in tatters. True to form, the fun-loving Aussie refused to wallow. 'When I got the word that my athletic career was over, I was stunned for 10 seconds, and then I started thinking about two things: staying alive and what's next. If there is a regret, I probably could've trained better. I was a lazy little bugger.'

Lazy so and so or not, Greg Welch was a formidable force throughout the nineties, winning the ITU World Championships in their Olympic, duathlon and long-distance guises and becoming the first non-American to win the Ironman World Championships. That and having plenty of laughter as the Clown Prince of Triathlon.

Welch was born in Campsie, just outside Sydney, in 1964. Sporting genes were in the family, with his dad a major league rugby player and his mum a dab hand with a tennis racquet. Welch's sporting diet consisted of surfing, rugby, tennis and cricket, and he showed promise as a cross-country runner. His move into triathlon came in 1985, and he was soon racing at Ironman Hawaii, placing 45th in 1987 and 19th a year later.

As it had for Mark Allen, everything clicked for Welch at Hawaii in 1989. 'In the history of the sport, 1989 was a magnificent year. Mark Allen took the first ITU World title and finally got the monkey off his back to win the Hawaii in the classic Iron War,' says Welch. 'If you want to add another to that list, an age-grouper builder went 8:32:16 in Hawaii to come third! I won $8,000 that day, and it gave me an air ticket to start my pro career.'

In 1990 Welch moved to San Diego. 'I left Sydney to pursue a dream. Me and Brad Beven shared a condo, but we tried not to go to the same races! We'd bring home a good wad of cash and got on like a house on fire. We were young and having fun!'

Having finished 39th at the ITU Worlds in 1989, Welch's preparation for the 1990 Orlando event was far from ideal. 'I fell and separated my shoulder and couldn't train for five weeks. It was a rocky build-up, but the course was set up for me – although coming through Magic Kingdom in Disneyland was quite surreal!' He broke the tape a minute before Beven in 1:51 hrs, with Stephen Foster completing the Aussie clean-sweep. Australia had arrived as a major force in triathlon, and Welch would take to the close-knit pro scene like a duck to water.

'I slept on Paula Newby-Fraser's sofa for a while. She was a garbage guts herself and would eat pizza the night before a race and consume Snickers like they were going out of fashion. But she was very scientific in her approach to the race day formula, and I learnt a lot about race nutrition from her.'

While Brad Beven found huge success in Olympic-distance racing, the diminutive 5ft 6in, 59kg Welch became famous for being distance-agnostic, taking silver at Hawaii in 1991, scooping two Escape from Alcatraz titles and winning the ITU Duathlon World Championships in 1993, the year he married fellow pro triathlete Sian Welch (who became one of Hawaii's famous crawlers in 1997). His most famous triumph would come on the Big Island in 1994, holding off the returning 42-year-old Dave Scott to win his only Hawaii crown. 'Kona was the biggest highlight of my life. I still see Hawaii as being the sport's premier race, with the Olympics.'

'I knew Dave would be strong but not that strong,' Welch continues. 'Jürgen Zäck sprinted for the $1,500 premium at 85-miles, and I went to get up out of the saddle and Dave just says, "Greg, Greg, Greg … don't worry about that. The $25,000 cheque is back here." I didn't know if he was joking, but he's won six times so I was going to race him!

'On the run I had a 24sec lead over Dave for the first 30k. Dave always said the race was won or lost at the Energy Lab. That day I got a split in the Energy Lab to say the gap was 32secs. I'd beaten the master in the Energy Lab!'

Welch would cross the line in 8:20 hrs to break America's hold on Hawaii.

He also became notorious for his partying ways, breaking his collarbone while celebrating his 1994 Hawaii win. 'I wasn't going to let a hangover the next day get in the way of a good time. Some of the stories get blown out of proportion; we'd have a couple of beers, go to a nightclub, but we'd never get into any trouble. Karen Smyers and myself were the two to call if you ever wanted a beer.'

In 1996 at the ITU Long-Distance Worlds, Welch became the first man to complete the Grand Slam – Hawaii and ITU world titles in the Olympic, Duathlon and Long-Distance formats – when he beat Spencer Smith and Luc Van Lierde. 'I was on fire that day!' is his verdict.

Welch continued to pick up titles as the 1990s progressed, as well as reportedly introducing a 15-year-old Chris McCormack to tri. The final piece missing in the Welch jigsaw was Olympic Games gold. Welch ended the 1999 ITU season as the top-ranked athlete, ensuring he'd have the number one vest in Sydney. Then disaster struck at October's Hawaii race.

After nine open-heart surgeries from 2001 to 2003, Welch now has a pacemaker in his chest, lives a life free from alcohol, and works for Californian eyewear maker Oakley. 'No way do I deprive my kids of a daddy because I felt like having a beer. Life is so fragile and worth protecting.'

▽ Welch's strength on the bike was fundamental to his success across all distances of triathlon

▷ The Clown Prince becomes the first non-American man to win the Ironman World Championships in 1994

Paula Newby-Fraser

▽ Paula Newby-Fraser takes her fifth Ironman Hawaii title in 1992, the last while racing under the Zimbabwean flag

Eight Hawaii titles, 24 Ironman wins, the first woman to break 9 hours in Kona, long-standing Roth records, an iconic bonk and one of triathlon's most famous rivalries – it's a deluge of iconic moments etched into the history of the sport. From beginnings in Southern Rhodesia to the lava fields of Hawaii, Paula Newby-Fraser's career is one of the greatest ever witnessed in triathlon.

Along with Julie Moss, Newby-Fraser is often cited as the first triathlete to transcend the sport, with the *Los Angeles Times* and ABC's *Wide World of Sports* proclaiming her the 'Greatest All-Around Female Athlete in the World', and a CNN and USA Today poll positioning her amongst a host of tennis stars – Martina Navratilova, Steffi Graf, Chris Evert and Billie Jean King – as one of the top five professional women athletes of the last twenty-five years. Mainstream adulation has been followed with a successful late career in ultramarathon, yet Newby-Fraser has forever remained committed to promoting the virtues of triathlon, pioneering online coaching with the Multisports.com project and working for Ironman in both a Pro Liaison position and as Director of the Ironman Foundation.

Newby-Fraser was born on 2 June 1962 in the African country of Southern Rhodesia (now Zimbabwe), and by the age of four had moved to apartheid-era South Africa. Educated at a strict all-girls' school, she found her refuge in sport, showing promise as both a nationally ranked swimmer and a classical ballerina in her childhood years. In 1984, intrigued by a local triathlon, Newby-Fraser bought a bike and, eight weeks later, won the women's event, breaking the women's course record and coming fourth overall in the process. Later that season she won the women's division of the South African Triathlon. The prize? An expenses-paid trip to the USA to compete in Ironman Hawaii.

Despite having never swum 3.8km, cycled 180km or run a marathon, Newby-Fraser scooped third place on her first experience at Kona in 1985, finishing just 5 minutes behind Joanne Ernst. Crucially, on its way to Hawaii, Newby-Fraser's plane stopped en route in San Diego – the home and epicentre of triathlon – where she was able to experience first-hand the sporting culture that had attracted the likes of Big Four athletes Scott Tinley and Mark Allen to the southern Californian city.

After discussions with her parents (her father owned a paint factory, her mother was a lecturer at an all-black college), Newby-Fraser swapped Durban on the Indian Ocean for America's Pacific coast and moved into an apartment in San Diego. In her second venture on the Big Island in 1986 she became the first woman to complete Ironman Hawaii in under 10 hours. Yet the finish-line celebration was rather anticlimactic, as Patricia Puntous – one of Canada's formidable Puntous twins who had dominated Hawaii in the mid-eighties – had crossed the line 2 minutes before her, only to be disqualified for drafting.

Hawaii 1987 would be Newby-Fraser's first Kona duel with Erin Baker, the rebellious and combative Kiwi athlete. While Kona history has been littered with heavyweight clashes – Dave

Scott and Mark Allen, Chris McCormack and Normann Stadler – the Newby-Fraser/Baker rivalry had another level: Newby-Fraser, having spent her formative years in South Africa, became an object of Baker's political fire.

In the hot 1987 showdown, Newby-Fraser broke her own course record by 9 minutes but still trailed in third, with Sylviane Puntous taking second, and Baker clocking a 3:11hr marathon split to break the tape in 9:35:25. The result led Newby-Fraser to devote even more attention to the sport, and in 1988 she finished 11th overall and won the women's race, blitzing Baker by over 11 minutes and smashing the women's course record by 25 minutes in 9:01:01.

In 1989 she went a minute better than in 1988, although her 21-minute victory over Sylviane Puntous would be overshadowed by Scott and Allen going head-to-head in the Iron War. Another noticeably hot year in 1990 saw Baker top the podium once more, but Newby-Fraser struck back again and won the next four consecutive Ironman World Championship titles.

Both the winds of Kona and Erin Baker were absent in 1992, and Newby-Fraser took control on the bike with a 4:56hr split. In taking her fifth Ironman Hawaii title, she posted the day's fastest female swim, bike and run splits to become the first woman to break the 9hr barrier at Kona. Her 8:55:28 time remained the Kona record for 17 years until Chrissie Wellington's similarly dominant 2009 performance.

Newby-Fraser's unbeaten stretch would end in the most dramatic fashion in 1995 with a fourth-place finish. She went into T2 with a 7-minute lead over the USA's Karen Smyers and held on for the majority of the marathon. With 300 yards to go she entered Ali'i Drive to the sound of the PA declaring her the victor. Then dehydration kicked in, and she famously hit the wall, leaving Smyers to take the Hawaii crown. she crossed the line over 20 minutes later but still finished fourth.

In 1996, though, she bounced back again to beat Natascha Badmann by 5 minutes and secure her eighth Hawaii crown, a record that still stands today (Allen, Scott and Badmann all have six titles) and quite possibly will do so for eternity.

△ Newby-Fraser transcended the sport of triathlon and still works for Ironman today

◁ On the cusp of taking another Hawaii title in 1995, Newby-Fraser hit the wall 300 yards from the finish line

Highlights

- Ironman World Champion, 1986, 1988, 1989, 1991, 1992, 1993, 1994, 1996

- 24 Ironman career wins

Natascha Badmann

△ Badmann places second to Paula Newby-Fraser at Ironman Hawaii on her first venture on the Big Island

Born in Basel, Switzerland, in 1966, Badmann was far from being a sporting child prodigy and took an unconventional route to the top of the triathlon tree. She was 17 in 1984, when her daughter Anastasia was born, and in her early twenties she was an 'overweight, smoking secretary' when co-worker Toni Hasler entered, and subsequently changed, her life forever. Spotting a raw talent, Hasler became Badmann's partner, coach and nutritionist. By 1989 Badmann's multi-sport career began with a sixth place finish at the inaugural Powerman Duathlon Championships: a race she and the Swiss would come to dominate.

She entered a number of Olympic-distance ITU races in the early nineties, leading to silver at the ETU European Championships in 1995 and a sixth place finish at that year's ITU World Championships (won by the similarly tough-as-nails Karen Smyers). That same month, also in Cancún, the diminutive 52kg, 5ft 5in Badmann scooped the World Duathlon Championship, the first of her countless world titles. The next year she took the Powerman Duathlon Championship title in Zofingen.

In October 1996 she first raced Kona, clocking a sub-5hr bike split to finish an impressive second behind Paula Newby-Fraser, who won her eighth and final victory. In 1997 another Powerman World title followed (Badmann would scoop her third in 2000), along with the Olympic-distance European Championship title. Producing her best Kona swim of 56 minutes and the day's fastest bike split, Badmann held off Lori Bowden on

Fondly remembered by boys of a certain disposition and generation if few else, the plot of John Hughes' 1985 film *Weird Science* involves two high school geeks creating their dream woman on a computer. The result finds Kelly LeBrock entering their lives. Swap those two computer nerds for a pair of discerning triathlon fans and the resulting creation could well have been Natascha Badmann.

With a smile that could melt a thousand hearts, the multilingual, gutsy, über-biking, ever-popular Swiss star Natascha Badmann is about the most perfect representative a sport could hope to produce. Her career résumé – still being added to at the age of 48 – includes a Dave Scott/Mark Allen-equalling six Ironman World titles and multiple world duathlon championships., But it is also full of drama, from one of Kona's most heart-breaking bike crashes to being a victim of Ironman Hawaii's biggest doping scandal.

Highlights

- Ironman World Champion, 1998, 2000, 2001, 2002, 2004, 2005

- Powerman Zofingen Champion, 1996, 1997, 2000

- ITU World Duathlon Champion, 1995

the run in 1998 to become the first European woman to win in Hawaii. She missed Hawaii in 1999, thanks to an unsuccessful attempt to race the Sydney Olympics, but returned to Kona in 2000 to win another duel with Canada's reigning champ Lori Bowden. Unusually, it was Badmann's swim that made the difference; she gained 15mins on the bike but lost the same time on the run. Bowden broke Badmann's winning streak in 2003 before the Swiss Miss took another title in controversial circumstances in 2004.

On that occasion Germany's Nina Kraft was the first across the Hawaii finish line, with a 17-minute victory over Badmann; a month later, though, Kraft was found guilty of EPO use. The 2004 Hawaii title would now be Badmann's, but the victory left a bitter taste. 'The most hurting was not getting flowers. Some people say, "C'mon, she got her pay cheque." That's not what I race for. Coming down Ali'i Drive, *this* is the pay cheque.'

Badmann and the ITU-conquering Michellie Jones produced a Kona classic in 2005, with Badmann unleashing her finest run on the Big Island to pass Jones at mile 18. Her 3-minute margin of victory afforded Badmann the chance to soak up the adulation of Ali'i Drive for her final Kona victory.

Stomach issues led to a 10th at Hawaii in 2006, yet Badmann still went into the 2007 edition as one of the pre-race favourites after breaking her course record at Ironman South Africa by 20 minutes. As was customary, Badmann was travelling through the field at 60km/h nearly 20km into the bike leg, when she hit a traffic cone on the Queen K. The crash left her famous Cheetah time-trial bike shattered, and Badmann nursing a broken rib, torn shoulder tendons and multiple bruises and abrasions. Undeterred, she mounted a replacement bike, cycling for another 50km before Hasler convinced her to stop. The crash deprived watching triathletes of the chance to witness Badmann going toe-to-toe with the new smiling kid on the block, Chrissie Wellington, in what could have been a Kona classic for the ages. More importantly, it saw Badmann undergo numerous operations and extensive rehab, with speculation that she'd hang up the tri-suit for good.

◁ Natascha Badmann aboard her famous Cheetah bike. The Swiss star's formidable bike prowess saw her scoop six Ironman world titles

Eighteen months later, in the muggy, southern heat of New Orleans on 5 April 2009, the watching hordes were treated to Badmann pacing down the Ironman 70.3 New Orleans finishing chute to claim a course record. While her six Kona titles and multiple duathlon championships may occupy pole position on the Badmann mantelpiece, the New Orleans title surely marks one of her most remarkable feats, beating a stellar field ten years her junior in the process.

Now a social worker, she underwent further injury struggles in 2010, yet she returned again in 2011 to produce a bike course record and place second at Ironman Lanzarote. In 2012, at the age of 45, she won Ironman South Africa (which she had already won three times) to become the then oldest female winner of an Ironman, and followed that with sixth place in Hawaii.

Here's 2014 Kona winner Mirinda Carfrae's take on the Swiss marvel. 'Natascha Badmann is my hero. When I first came to race in the US I raced her twice at Eagleman and Buffalo Springs. Both races she was smiling all day long and just killing it! She had to be 40 then, and I was in my mid-twenties. She's just an impressive human being and has so much positive energy. I just love her!'

▽ Badmann would finish behind Nina Kraft at Hawaii in 2004, only for Kraft to admit to doping a month later

Karen Smyers

△ Smyers becomes the Ironman World Champion in 1995 after posting one of the fastest Kona marathons of the decade

If there was an award for triathlon's toughest ever athlete then Karen Smyers would likely be battling Brad Bevan and Mike Pigg in a three-way duel for top honours. It took 17 years for Smyers to DNF in a race (and that was due to a broken collarbone), with 18-wheel trucks, collapsed lungs, a storm window slicing through a hamstring and thyroid cancer all failing to stop a career that is still up and running today.

Such are the Pennsylvanian's dogged triumphs over the odds that life kept throwing her way that her remarkable achievements on the race track can sometimes be overlooked – something not lost on Smyers. 'I got more attention from having cancer and getting hit by a truck than all my races. People sure love comeback stories!' But what achievements they are. Six US Pro titles, one

overall ITU World Cup series title and two ITU World Championship titles all grace the Smyers trophy cabinet, and in 1995 the stellar runner became the first and only woman to win Ironman and ITU World Championship titles in the same year. She is in lofty company: Mark Allen is the only man to achieve the feat.

Smyers was born on 1 September 1961 in Corry, Pennsylvania, and raised in Connecticut. She entered the world of triathlon in 1984 after graduating from Princeton University the year before. 'I was finding my way in a new city like Boston and looking for a way of keeping sports in my life, as I swam and ran on the track at college. I had two of the three disciplines already, but it took a long time to learn biking. I could've shortened my learning curve if I'd had the foresight to hire a bike coach; I was cycling four miles to work and I thought that was enough!'

Although located 3,000 miles away from the fledgling triathlon scene in San Diego, Smyers still had encouragement from the West Coast royalty. 'I was a little isolated, but Paula Newby-Fraser was hugely encouraging, saying, "Smyers, come quit your job!" Triathlon wasn't a full-time job until 1989 when I came fourth at the ITU World Championships in Avignon and thought, "Hey I can do this".'

Kiwi Erin Baker would dominate that year's ITU's debut World Championship showcase, finishing 3 minutes ahead of Smyers in Avignon, France. But the positions would be reversed a year later in Orlando, with Smyers breaking the tape 15 seconds ahead of Canada's Carol Montgomery to secure her first major triumph.

'If Erin Baker had a good day, then you'd just forget it. But I soon got more confidence and realized, if *I* had a good day, then no one was completely out of reach.'

The year 1990 also saw Smyers win the first of her six consecutive US Pro Championships, and in 1991 she took the overall ITU World Cup series title for winning four of her six World Cup races and coming second in the other two. Her ability to reach the podium continued throughout the 1990s. At Salford in 1993 she fell 2 seconds short of another ITU World title after making up 5 minutes on the run:

'I like the one and done method when I was racing Ironman, I'd focus on the short-distance stuff, and Hawaii would be my one race of the year,' was Smyers's approach to long-distance racing. After taking fourth on her Hawaii debut in 1993, she scooped silver in 1994 in a race dominated by Paula Newby-Fraser. Smyers's *annus mirabilis* would arrive in 1995. At Ironman Hawaii, Newby-Fraser went into T2 with a 7-minute lead over Smyers and held off for the majority of the marathon. With 300 yards to go, Newby-Fraser entered Ali'i Drive to the sound of the PA declaring her the victor, then dehydration kicked in, and she famously hit the wall, leaving Smyers to take the Hawaii crown. Lost in the drama was the fact that Smyers's 3:05:20 marathon was one of the fastest of the decade in Kona.

Five weeks later, Smyers took the ITU World Championship title in Cancún, Mexico, to claim the double. The race was the first in which drafting was legal, a move Smyers opposed, but, undeterred, she won convincingly against a field containing Jackie Gallagher, Natascha Badmann and Emma Carney.

She added another ITU World title in 1996, taking the Long Distance Worlds in Muncie (ahead of Badmann), proving a model of consistency in posting swim, bike and run splits all in the day's top five. Unknown to her at the time, this was to be her final ITU event for three years, for a trio of major challenges reared their heads.

The first came in 1997 when a window shattered and sliced through her hamstring, forcing her to miss much of the 1998 season also (in

the event, she gave birth to her first child in May 1998). Smyers was then aiming for a return at Hawaii in October 1998, but was on a training ride when an 18-wheel truck tried passing her on a country road, clipped her bike and left her nursing six broken ribs, a separated shoulder and a collapsed lung. Again she remained undaunted and set her sights on returning to Kona in 1999 and qualifying for triathlon's debut at the Olympics in 2000. This time, thyroid cancer intervened, and she had her thyroid removed in a six-hour operation in December 1999. Again she won through, and returned to the racecourse in 2001 to win her seventh National Champion title.

Smyers was already famous for not posting a DNF for 17 years, a determination she attributes to being one of seven siblings. 'I grew up in a big family, and I always had to work a bit harder for my brothers and sisters to let me play. I think my record of not posting a DNF stems from fear. It's a slippery slope; if you ever justify dropping out for something like not having a good day, then you're just dooming yourself. If you use that excuse once, then you could use it a hundred times.'

After a second maternity leave in 2004, Smyers returned to the Hawaiian Ironman in 2005 and at 44 posted another top 10 performance. Inductions into the USAT and ITU Halls of Fame followed. But she still isn't done on the track. 'I'm thinking of a return to Hawaii as an age-grouper in October 2015. I haven't made the switch to be an amateur yet, but I wanted to wait until the point when I'm not expected to win any more!'

△ Smyers on the bike at Cancun in 1995, where a 36:39min run secured her second ITU world title

△ Smyers becomes the first woman to do the double of winning both Ironman and ITU world titles in the same season

The Triathletes
Spencer Smith

▷ Spencer Smith was one of the most attacking, aggressive racers to have graced triathlon, winning countless domestic titles and two ITU Olympic-distance world titles

Back when Bryan Adams was hogging the singles chart in the early nineties, Spencer Smith was one part of a contrasting double act that dominated Olympic-distance triathlon. If Smith's great British rival – the South African émigré Simon Lessing – had the edge in ITU World titles, then Smith – the son of a used-car salesman – was a cult hero who provoked more devotion; the Andre Agassi to Lessing's Pete Sampras.

Committed, charismatic and confident, the name Spencer Smith still conjures excitement in fans of the sport (he's one of the few triathletes to have a biography published: the enjoyable *Transitions* by Vitruvian race organizer Mark Shaw).

Named after Spencer Tracy, Spencer Smith was born on 11 May 1973 in West Middlesex Hospital to Barbara and Bill Smith, a former footballer for QPR. He started swimming competitively at four and by 15 had achieved National Championship success. But already he was seeking a fresh challenge, and he joined the Thames Turbo Triathlon Club, the future home of British stars Tim Don and Stuart Hayes. He went on to win the National Junior Triathlon Championship in 1989 – edging Iain Hamilton into second place at Holme Pierrepont, the future home of Hamilton's Outlaw event – and the National/European Junior double in 1990 – accompanied by a familiar soundtrack: dad Bill shouting 'Go on, my son!' from the side-lines.

A chance encounter in autumn 1990 saw then volleyball coach Bill Black become the man tasked with elevating Smith's bicycling and running to his swimming level. Combined with the 17-year-old's

△ Smith pre-race at the Windsor Triathlon, one of his happy hunting grounds, where he took six titles

famous dedication, Black's magic soon reaped the rewards. A win at the inaugural Windsor Triathlon in June 1991 was followed by 13 other victories that season, including Ironbridge, the European Junior Champs (16–18) in Germany and the National Championships at Wakefield. Smith's tri season finished as a spectator at Ironman Hawaii, where he met his triathlon hero Mark Allen. 'He was my hero from the start and still is to this day. A true living legend that could win at any distance.' A seed was planted.

The next year started with wins at both the National and European Duathlon Champs (the boy could now bike), and then silver behind Lessing at the 220 Triathlon Series race in Swindon, which marked the start of Britain's most famous triathlon rivalry. After powering his way to the front on the swim, Smith led a British one-two-three at the European Championships in Belgium in July ahead of Lessing and Glenn Cook, before blitzing the ITU Junior World Championships in Canada.

Smith turned 20 in 1993 just as the Olympic Games-courting ITU were discussing dropping the non-drafting format, a move that would fundamentally change the dynamic of racing. Ironically, he was disqualified for drafting (and giving a draft-buster a volley of choice Cockney words) at the 1993 Euros before the ITU Worlds headed to England and a classic in Manchester.

Now a fearsome cyclist, Smith tore through the swim and the non-drafting bike leg in front of the BBC cameras and entered T2 a minute before Lessing and the chasing Olympic-distance greats Hamish Carter and Brad Beven. Those expecting the loping gait of Lessing to reel Smith in saw the Londoner extend his lead to batter the field by nearly 2 minutes. 'It was one of those days where you couldn't hurt yourself enough,' was Smith's judgement. He would also rank it as his greatest achievement, a race that 'made my mum and dad proud.'

Smith won his final ITU World Title in New Zealand in 1994, before boycotting the 1995 Worlds on account of the implementation of draft-legal racing. With triathlon making its Olympic debut in 2000, the ITU would feel vindicated in its decision but for a flat-out swim/biker like Smith, it hastened a departure to long-course racing. A bronze at the middle-distance ITU World Championships in 1996 came before another European Championships Olympic-distance title in 1997.

Both professionally and privately, 1998 was a mixture of major highs and crushing lows for Smith. His father died of cancer in the summer after a two-year battle, and one of triathlon's true characters exited the scene. Just two months later, on his debut at Ironman Hawaii, Smith came fifth to earn a still-standing British male record. He married his girlfriend Melissa days later before finding out that he'd tested positive for the banned steroid nandrolone. Initially he was cleared by the British Triathlon Federation, but the United States triathlon federation (USAT) appealed and took the case to the International Triathlon Union, which threw out the appeal. The Americans appealed a second time, and the matter was referred to the Court of Arbitration for Sport, the highest assembly in sport. It too cleared Smith after finding that the Los Angeles laboratory that analysed the urine sample had made some significant mistakes. Finally Smith was a free man, but the ordeal had seen him spend $100,000 in legal fees (as well as suffer a huge loss in earnings).

Disillusioned with the world of multisport, Smith opted to forgo any attempt to qualify for the Sydney Olympics in 2000, instead embarking on a brief break from triathlon in the world of cycling, namely the Linda McCartney Pro Cycling Team, in 1999. Returning to long-course triathlon, he placed eighth at Ironman Hawaii in 2000 before victories at Ironman Florida and Ironman Brazil in 2001 and 2002, respectively.

It was typical of his dogged determination that he recovered from a horrific training ride accident in 2005 to place second at Ironman Arizona in 2006. Now based in Florida, Smith scaled down racing as his S2 Coaching career took hold, with his passion still inspiring triathletes 25 years after a raw young talent flung open the doors of Thames Turbo tri club.

▽ Smith was a formidable biker, with his battles with Simon Lessing becoming etched in British triathlon history

Hamish Carter

▷ Carter with New Zealand team-mate Bevan Docherty and Switzerland's Sven Riederer on the Athens podium

▽ Hamish Carter battles the heat and hills at the Athens Olympics on his way to taking Olympic Games gold

Triathlon's toughest-ever Olympic Games bike course … relentless humidity and heat … a stacked field that featured Simon Whitfield and Tim Don. In the words of Aussie superstar Greg Bennett, who finished fourth that day at Athens in 2004: 'If you're going to get beaten, you want to be beaten by tough bastards. And that day New Zealand surely had the toughest men in the field.'

One of those Kiwi triathletes was Bevan Docherty, the reigning ITU World Champion and a formidable sprinter (witness his superhuman

finish at New Plymouth in 2005). The other was the 33-year-old Hamish Carter, in his last shot at Olympic glory, having finished a disappointing 26th at the 2000 Sydney Olympics despite being a pre-race favourite alongside Britain's Simon Lessing.

If the smart money was on Docherty as the two friends battled shoulder-to-shoulder well clear of the field, no one had told Carter. Five hundred yards from the line the Aucklander broke free to claim the second-ever men's Olympic gold medal and banish the memory of Sydney.

'Everything was on the line for that race,' says Carter,

At 33, Athens was my last shot at the Olympics, but I'd enough experience to rewrite the way I trained and approached the race. My coach stuck to the fundamentals and I brought the innovation. I trained less than everyone else but when I trained hard, I trained harder than everyone else.

Hamish Clive Carter was born on 28 April 1971 in Auckland. After competing twice at the national school championships in rowing, Carter moved over to triathlon, for which his slender 75kg, 6ft frame might be better fitted than it was for rowing. On his ITU debut at the 1992 World Championships in Canada he finished 60 places behind Simon Lessing. But within a year, at the ITU Worlds in Salford, Manchester, he was mounting a podium whose top two steps were occupied by Lessing and Spencer Smith after one of British triathlon's classic duels.

'I came into the sport when it was non-drafting. Transition would be a paddock somewhere, and it was often racing on open roads.' But, controversially, the sport of ITU racing would soon switch to draft-legal racing, something Carter initially resented.

The shift to drafting was a disaster for me at first! I was strong at the time-trial formats and when it moved to drafting I was on the verge on never winning a race again. I totally disagreed with the philosophy but those who were running the sport had a vision. I was lucky enough to adapt as an athlete to a changing sport.

Carter recorded his first of 11 ITU World Cup wins a month after Manchester, with the rest of the nineties seeing his consistency produce 22 podium places in 33 ITU race starts while battling the aforementioned Brits and the likes of Greg Welch and Brad Beven.

Racing Brad Beven every weekend definitely set me on a trajectory that I probably wouldn't have found if he wasn't there. I rarely could beat him, as he was incredibly consistent at a really high standard. He helped shape the sport at that time.

Going into triathlon's maiden appearance at the Olympic Games in Sydney 2000, Carter was in fine form, with a gold, silver and a top five in his three ITU races that season. The scene was set for an Opera House showdown with that old race nemesis Lessing. But it wasn't to be for either of them, with the Brit overcooking the bike and Carter succumbing to pressure. 'The desire to be successful can crush you. That was my mistake in Sydney; getting caught up in it all.'

If 2001 was largely a race year to forget for Carter, he was back to podium-hopping ways in 2002, with a string of top results leading to bronze at the Commonwealth Games in Manchester, finishing 7 seconds behind Whitfield. More wins followed before Athens 2004, where Carter grasped his last chance at Olympic glory. 'To be able to change as a person four years after Sydney was the most pivotal and satisfying part of my

career,' he says. 'It's not a normal race, funky things happen at the Olympics.'

The ITU World Championships was a title still missing from the Carter portfolio, and 2006 brought him closest to the gong, losing out to Britain's Tim Don on the home stretch in Perth.

It dawned on me that whether I won or not didn't matter. Winning the Olympics ruins you in that sense. You lose your desire, and I knew my time was up although I raced really well in 2006. I had a young family and wanted to experience a new kind of life.

After beating the world's best off-road triathletes to win the Xterra World Champs in October 2006, Carter retired in early 2007 after nearly twenty years as a racer. Business ventures and coaching have followed, but 2012 saw Carter join Welch in having heart problems when he was diagnosed with atrial fibrillation. His heart rhythm has been consistent since, but he's been told to expect the problems to return. In 2015 he divides his time between the sports rehydration brand SoS and working as the Performance Planning Manager at High Performance Sport New Zealand, imparting his world-beating advice to coaches and athletes in the run-up to Rio 2016.

▽ The Kiwi star recording his final ITU victory, at the Edmonton World Cup race in 2006

Brad Beven

▽ Brad Beven is one of the greatest Olympic-distance triathletes of all time, creating one of the sport's finest winning streaks in the early nineties

Ask racing greats Hamish Carter, Courtney Atkinson, Simon Whitfield and Simon Lessing who their triathlon hero is, and the man top of their list isn't a World Champion athlete but an Aussie farm boy without a World Championship title or Olympic appearance to his name. 'If you question the guys from the sport now, "Who's Brad Beven?", I'm sure they'd have no idea. He should be the [French five times Tour de France winner] Bernard Hinault of the sport,' Whitfield has passionately argued.

Yet to paint this North Queenslander as a loveable loser would be to do a great disservice to one of the most consistently brilliant Olympic-distance triathletes of all-time. Tap the name Brad Beven into the International Triathlon Union's online results archive, and the results are barely believable. From October 1993 to July 1997 Beven entered 15 ITU World Cup races – back when World Cups were the premium ITU series event. He won every single one of them, leaving a host of world-beaters in his wake. In Olympic-distance history, only his fellow Aussie Emma Snowsill's mid-noughties purple patch and Alistair Brownlee's CV come close in terms of dominance.

Brad Beven was born on 18 September 1969 in Miriwinni, North Queensland, a tiny town (population 200) ringed by sugar cane farms, rainforests and miles of South Pacific coastline. As with the Brownlees brothers' relationship with the roads and trails of Yorkshire, Beven's triathlon career was inextricably shaped by his surroundings, swimming in the croc-infested

swamps around his parent's farm, chasing his dad Ray's tractor through the cane fields and, at Ray's behest, running 10km to school and back barefoot with bricks in each hand in a bid to build up his 'puny' physique.

'I was always on the run, and took up triathlon when I started cross training for my running and swimming training,' Beven says. He entered his maiden race, Cairns' first-ever triathlon in 1982, at the age of 14. From that point he 'would never look back,' racing early incarnations of the Noosa Tri and, by the age of 19, placing sixth after Mark Allen at 1989's inaugural ITU World Championships in Avignon. Self-coached throughout his career, Beven came second to Rick Wells at the Commonwealth Games in January 1990 – where triathlon was making its debut as a demonstration sport – in a race that witnessed the start of his major championship heartache.

Along with Greg Welch and Miles Stewart, Beven helped establish triathlon in the Australian sporting consciousness. Welch and Beven would form part of an Aussie clean sweep with Stephen Foster at the 1990 ITU World Championships in Orlando, USA; a formidable swim was enough to see Beven leading into the run before being passed by his superstar compatriot Welch. The latter soon went on to succeed in his crusade to take Ironman Hawaii gold, while in 1994 Beven became unstoppable in Australia's crack domestic scene, winning five Australian Triathlon Championships and seven Australian Grand Prix Champs in his career.

The stone-cold classic 1993 ITU World Championships in Salford, Manchester, was dominated by Spencer Smith, who obliterated the other contenders, and Beven trailed in fourth. A year later at the ITU Championship final in New Zealand, Smith was again the nemesis, edging Beven into second even though the Aussie made up a minute on the run.

Another British legend, Simon Lessing, stood in Beven's way to ITU World Championship glory at Cancun in 1995. Yet on the ITU World Cup circuit Beven was unstoppable, winning the overall Series title four times. 'We'd race 30 times a year, and the World Cup winner would be the most consistent for the year, and that was satisfying for me,' says Beven. 'As they say, it's easy to get to the top but harder to stay there. Consistency is tough when there are so many great athletes out there.'

Two of those were future Olympic champions Hamish Carter and Simon Whitfield. 'It was at a time when we were all trying to grab a little piece of it, but we were also together, getting swept along with the progression of the sport,' says Beven. 'We were all in the same arena competing for the same titles, dollars and sponsors, but the rivalry didn't get in the way until race day. They weren't ratbags as well.'

Simon Lessing, a man with huge respect for the Aussie, finally ended Beven's four-year World Cup winning streak at Stockholm in 1997, which would be the last time the Aussie graced the ITU podium. A torn calf muscle led to a fallow period as triathlon geared up for its Olympic Games debut at Sydney 2000, and then, as Beven's form returned, his chance of Olympic glory was snatched away. On his way to an interview with Mark Allen, he was hit by a car at a pedestrian crossing on the eve of a key Sydney qualifier.

'Missing my chance to go to the Olympics is definitely my greatest regret, as being an Olympian is something that any layman can respect. It was hard to swallow, as I was in good shape, and it [the Olympics] was taken from me,' says Beven 15 years on. 'I watched the qualifier from a hospital bed with eight broken ribs. Circumstances dictated that I didn't get my shot; I could hear echoes of that movie – "I could've been a contender". But I had to put it in perspective: I came out of a bad situation relatively in one piece, even though it ended my career in the blink of an eye.'

Since watching Simon Whitfield – one of countless ITU racers he inspired – take gold at Sydney, Beven has moved into coaching age-groupers with his BBT coaching outfit. 'The Type A Alpha, training-obsessed, techno junkie is triathlon's greatest asset,' Beven says from his base in Brisbane. 'It never ceases to amaze me the people that are attracted to the sport. Let's hope this continues.'

◁ Despite his World Cup pedigree, sadly a major championship title and Olympic appearance alluded Beven in his decorated career

The Triathletes
Leanda Cave

▷ Leanda Cave has won world titles at every level of triathlon in a long and illustrious career

▽ A decade after winning the ITU Worlds, Leanda Cave won the Ironman World Championships at Kona in 2012

She may not have reached anything like the household-name status achieved by the Brownlees and Chrissie Wellington in the UK, but Leanda Cave has a genuine claim for the title of Britain's most decorated triathlete in history. World Championship titles at ITU, Ironman, Ironman 70.3 and ITU Long Distance all decorate Cave's wincing mantelpiece, nestling alongside silver medals from the Commonwealth Games and European Championships and four Escape from Alcatraz titles. But to call Cave versatile almost does her a disservice.

Like Simon Lessing – a fellow British legend whom she notes as a key influence on her – Cave's career has been that of a globe-trotting athlete. Born in Lincolnshire in 1978 to a Welsh mother, Cave spent her early years in Queensland, Australia, entering her first triathlon at the age of 14 before returning to the UK at 19 to train and race.

Based in Bath, she took the U23 world title in Carlsbad in 2001 before a breakthrough 2002 season. A second-place finish at the ETU European Championships in Hungary preceded the Commonwealth Games in Manchester, which led to what Cave calls the 'proudest moment of her career'. In front of her watching family and a partisan crowd, Cave – racing in the colours of Wales – beat the fancied Australian ITU World Champions, Michellie Jones and Nicole Hackett, to take silver 19 seconds behind the Canadian veteran, Carol Montgomery. Ten years later, Cave still holds that silver in the highest regard, even placing it above her Ironman World titles. 'My family was there. It was on home soil. After the race, my Mum said something that shaped me until this day: "We never thought you would be this good." It validated my achievement and it's enabled me to believe in myself ever since.'

The year 2002 culminated in Cave becoming the ITU World Champion in Cancún, Mexico, edging a stellar field that included Michellie Jones again, Loretta Harrop and Cave's future coach, Siri Lindley. An injury-disrupted 2003 followed, before one of the lowest points of Cave's storied career –being controversially overlooked for the 2004 Athens Olympics in favour of Jodie Swallow, who'd barely raced that season. Cave moved to middle-distance racing in 2006, before 2007 saw wins at Escape from Alcatraz (she'd go on to take four Alcatraz titles), the ITU Long Distance World Championships and a top 10 in her maiden Ironman World Championship race. In 2011 she reached the Hawaii podium for the first time – in a women's race best remembered for Chrissie Wellington's heroic victory – before scoring her first full Ironman title at Arizona in November.

A decade on from her breakthrough season, Cave (now bearing the nickname Superbird) made 2012 another year to remember with a win at the Ironman 70.3 World Championships in Vegas in September. A month later she took victory on the lava fields of Kona, passing Caroline Steffen with three miles of the run remaining, to take the title by just 62 seconds.

Less than six months after becoming the first woman to do the Ironman double, Cave was diagnosed with basal-cell carcinoma, a skin cancer considered malignant. The shock diagnosis changed her outlook on training, and she now begins her day at 4.30 a.m. to minimize training in direct sunlight and uses indoor training facilities when possible. A hamstring tear and the demands that come with being a double world champion also disrupted her Kona prep in 2013, with a respectable 13th place overshadowed by the podium-hopping exploits of Brits Rachel Joyce and Liz Blatchford. By the end of the year Cave's motivation to train had hit 'an all-time low'.

Not for the first time in her career, she had a turbulent season in 2014. After four years with Siri Lindley, Cave moved back to Cliff English (who had coached her in 2005–06) in Tucson, Arizona. The initial aim was a return to her short-course roots and a spot in the Welsh Commonwealth Games dream team of Non Stanford and Helen Jenkins at Glasgow in July. But she was snubbed by the Welsh Triathlon selectors – the latest high-profile omission of her career – while fellow World Champions Stanford and Jenkins also missed out due to injury.

The decision was tough to take for British triathlon fans hoping for a rare opportunity to watch her in the flesh, and the 36-year-old Cave publicly criticized the Welsh federation.

'I'm a totally able-bodied athlete without injury, prepared to put it on the line for my country … I'm in the shape of my life. I've not been this fit for many years. We could have had the best team in the world.'

A disqualification for losing her race number while leading at Ironman France continued Cave's ill-luck, but August saw her back to her best. She finished second at the Ironman 70.3 European Championship, then demolished the field at Ironman Sweden a week later, producing the day's fastest female swim, bike and run splits to break the tape in front of 50,000 spectators in Kalmar in 8:56:50 – some 33 minutes ahead of the nearest competitor.

She went into the October 2014 Hawaii race as one of the athletes tipped to challenge Mirinda Carfrae's dominance on the Big Island. After being the last pro athlete to enter the water, Cave came out of the swim in seventh, and the bike in 12th but dropped back on the run for a finishing place of 18th. 'Every dog has its day, and this was definitely not mine,' she said after the race. Cave turned 37 in March 2015 and still has time on her side for continued long-course success. Whatever happens, it will certainly be worth following.

▽ Cave celebrates her Hawaii crown by doing the Blazeman roll, in honour of the American triathlete Jon Blais who lost his battle with ALS (also known as Lou Gehrig's Disease) in 2007

The Triathletes

Emma Snowsill

Highlights

- Olympic Games Champion, 2008

- ITU World Champion, 2003, 2005, 2006

- Commonwealth Games champion, 2006

▷ Snowsill secures victory over her great rival Vanessa Fernandes at the 1996 ITU World Championship in Lausanne

As big game triathletes go, Emma Snowsill is right up there alongside (and arguably eclipsing) Alistair Brownlee and Simon Whitfield as the best Olympic-distance racer triathlon has ever seen. In a formidable period from 2003 to 2008 the Australian won 15 of her 23 races and stood on the podium a scarcely believable 21 times.

For a woman who's won the holy trinity at Olympic-distance level, it feels strange to add that Snowsill might have achieved even more in her career. Had Triathlon Australia not controversially overlooked her for both the 2004 and 2012 Olympics, the tale of the girl from the Gold Coast might have been even grander.

Born in the triathlon heartland of Australia's Gold Coast in 1981, Emma Laura Snowsill joined Australia's great lineage of ITU World Championship-winning women, which already numbered Michellie Jones, Emma Carney, Jackie Gallagher, Loretta Harrop and Nicole Hackett. At the age of 19 she won the ITU junior (16–20) World Championships in a major year for both herself and triathlon. 'I did my first Olympic-distance race in 2000 and went to watch the triathlon at the Sydney Olympics. Witnessing that was what made me think it was something I should aspire to.'

A gold at the 2001 Sydney Youth Olympic Festival followed a year later before tragedy struck in 2002 when her boyfriend and fellow triathlete, Luke Harrop, was hit and killed by a woman driving a stolen car. It sent Snowsill into depression and away from the sport until Harrop's sister, Loretta, convinced her to start training again.

'My hero of triathlon has got to be Loretta Harrop. I admired the way she raced and, as I got to know her, I came to understand the mental aspect of competing even more,' says Snowsill.

Snowsill's elite breakthrough arrived in 2003 with her first ITU World Cup victory swiftly followed by her maiden World Championship title at Queenstown, New Zealand, in December of that year. With a 36-minute run split well over a minute faster than any of the women's field, the diminutive 5ft 3in Snowsill's reputation for having the most fearsome run in triathlon was forged.

Early 2004 saw Snowsill (and Michellie Jones) being controversially passed over by the Australian selection panel for the 2004 Olympic Games in

Athens. The same thing happened in 2012, when Snowsill was overlooked in favour of Emma Jackson, a decision that once again created a backlash from a number of professional athletes.

Her six ITU podiums out of seven in 2005 included another ITU World Championship title in Gamagori, Japan, before a formidable year in 2006 saw Snowsill win five out of her six ITU races (her only loss won her a silver medal). She fought off a triple-pronged Kiwi assault from Sam Warriner, Andrea Hewitt and Debbie Tanner on home soil at the Melbourne Commonwealth Games in March, and victory over Portugal's Vanessa Fernandes at the ITU World Championships in Lausanne followed in the autumn.

In 2007 she was affected by asthma and injuries, and at the behest of her coach, Bill Davoren, reluctantly spent the season in the shadow of her great sporting rival Fernandes, before an undefeated *annus mirabilis* in 2008 for the Aussie. The year started with two ITU World Cup victories and a win at triathlon's biggest payday in Des Moines before the great showdown of the Snowsill/Fernandes years: the Beijing Olympics. The pair would exit T2 together before Snowsill, with her asthma inhaler tucked into her top, once again unleashed the day's fastest run split to beat Fernandes by over a minute to become Australia's first and only Olympic gold medallist in triathlon. A day later her future husband, Germany's Jan Frodeno, took the men's title.

The next season saw the ITU establish its World Triathlon Series over the one-off World Championship, a move that perhaps didn't suit the big-day player. 'A big change in Olympic-distance racing is the ITU making the World Championships a series instead of a one-day Championship,' Snowsill believes. 'I'd love to see the World Championships go back to a one-day race.'

Although great victories have still been scored – notably at the 2010 ITU Grand Final in Budapest – Snowsill, like her Beijing rival Fernandes, has since been unable to add to her World Championship collection. She hasn't raced competitively since 2012, and recurrent immune-system issues, picked up after holidaying in Bali, led her to retire at the age of 33 in 2014. 'Coming to a decision is often the hardest, and my process hasn't been the easiest one either, but now is the right time,' Snowsill announced on her website. 'Truthfully, my health has really struggled over the last four years, and ultimately my body helped make the decision for me that it didn't have what it needed to compete at the highest level on the world stage any more.'

Snowsill is currently based in Girona with Frodeno, yet her involvement in sport and triathlon continues, and she is now studying online at the Institute of Integrative Nutrition, with her media work taking in the Commonwealth Games and the Nanjing Youth Olympic Games.

△ Emma Snowsill's devastating run speed saw her land both Olympic and ITU world titles

▽ On the Olympic podium in 2008 with Portugal's Vanessa Fernandes and Aussie compatriot Emma Moffatt

Simon Whitfield

Highlights

- Olympic Games Champion, 2000

- Olympic Games, 2008, silver

- Commonwealth Games Champion, 2002

▽ Whitfield became the first male Olympic champion in triathlon and an icon in the sport

Proof that nice guys don't always finish last is Simon Whitfield, one of the most popular performers ever to step on a starting pontoon in triathlon. Yet behind the smiles and affability is one of the triathlon athletes most dedicated to training, famous for his relentless pursuit of sporting excellence (so much so that the term would become his catchphrase).

The Canadian would become famous for his tactical knowhow and big-race ability, his achievements including 11 ITU World Cup victories, nine Pan American Cup wins, a record four Olympic appearances and, of course, becoming triathlon's first-ever male Olympic and Commonwealth Games champion. The countless number of triathletes he's inspired includes Ironman Hawaii champion Craig Alexander. 'I still get shivers whenever I recall Simon taking Olympic gold in Sydney. He's contributed so much as an athlete, ambassador and role model. Seeing Simon Whitfield in full flight on the run, in my opinion, is the greatest spectacle in the sport.'

Simon St. Quentin Whitfield was born in Kingston, Ontario, in 1975. He made his triathlon debut at 11 in a race organized by a friend in Ontario, reportedly racing in boxer shorts and a Mickey Mouse hat. He quickly showed promise in Canada's Kids of Steel events. He was in his teens when he said, 'My goal was always to be the best in the world at something,' and he moved to Australia at the age of 17, where his hero Brad Beven was ruling Australia's formidable domestic scene. He teamed up with future Aussie star

Greg Bennett and was soon benefiting from Bennett's work-rate and guidance.

Simon returned to Canada in 1997 to co-found the National Triathlon Training Centre with his then coach Barrie Shepley. A smattering of decent ITU results followed, most notably two top 10 finishes at the ITU World Championships, plus an ITU World Cup podium in Rio that secured his Olympic spot for Sydney 2000. But there was little to suggest to outside observers that a gold medal was imminent at triathlon's Olympic debut. In hindsight, however, the race-best run split at the ITU World Cup race in Corner Brook six weeks before Sydney was a sign of an athlete peaking at the optimum time.

During the lead-up to Sydney, the media were mostly citing British multiple World Champion Simon Lessing as the man to beat. For Whitfield, the pressure was off. 'Lessing just did not seem to be enjoying the occasion,' he recalls, 'but I was having a blast!'

Whitfield came out of the Sydney Harbour waters 30 seconds behind the favourites, Lessing and the Kiwi Hamish Carter, and left T2 in 25th place after a bike collision nearly wiped him out. 'The crash was almost the perfect stimulus to fire me up,' he says. With Lessing overcooking it on the bike, Whitfield charged out of transition to leave a host of world-beaters in his wake.

With 2km to go, Germany's Stefan Vuckovic had control of the race, at one point opening a 20m gap between himself and the chasing Canadian. 'I was thinking, silver at the Olympics is actually quite awesome,' Whitfield adds, 'and then

I looked over my shoulder and saw third and fourth stacking up behind and thought that fourth would be terrible, so I upped the pace.' With the Opera House finish line in sight, Whitfield passed the German to win by 13 secs and enter triathlon immortality.

Now 26 years old, Whitfield continued his stratospheric progression after the Olympics, winning three ITU races in 2001. More World Cup wins followed in 2002 before Whitfield became the first male triathlete to win the Commonwealth Games title, overcoming the Aussie Miles Stewart by just 2 seconds in Manchester.

Both the 2003 and 2004 seasons shared ITU victories aplenty building up to a disappointing finish at the season's end ITU World Championships. If there's anything anticlimactic about Whitfield's career, it's his ITU World Championship record. His best place is a fourth at Hamburg in 2007, leaving him, like Hamish Carter and Brad Beven, as a serial winner who never won one of triathlon's most famous accolades.

Always a forward thinker, Whitfield was behind triathlon's most famous use of a domestique at the 2008 Olympics, when his fellow Canadian, Colin Jenkins, acted as his pace man and protector on the bike. The tactic took Whitfield to within 200m of his second Olympic gold before Germany's Jan Frodeno, in the race of his life, edged him on the home straight to win by 5 seconds.

Whitfield went into the 2009 Hy-Vee ITU Elite Cup event after a run of bad form, and nearly boarded an early plane home, only to end up as the victor of a triathlon classic for the ages (and winner of a giant $200,000 cheque). The final 50 metres saw him fighting Kris Gemmell, Brad Kahlefeldt and Jan Frodeno for the title, before he broke free on the blue carpet to take revenge on his Beijing nemesis.

Whitfield went into the London Olympics as the Canadian flag bearer, a record four-time Olympic triathlete and with pundits still tipping him as a potential medallist. Sadly his race-ending bike crash wasn't the Olympic denouement he would've scripted, and the outpouring of sadness from his watching family, the press and spectators confirmed the enduring fondness he inspired in followers of the sport.

Along with Bevan Docherty and Tim Don, Whitfield was one of the post-2012 Olympic ITU émigrés expected to challenge for honours in the world of long-course racing. But in 2013 he revealed that he'd hung up the tri-suit to spend more time with his daughters. 'I'm done. I don't know how to do it at 90%; if I went back I'd like to have a crack at beating the Brownlees, but that level of commitment would be too much.'

△ Whitfield is a master tactician and wily racer, who won both Olympic and Commonwealth Games titles

▽ Showing the guns with friend and fellow multi-Olympic medallist Bevan Docherty

Javier Gómez

▷ Javier Gómez is world-class across all three disciplines and is heavily-tipped for Ironman success after Rio 2016

▽ Gómez faces-off against his major rival Alistair Brownlee at Australia's Gold Coast in 2009

Four ITU World Championship titles, the Xterra World title, three European Championships, the Ironman 70.3 World title, an Olympic silver medal … The scary thing about Javier Gómez Noya is that there could be much more to come from one of the best all-round athletes to grace the sport of triathlon. By 2017 he could realistically be the first man to own both Olympic and Ironman World Championships titles (unless Jan Frodeno beats him to it once again, of course). And, yet, one of triathlon's greatest careers so nearly never took flight, and the early battles of Gómez's career were fought not on the race track, but in the sporting courts.

Javier Gómez Noya was born in Basel, Switzerland, on 25 March 1983. His parents returned to Spain in July that year: to Ferrol, on the north-western coast above a Coruña, where Javier would spend his formative years. A sporty childhood of football, mountain biking and swimming led Gómez to discovering triathlon at the age of 15.

Under the tutelage of long-term coach José Rioseco, the prodigious teenager dominated the local junior scenes in both swimming and triathlon.

In December 1999 the rug was pulled from under his feet however when the medical services of the Consejo Superior de Deportes (CSD), the Spanish government agency for sport, detected a cardiac anomaly. His international race licence was revoked, and seven years of court cases and visiting cardiology specialists worldwide began.

Throughout this period his international race licence would be intermittently reinstated, but his racing was largely restricted to Iberian events.

A move to university to study engineering was swiftly curtailed, and Gómez moved to Pontevedra to concentrate on his professional triathlete dreams.

His debut ITU race took place at the Estoril European Cup race in 2002, where he finished sixth, outpacing past and future Belgian Ironman Hawaii greats, Luc and Frederik Van Lierde, yet falling some way short of British legend Simon Lessing at the head of the field. Little did Lessing know on that midsummer day in Portugal that the 19-year-old crossing the line 80 seconds after him would one day equal his record of four ITU World Championship wins.

Further licence problems followed in 2003, yet Javier was cleared to race at December's ITU U23 Worlds in New Zealand. Undertrained and lacking race practice, he nonetheless triumphed in Queenstown, beating a field that contained future rivals Steffen Justus and Luke McKenzie to take his first major title. An attempt to qualify for triathlon's second Olympic Games outing in Athens followed, but Gómez was controversially excluded from the process on account of his heart anomaly by the Federación Española de Triatlón (Fetri).

In 2005 Gómez hit his lowest ebb, barred from boarding the plane to World Cup races in Mexico and Hawaii by the CSD. But early 2006 saw him finally regain his race licence for good, and one of triathlon's most prolific periods could begin.

In 85 ITU-sanctioned races from 2006 to the end of 2014, Gómez was amongst the top ten 79 times, amassing 34 victories and 64 podiums along the way. If two brothers from Yorkshire hadn't shown up, the groans from his overstocked trophy cabinet would have been even greater.

The eight-year period saw Javier scoop ITU World Championship titles in 2008, 2010, 2013 and 2014, and three ETU European Championship gongs. Alongside this, two mega bucks Hy-Vee titles and the 2013 Escape from Alcatraz gold have all headed to Galicia. The Olympic title is the only one to have brought heartache.

After his exclusion in 2004, Gómez went into 2008 as the favourite for the Beijing title but came out the loser in a showdown with Jan Frodeno, Simon Whitfield and Bevan Docherty, finishing fourth. At the 2012 Olympics in Hyde Park, Gómez took the silver medal, finishing 11 seconds behind a dominant Alistair Brownlee on home soil.

While his record against Jonny Brownlee is favourable (he held the upper hand in all of 2014's Olympic-distance races), Gómez rarely gets the better of a fit and focused Alistair. But to win at Rio 2016 he knows what he has to do to shake off the Brownlees or Spain's other great hope, Mario Mola.

'Cutting 30 seconds off my 10km run is the dream. I've completed many workouts running up- and downstairs to work on my weakness – the sprint – and it seems to be paying off. It's exactly what I'll be working on ahead of Rio.'

Ominously for the long-distance world, Gómez also has eyes for another of triathlon's greatest prizes. He went to Ironman Hawaii in 2011 to witness Craig Alexander's final triumph and vowed to return.

His first middle-distance race in May 2013, at Challenge Half Barcelona, saw Gómez trounce the two-time Ironman World Champion, Chris McCormack, to take the title. In February 2014 he broke the tape first at Ironman 70.3 Panama before going on to win the Ironman 70.3 World Championships at Mont Tremblant in September, getting his revenge on Jan Frodeno and winning by a minute. Even before his stunning Ironman 70.3 World triumph over a field of more experienced athletes, many had tipped the Spaniard as the future king of long-course racing, with Spencer Smith labelling him 'the next sensation in triathlon in long-distance racing'.

▽ After silver behind Ali Brownlee sat London 2012, the Olympic title is missing from the Gómez trophy cabinet, with Rio 2016 his final chance at Olympic glory

Vanessa Fernandes

△ Vanessa Fernandes celebrates winning the 2007 ITU World Cup in Beijing

A month after taking silver at the Beijing Olympic in 2008, Vanessa Fernandes went to Pulpi in Andalusia to take the European U23 Championship title. That she was still just 23 years old was barely fathomable to anyone who had watched her dominate the sport during the decade with Emma Snowsill. For here was a complete swim, bike and run athlete with two Olympic appearances, a record 20 ITU World Cup victories and an ITU World Championship to her name. And yet Fernandes' fall was as swift as her prodigious rise. The U23 title in Pulpi was followed by just two more ITU career wins before she vanished as a force in triathlon, seemingly burnt out at the age when most careers start reaching top gear.

Vanessa de Sousa Fernandes was born into a sporting family in Perosinho, just south of Porto in northern Portugal, in 1985. Her father was a professional cyclist who became the inspiration for her to start cycling and triathlon. By the age of six she was swimming, by the dawn of her teens she'd joined a track cycling club, and at the age of 15 she'd entered the world of triathlon.

A host of junior triathlon and duathlon titles would follow, before she beat ITU World Champions Emma Snowsill and Sheila Taormina to win her first World Cup at Madrid in 2003, on a course where she would prove victorious for the next six consecutive years. Her first European Championship title would follow in April 2004, and then she finished an impressive eighth after posting the fifth fastest run split of the day in the Athens Olympic Games at the age of 18.

The next four-year Olympic cycle would see Fernandes enter 37 ITU races and win 30 of them, garnering four consecutive European Championship gold medals, plus ITU World titles in duathlon (2007 and 2008) and triathlon (2007) in the process. In a sport previously dominated by North Americans and Antipodeans, Fernandes (along with Spain's Ivan Rana) also helped put Iberia on the triathlon map.

Fernandes' adversary throughout this period was Snowsill, and she lost twice to the Aussie at the ITU World Championships in 2005 and 2006, before gaining the upper hand at Hamburg in 2007. At the Beijing Olympics in 2008 the scene was set for a classic showdown between two of the sport's most consistent performers.

As the sporting world's eyes focused on Beijing, and triathlon made its third Olympic Games appearance, the superstars of women's triathlon were inseparable for the first two

disciplines of the race. After exiting T2, Fernandes would produce the day's second fastest 10km split of 34:21mins, only for Snowsill to overpower her on the run, to break the tape more than a minute ahead and leave her Portuguese rival to settle for silver. As one of Portugal's two medal winners at the Games, though, Fernandes was the flag bearer for Portugal at the closing ceremony.

At just 23 Fernandes had time on her side to eclipse Snowsill in the next Olympic cycle, and she started well, winning both that European U23 title and the ITU World Duathlon Championships after the Games. Yet the Portuguese starlet was never to reach such heights again after 2008. She was hit by a series of injuries (Achilles), illnesses ('flu-like symptoms') and, by most accounts, a turbulent coaching relationship with Hugo Sousa (reports suggested that Fernandes kept pushing her body even when she was injured), making the former prodigy a pale shadow of her former self.

Having spent most of 2009 on the sidelines, Fernandes made a return to that happy hunting ground in Madrid in June 2010. After flickering briefly, she finished 10th overall. After another brief return (and 26th position) at the ITU World Series in Yokohama in 2011, Fernandes informed the Portuguese Triathlon Federation that she was to take a break from the sport.

'There are moments in life when we must face choices that are difficult, and sometimes it is tough to escape them,' she said. 'Triathlon has always been part of my life, and, despite the anguish I feel in making this decision, I think it is the best way to preserve the past.' At the time the Perosinho prodigy said it would be a temporary hiatus but four years later the triathlon world is still awaiting the return of Vanessa de Sousa Fernandes.

△ The 2007 ITU World Cup in Rhodes, a season in which Fernandes dominated Olympic-distance racing

▽ Fernandes at the 2008 Mooloolaba ITU World Cup race, where she would be beaten by a familiar foe in Emma Snowsill

Bevan Docherty

△ Two-time Olympic medallist Bevan Docherty takes victory at the Edmonton ITU World Cup in 2007

Highlights

- ITU World Champion, 2004

- Olympic Games, 2004, silver

- Commonwealth Games, 2006, silver

Anyone wanting to witness the brilliance of this Kiwi Olympian should tap the words 'Bevan Docherty sprint finish' into YouTube. The location, New Plymouth, might not roll off the tongue in the manner of Kona, Nice and Roth, but this North Island town was the setting for one of triathlon's most inspiring finishes. With 5km of the run left to go, a collection of the world's best athletes – including Kris Gemmell, Courtney Atkinson and Brad Kahlefeldt – came together to jostle for positions.

The sparring lasted until the finish line was just 300m from view, when home favourite Gemmell made a seemingly decisive break. The motorbike cameraman (90,000 viewers were watching on the ITU's website) followed Gemmell to the edge of the blue carpet when – with a running gait not unlike the Mercury Man in *Terminator 2* – Docherty came from nowhere to power past his stunned compatriot on the blind side and win by 3 seconds. After nearly two hours of racing, Docherty's sprint earned him a healthy share of the $100,000 prize pot and has since garnered 500,000 views. It also typified the determination and athletic prowess of one of triathlon's most consistent performers.

Born in Taupo on New Zealand's North Island in 1977, Docherty (whose sister Fiona was to become a World Duathlon Champion) began his immersion in triathlon in 1994 as he 'needed a break from running,' having represented New Zealand at cross-country. Coming 21st at the ITU Junior Worlds in 1997 barely hinted at things to come, and by the turn of the century Docherty was regularly placing on the podium in ITU cup races around the globe. A disappointing 42nd at the 2002 ITU World Championships in Cancún was followed by the most successful period of Docherty's short-course career: he rarely finished off the podium in 2003 and then hit the peak of his powers in 2004.

He went into the 2004 ITU World Championships in Madeira as one of the favourites. The race would become an ITU World Championship classic; from a field containing past and future world-beaters Tim Don, Hamish Carter and Javier Gomez, only Docherty and Ivan Rana broke the 30min barrier on the run. It came down to a sprint finish on the blue carpet, where the 6ft 2in Docherty edged his Spanish rival by one second to take his only ITU World Championship title.

Three months later, under 29°C heat in Athens at triathlon's second Olympic Games appearance, it was Docherty's turn to be out-sprinted, Kiwi compatriot Hamish Carter breaking free with 500m to go and edging him into silver by just 6 seconds. Defeated but not dejected, Docherty would later rank the result as the greatest of his career.

That New Plymouth sprint finish aside, the year 2005 was a post-Olympic comedown for Docherty, but he fared better in 2006, taking silver behind the Aussie Brad Kahlefeldt at the Commonwealth Games in Melbourne. Seven podiums in 10 races followed in 2007 before another Olympic year, with the world's eyes turning to Beijing and triathlon's third appearance at the Games.

Docherty went into the race in fine fettle, scooping silver behind Gomez at the ITU Worlds in Vancouver. Beijing would witness another

△ Docherty at the 2008 ITU World Cup race in Kitzbühel, a month before taking Olympic bronze in Beijing

Olympic classic, with four contenders – Docherty, Simon Whitfield, Javier Gómez and the unfancied Jan Frodeno vying for triathlon immortality late in the run. If the vast experience of former Olympic medallists Whitfield and Docherty was expected to prevail, the youthful Frodeno was having none of it; he pushed past his rivals to leave Whitfield and Docherty with the silver and bronze medals, respectively.

Docherty became a three-time Olympian at London 2012, placing 12th as an era ended for the likes of Docherty, Whitfield, Kahlefeldt and Gemmell. The new order of the Brownlees, Gómez and Co. was now firmly established. Immediately after the Olympics, Docherty was one of the first Olympic veterans to join the world of long-course racing. The America-based athlete immediately placed third at the 1.9km/90km/21.2km Ironman 70.3 World Championships in Las Vegas before successfully adapting his short-course powers into the slow-twitch endurance needed for 226km of racing by taking his first long-course victory at Ironman New Zealand in 2013. Stomach issues resulted in a DNF at his maiden Kona venture later that year, and following another DNF in Hawaii in 2014 the BeeDoc announced his retirement from professional triathlon in January 2015.

◁ After exiting the ITU's draft-legal racing, Docherty made a winning start to his long-distance career

Mike Pigg

Highlights

- Ironman World Championships, silver, 1988

- Xterra World Champion, 1997

- Four-time USA National Champion

▷ Mike Pigg broke the Big Four's dominance of the sport in the late eighties

Chris McCormack has labelled him the most hard-core triathlete who ever lived, while Simon Lessing ranks him with Brad Beven and Spencer Smith as the toughest competitors he ever faced. Even his name sounds cool. So what is it about Mike Pigg that earns him such devotion amongst triathletes?

Pigg was raised in Arcata, a college town in Humboldt County on the north Californian coast (he still lives five miles north of Arcata in McKinleyville). 'I wanted to be outside. It was calling me all the time,' he has said. In his youth he was a competitive swimmer and was soon earning money assisting a mechanic at a trucking company, cleaning the workshop and changing tyres, already demonstrating a work ethic

that would take him to within two minutes of Ironman Hawaii glory.

Cross-country running was his passion during his college years, but he was lured to triathlon, watching highlights of the 1983 Ironman Hawaii, where he caught sight of Dave Scott.

He was so fit. His ribs were showing. And he had these big old lats sitting on top of his ribs. You could see the full anatomy of his legs. He was just doing the ultimate challenge, challenging the whole body, and that intrigued me from the start.

A move to full-time triathlon soon followed, with an average training week consisting of swimming 20,000m, riding 350km and running up to 80km. In his first year as a pro in 1985, he finished fourth at the inaugural Ironman in New Zealand. The same year saw the first of five consecutive adventures on the Big Island in Hawaii, when he finished seventh in a race won by Scott Tinley. Thereafter he achieved a steady progression in Hawaii, finishing 9th in 1986, 4th in 1987 and 2nd in 1988, in what would – with both Dave Scott and Mark Allen out of the reckoning – remains his best shot of scooping the big prize. Pigg's bad luck was that another member of the Big Four, Scott Molina, was on hand to edge him on the run by just 2:11mins (at that time the second-closest men's finish in the Hawaii event's history). Pigg's 8:33hrs would have been a winning time in all but one of Hawaii's previous editions.

As Pigg was reaching the peak of his powers in Hawaii, a bacterial infection hit him, and he was unable to fuel sufficiently on the fly. Just as Mark

Allen and Dave Scott were rewriting the record books, Pigg struggled round Kona to finish 15th in 1989. *Competitor* magazine founder Bob Babbitt is just one industry titan who believes Pigg was destined for Kona glory. 'If he didn't have the digestive problem, could he have won Hawaii? No question.'

While he was trying to deal with his digestive difficulty, Pigg took a four-year sabbatical from Hawaii. Far from taking a break from triathlon, though, he was already experiencing huge success in Olympic-distance racing. His fearsome bike prowess blitzed the 40km bike leg to win him 15 of his 20 races in 1988 (he is said to have won over 50% of his 150 career races) and four USA National Championships. His short but sweet ITU career saw him post the fastest bike split of the day in the 1990 and 1991 ITU World Championships (he finished 11th and 3rd, respectively). 'Knocking off the Big Four one at a time,' he beat Greg Welch by just one second to win the 1991 ITU World Cup race at a classic in St Croix that was the ITU's first-ever ITU World

Cup race; Mark Allen followed 3 minutes later. He is still believed to hold the record for ascending St Croix's notorious Beast climb.

Pigg would return to Hawaii for his fifth and final time in 1993, finishing a dejecting 16th to just beat Paula Newby-Fraser to the line. However as with Brad Beven, the lack of a major championship win has only heightened his cult athlete appeal. And Pigg himself is philosophical about his near-misses on the lava fields of Hawaii. 'I don't have nightmares about it. My philosophy is you have to give it your 100 percent, and you're a winner. That was my 100 percent.'

A father of twin girls, Pigg has intermittently dipped his toe back into triathlon in the years since he terrified athletes on the bike in his pomp in the 1980s and 1990s, but he has largely preferred marathons, occasional adventure races and coaching basketball to the world of multisport. And what does this hard-core, pedal-to-the-metal AC/DC-loving cult hero currently do as a day job? He sells real estate. Proving that sometimes it's better to print the legend than the fact …

△ Pigg was a world-class and much-feared cyclist, yet stomach issues were his downfall at Ironman Hawaii

△ The popular and powerful Pigg aboard a Softride tri-bike

The Triathletes
Eneko Llanos

Three-time XTERRA World Champion, ITU Long Distance World Champion, Ironman Lanzarote and Ironman European Champion winner and a double Olympian. So why is Eneko Llanos still under the radar when it comes to triathlon greats? Perhaps it's his unassuming personality or that his pure longevity has ensured he'll never be the hot new kid on the block. Or maybe, just maybe, it's down to the painful truth that – despite near misses – Ironman World Championship glory has so far eluded him.

Born in 1976 in Vitoria-Gasteiz, the capital of the Basque country in northern Spain, Eneko

▽ Llanos on the bike at the Ironman Asia Pacific Championships in 2013

Llanos Burguera was quickly thrust into a sporting life. Hiking by three, summer holidays spent scaling the Pyrenees into his teens and a promising career in Basque *pelota* were his prelude to multisport.

I grew up two hours from the Pyrenees, so I spent plenty of time in the mountains. I was involved in many different sports like judo, trekking, swimming, rock climbing and Basque pelota, where you play against another player and hit a ball with your hand against a wall. I also owned one of the first mountain bikes in my city.

In 1992 his brother, fellow pro Hektor, introduced Eneko to triathlon, and one of the sport's longest careers would begin. Throughout the nineties Eneko's ITU career was modest, punctuated by the odd top ten performance and 23rd position at triathlon's Olympic debut in Sydney 2000. The first major result of his career was a win at the ITU Long Distance World Championships in 2003, beating a field containing Normann Stadler and Torbjørn Sindballe. The first of his three Xterra World Championship titles followed in October, with two more off-road world titles won in 2004 and 2009.

After taking silver at the 2004 ETU European Championships (9 seconds behind Rasmus Henning) and 20th at the 2004 Olympics in Athens, a move to long-course racing was inevitable.

After the 2004 Olympics I started Ironman, and it took me a while to adjust to the training. I didn't finish my first two Ironman

races and I also had another really bad DNF at Ironman Canada. We [Llanos and his then coach/training pioneer, Iñigo Mujika] questioned whether we had taken the right decision, but we knew that it was just a matter of time. Soon I would finish second at Ironman Western Australia in 2005.

Llanos's first Ironman win would come at Lanzarote in 2007, and it made him the first Spanish man to win the race on his wife's home island. To date, his big chance at Kona glory came in 2008. 'That was the big chance. It was close, really close,' says Llanos ruefully today. Llanos left T2 with a four-minute lead over the Australian Craig Alexander but would lose his advantage to trail him home by 6 minutes.

Stomach problems led to a disappointing 14th on 'a very bad day,' at Hawaii in 2009, but a win at the maiden Abu Dhabi International Triathlon in 2010 saw him take a healthy share of the $250,000 prize pot back to the Basque country. Llanos would win the ETU Long

Distance Triathlon European Championships in his hometown in 2010 before joining new coach Dave Scott in late 2012. The results were instant, with the 2013 season witnessing wins at the Ironman Asia-Pacific Championships in Melbourne and the Ironman European Championships in Frankfurt, yet his Kona frustrations continued with an 11th position in October.

A vegetarian for the past two decades ('It's for moral reasons, and it's been good for me. When you become vegetarian you start taking care of what you eat,' he says), Llanos came home third at Challenge Roth in 2014, shaping up smartly for another assault on the podium at Ironman Hawaii. But come October, his Kona curse struck again. 'He was in good shape, but he then had a cold, which turned into a fever and compromised his preparation and race,' says Dave Scott. 'It was catastrophic for him, as he'd been in great shape in the two months before the race, and the athletes knew he would have been a force to be reckoned with. It was wickedly frustrating.'

At 38, Llanos finds time is running out for him on the Big Island, yet Scott remains upbeat. 'Kona is a different beast, and the temperament is different. But I'd like him back in Kona, he has good Spanish blood and he's done it before in hot races. I've seen his numbers in training and I'm optimistic that he can take the day in Hawaii.'

◁ 2013 was a high for the Spanish athlete, winning major Ironmans at Frankfurt and here at Melbourne

▽ Celebrating his Melbourne victory. A gold in Hawaii is still missing from the Llanos medal collection

The Triathletes
Dave Scott

▷ Dave Scott has been a formidable force in triathlon almost from the get-go, winning Ironman Hawaii a record six times

Six-time Ironman World Champion, coach, guru, inspiration, influence, innovator, statesman, Iron War protagonist ... Dave Scott has been a towering presence in triathlon since the dawn of the sport. Arguably, no other person has been as influential in establishing Ironman in the worldwide sporting consciousness as this Californian. His rip-roaring Kona victories, epic battles with Mark Allen, unparalleled pain threshold, even his rinsing of cottage cheese, all have gone down in triathlon folklore. Quite simply, he is The Man.

Born on 4 January 1954, Scott grew up in Davis, a college town 20km west of Sacramento. By his teens, his relentless appetite for sport saw him starring in baseball's Little Leagues, on the basketball court and in the swimming pool, with his parents fitting an 11m pool into their garden to keep their endurance devotee active when the local club was shut.

After graduating in physical education at UC Davis, Scott started a swim club in Davis that quickly gained a very large membership. Scott's first triathlon came as early as 1976, when his fitness and endurance base earned him second place at the Turkey Triathlon in San Francisco. Scott's prize for his feat was, naturally, a frozen turkey, appropriately perhaps for the 182cm athlete, who was already becoming infamous for his ferocious appetite combined with an informed approach to food. He consumed 25 pieces of fruit a day and rinsed his cottage cheese to remove the excess fat in a bid to fuel the reported 5,000 calories he burned each day in training.

After finishing ninth at the Waikiki Roughwater Swim in Hawaii in 1978, Scott was handed a flyer for the second-ever Ironman Hawaii race by the race creator John Collins. Intrigued but no more, he eventually threw the flyer away and moved on to other things; subsequently, though, he saw Barry McDermott's famous account of the 1979 race in *Sports Illustrated* magazine and vowed to return to Hawaii in 1980. After performing a mock Ironman in training, Scott obliterated the competition in February 1980, winning by over an hour and becoming the first man to go under 10 hours (9:24:33), and all in front of the ABC *Wide World of Sports* cameras. The Man nickname was born.

Injury caused him to miss the 1981 Hawaii event (the first to be held in Kona); then, in February 1982, he saw his course record broken by the new star of 226km racing, Scott Tinley, to whom he finished second. That loss lit a fire in Scott for the next Ironman Hawaii event, held in October 1982 as the race was moved to the autumn.

Highlights

- Ironman World Champion, 1980, 1982 (Oct), 1983, 1984, 1986, 1987
- Ironman World Championships, silver, 1982 (Feb), 1989, 1994
- Ironman Japan Champion, 1989

Back then no one could control my fate better than myself. I didn't have a coach or a mentor, and I found that I was my hardest judge. I didn't have the tools that athletes have now. I didn't have heart rate monitors or a power meter. So I used my wristwatch, so I would smash everything based on my watch.

And smash everything Scott did, beating Tinley by 20 minutes to reclaim his Hawaii crown in an event that also featured other future Big Four members Scott Molina and Mark Allen. That win started a trail-blazing winning streak; Scott was unbeaten at Hawaii until 1989 (though he boycotted the 1985 event due to the lack of a prize purse and missed 1988's through injury).

As well as demonstrating his athletic strength across all three disciplines, his victories in Hawaii showcased Scott's famed mental fortitude and never-say-die attitude: in 1983 he made up a deficit on the bike to beat Tinley by just 33secs; he broke the 9hr barrier to pummel Allen in 1984, did the same again in under 8:30hr in 1986, and passed his increasingly despondent rival with 7km to go in 1987. And all this despite being the sport's biggest scalp:

'I knew at Hawaii I was the bumblebee; I was the bullseye. They wanted to knock off Dave Scott, but I sensed it and relished it. Even in 1989's duel, I liked my position throughout the race – apart from at the finish line.'

In that 1989 classic the 35-year-old Scott produced a 2:41hr marathon on the way to smashing his course record by 18mins with a time of 8:10:13. Unfortunately for him, though, Allen – five years his junior – had matched him every stroke, pedal and stride for 223km before breaking free with 3km to go to win his first Kona title at the eighth time of asking. But, looking back, Scott says,

Coming across the line, I thought, 'Damn,' I hate to lose this one'. In retrospect, it was a stellar day for both of us. Over the years, the numbers that we did have stood the test of time. And if we had the faster equipment the athletes have today, we would've gone a helluva lot faster.

Scott's grip on the Ironman Hawaii title may have ended on that unforgettable day, now known as the Iron War, but he returned to Hawaii in 1994 at the age of 40 to push Greg Welch all the way and finish second. Then two years later he clocked a 2:45hr marathon to come fifth.

Since he retired from elite racing, Scott has become an elite coach (his athletes have included Chrissie Wellington, Rachel Joyce, Eneko Llanos and his son Drew, a rising American star of Ironman), a motivational speaker, a certifier of coaches, commentator and all-round inspiration. Is the lure of racing Hawaii still there, though?

Yeah, if someone paid me a lot of money! Seriously, though, I've got a host of injury things. I was hit by a car five years ago and got hit by a truck again recently! So I wouldn't want to go in and do it haphazardly at my seasoned age – I'd want to go in and be respectful. So I'll say it's always open.

▽ After a five-year hiatus, Scott returned to Hawaii in 1994 to finish second at the age of 40

Michellie Jones

△ Michellie Jones' consistency across all three disciplines saw her take both ITU and Ironman world titles

Triathlon Club while studying physical education at university in Wollongong.

Jones qualified for the 1989 Worlds in Avignon but couldn't afford the flight ticket; by 1990, though, she was making a living from the sport and represented Australia at the ITU Worlds in Orlando. She won her first ITU World Championship title at Muskoka, Canada, in 1992 by virtue of her strength across all three disciplines. A year later she repeated her win in Salford, England, this time producing the fastest bike split of the day by a staggering four minutes and then overtaking America's Karen Smyers late on the run to win by two seconds. Says Smyers today:

> I loved racing Michellie Jones because she never seemed to have a bad day. On a flat course, I couldn't catch her on the bike but I could sometimes beat her if we started the run together. I had boundless energy at Salford and was sure I could outrace her in the sprint … and she zoomed right past me.

Over the next four years Jones stayed away from the ITU circuit, largely in protest at the implementation of the draft-legal format in 1995, yet, basing herself in San Diego, she racked up the career wins in America with seven victories at the Chicago Triathlon, eight Escape from Alcatraz titles and seven St Anthony's Triathlon wins.

An Xterra world title in 1996 proved that she could handle all-things off-road as well, and a return to the ITU circuit in 1997 produced plenty of World Cup victories, if no more ITU World Championship titles.

Michellie Jones is reported to have more career wins than any other female athlete in history, with an extraordinary 175 career wins. Most athletes will never enter 175 races in a lifetime, so to win that many testifies to the all-round brilliance, consistency and versatility of the ITU, Ironman and Xterra world champion.

Michellie and her twin sister Gabby were born on 6 September 1969 in the Sydney suburb of Fairfield. As with Brad Beven (another world-beating Aussie born 12 days later), a rural farming upbringing instilled a love of the outdoors, and she was swimming and running (not to mention developing a still-standing love of riding horses) from a young age. She was initially identified as a talented race-walker, but she joined the Cronulla

Highlights

- Ironman World Champion, 2006
- ITU World Champion, 1992, 1993
- 175 career wins

To say that the Australian women dominated the ITU circuit in the nineties would be an egregious understatement. They won seven of the decade's ITU World Championships, with titles shared out between Jones, Emma Carney, Joanne King, Jackie Gallagher and Loretta Harrop. This dominance peaked at the 1999 ITU Worlds in Montreal, where the Aussie gang took the top five places, with Harrop out-swimming her compatriots to win the title.

Yet the rivalry pushed the athletes to such a level that few other nations got a look-in during this period. As Jones explained to the ITU in 2014:

A lot of people don't realize just how strong the Australian women were in the nineties and going into 2000. And it wasn't just two or three, or five or six of us. We got the first five places at the ITU World Championships in 1999, with all of us vying for just three Olympic spots.

Make the team Jones did, winning the Sydney World Cup races/test events in May 1999 and April 2000 to establish herself as the favourite going into triathlon's first ever Olympic Games race on 16 September 2000 in Sydney Harbour. On home soil and in front of an expectant crowd, Jones and Switzerland's Brigitte McMahon would be level pegging throughout until the Swiss broke free late in the run to break Australian hearts and become triathlon's first Olympic champion. McMahon's victory may not have been the bolt from the blue some have suggested (she had beaten Jones in Lausanne a month before), although she never scaled such heights again and retired from the elite circuit in 2005 after testing positive for blood-boosting EPO.

'Hopefully I'll be at the next Olympics,' said an elated and defiant Jones at the Sydney finish line. It wasn't to be, though; for Athens 2004 the Triathlon Australia selectors overlooked Jones (and Emma Snowsill) in favour of the rookie athlete Maxine Seear. Jones's omission, overlooking her victory in the Athens test event, led her to move to non-drafting long-course racing (despite vowing never to do such a thing after witnessing the scenes in the Ironman Hawaii medical tent as a spectator in 1995).

△ The familiar sight of Jones celebrating on the blue carpet, with the Aussie racking up 175 career wins

Famous for her training volumes and professionalism, Jones was quick to score success in Ironman, winning her debut race at Florida in 2004. As Craig Alexander, who trained with her in America, noted:

Michellie had good genetics but she also had an unbelievable work ethic. She was smart, she ate well and knew when to take a day off. A lot of us thought we were professional in our training but she brought that to the sport. She was the ultimate professional.

Her Kona debut in 2005 was a classic. Guided by her coach and husband Pete Coulson, himself a track cycling champion, the Hawaii rookie did the unthinkable and outdid the reigning Queen of the Hawaii bike course, Natascha Badmann. Jones left T2 with a 10-minute lead over the Swiss star, yet couldn't hold her off on the run, where Badmann produced her fastest marathon run in Kona to win her sixth and final title.

A year later Jones was back in Hawaii to become one of the small number of women to win both ITU and Ironman world titles, her convincing victory founded on a dominant 54min swim. This was the last major title of Jones' career, yet she's still racing and winning today as a coach and age-group athlete. That and riding her beloved horse.

The Triathletes
Erin Baker

The life of combative and combustible Kiwi athlete Erin Baker has been punctuated by controversy – whether throwing explosive devices during the South African rugby tour of New Zealand in the apartheid days, fighting gender inequality in triathlon or railing at the 'useless corrupt old men' at the International Olympic Committee. Sometimes her rebellious ways have overshadowed her significant (indeed landmark) achievements on and off the race course. These include becoming the first female ITU world champion in 1989, the first antipodean winner at Ironman Hawaii in 1987 and being cited as a major factor in the sport's establishment of equal prize pots for men and women.

Erin Margaret Baker was born in 1961 in the small South Island town of Kaiapoi on New Zealand's eastern coast. From 'a big, working-class family', she was one of eight children, with her sisters Kathy and Maureen winning national titles in swimming and aerobics respectively and Philippa being a world champion rower. Baker's first sporting successes came in cross-country running, and she proved so fast in her debut race that her family missed seeing her cross the finish line by 15 minutes.

Her first brush with infamy came in 1981, when she was convicted of throwing explosive devices while protesting against apartheid during the South African Rugby team tour of New Zealand. This was to affect her triathlon career because she was banned from entering the United States for some years, and so could not compete in competitions there, including Ironman Hawaii.

Baker's first tri race and victory came in 1984 in Sydney, where she was working as a radiographer, and a year later she would take the first of her three titles at the middle-distance Nice International Triathlon. Wins at Ironman New Zealand in 1986 and 1987 followed, and then, after lobbying by the race organizers, her first venture on the Big Island of Hawaii came in October 1987. In the tightest battle for podium places that the event had witnessed, Baker fought off previous winners Sylviane Puntous and Paula Newby-Fraser deep into the run, becoming the first athlete from Down Under to win the Hawaii crown and smashing Newby-Fraser's course record by 14 minutes in the process.

A rejuvenated Newby-Fraser got her revenge in 1988 when she reclaimed her title, but the rivalry between the pair extended beyond the Ali'i Drive tarmac. Newby-Fraser's formative years, spent in South Africa, reportedly made her an object of Baker's political fire. As Newby-Fraser told the American journalist Timothy Carlson in 2010, 'She dehumanised me. To her, I just represented the South African government. I took the brunt of all her political stance against the government. I became the scapegoat.' Baker's activism would lead to countless positive developments throughout her career, however: for example, forcing the Nice International Triathlon organizers into an about-face over their policy for only handing the male winners a new car at the event. The former ITU President, Les McDonald, also sees one of the reasons for the move to equal prize money in the sport as being down to athletes like Baker failing to take no for an answer.

Baker's versatility across all distances propelled her to numerous titles across all levels of the sport and, after being talked out of retirement in 1988 by her future husband and fellow triathlon legend Scott Molina, in 1989 she joined Mark Allen as the inaugural winner of the debut ITU World Championships in Avignon, France. She was now famous on the circuit for her relentless training around Boulder, Colorado. Dave Scott was just one athlete astonished by her pace and mileage. 'Erin Baker was phenomenal,' he says

today. 'She'd go out on rides with the men, and it'd take everything we had to drop her!'

In early 1990 Baker took gold at triathlon's demonstration event at the Commonwealth Games and broke the course record at Ironman Canada after a 2:49hr marathon run split, faster than every man that day bar Molina. In October her rivalry with Newby-Fraser was rekindled in Hawaii. This time it was Baker's day, and she produced a record 3:04hr marathon as athletes dropped like flies in some of the hottest race-day conditions Hawaii has ever witnessed.

The 1990 title was Baker's last in Hawaii, but she continued to rack up the victories across every level of multisport, winning the ITU World Duathlon Championships in 1991 and Powerman Zofingen in 1992 and 1994 to amass a total of 104 wins in the 121 races she entered, including four wins at Ironman New Zealand and two at Ironman Canada. In 1994, soon after the birth of her first child with Molina, she hung up her tri-suit for good, yet the accolades kept coming. *Triathlete* magazine named her their 'Triathlete of the Decade' in 1999, adding, 'We've stopped trying to figure Erin out. We just accept her as the best female triathlete that ever lived,' and in 2014 she became one of the first athletes inducted into the ITU's Hall of Fame.

◁△ Erin Baker had incredible versatility across all distances, winning both ITU, Ironman and duathlon world titles

▽ Baker won 104 of her 121 career races, with the pinnacle being her two victories at the Ironman Worlds in Hawaii

The Triathletes
Chrissie Wellington

Highlights

- Ironman World Champion, 2007, 2008, 2009, 2011
- Challenge Roth winner, 2009, 2010, 2011
- Ironman world record holder, South Africa 2011

△ Wellington becomes the fastest Iron women in history at Roth in 2011

'I want to cross the finish line feeling like I've given it physically and mentally absolutely everything. This year, I couldn't have given any more.' After three wins in a row at the Ironman World Championships in Hawaii (2007–9), that seems a strange thing for British racing great Chrissie Wellington to say in 2011 – but she had finally got her wish.

Two weeks before the 2011 race, the 34-year-old was in the 'best shape of my life'; then a training ride crash left her with a battered body and a torn pectoral muscle. Ten days before the race, her infected leg was twice its normal size. With five days to go, she had to be lifted, weeping, out of the pool by her coach, Dave Scott, and boyfriend, Tom Lowe.

In Kona on 8 October Chrissie (who hadn't started in 2010, due to pneumonia) was four minutes behind reigning Ironman world champ Mirinda Carfrae after the swim in Kailua Bay. Suffering from hip, back and calf problems, she plugged away on the bike and entered T2 in sixth, three minutes ahead of run course record-holder Carfrae.

Wellington went through the first half marathon in 1:22hrs before Carfrae started chipping away at the deficit. 'Chrissie's body was finally starting to shut down. She just had to hang on,' Dave Scott observed from the sidelines. Inspired by Rudyard Kipling's 'If' inscribed on her water bottle, she dug deeper into her mental and physical reserves than ever before.

Only at the top of Palani Hill late in the run could Chrissie start to acknowledge her victory. In spite of the physiological and psychological toil, her 8:55:08 time was only a minute off her own course record. 'Hopefully this has shown that I'm human,' she said after reaching the finish and before being hooked up to an IV drip (and then later devouring the best chicken nuggets and chips that Kona could offer).

That epic encounter was to be Wellington's Ironman finale: her unprecedented thirteenth victory in thirteen Iron-distance starts. 'As I crossed the line I felt a weight lift off my shoulders, and not just because I'd won: because I'd defied what I thought I could achieve', as she wrote in her retirement statement.

If Chrissie Wellington's career was relatively short in comparison to fellow Hawaii immortal Paula Newby-Fraser's, her lasting impact was incalculable. She showed the political passion of Erin Baker when promoting women's sporting equality and the smiles of Natascha Badmann on the race course, and she proved that the girls could beat the boys at sport with her reliable ability to 'chick' all but the very top male athletes. She also gave Britain's female Iron contingent a shot in the arm. Before her 2007 Hawaii victory, there'd been just one British medal in 29 Hawaii editions; since 2007 the British women have never been off the podium.

Born in 1977, Chrissie had a sporty childhood in rural Norfolk, swimming for her local club in her teens. After gaining an MA in development studies she worked as a government adviser for international development policy at the age of 25. A sabbatical followed in 2004, soon after her first triathlon at Dorney Lake (where she finished third), which involved moving to Nepal to oversee a community-based project in Kathmandu. Here she would embark on off-road runs and mountain biking in Nepal's hilly terrain, reaping the benefits of training at altitude and once completing a 1,400km journey to Mount Everest's Base Camp.

She returned to her development job in 2006 and picked up her age-group triathlon career again, winning the Olympic-distance Shropshire Triathlon to qualify for the ITU Age-group World Championships in Lausanne, Switzerland, that September. In an early example of her famous motivation, she trained 20 hours a week for the race – which paid off when the 29-year-old won by over four minutes.

In January 2007, Wellington made the life-changing decision to pursue a professional triathlon career, joining Team TBB under the watch of the tough Aussie coach Brett Sutton. Although she initially struggled in the ultra-competitive environment, she won a handful of short-course races in early 2007, before taking on the Alpe d'Huez Triathlon in August – which she won by 29 minutes.

Sutton sent her off to Korea later that month to compete in her debut Ironman; in a sign of things to come, she won by 50 minutes and beat all but six of the men. That win enabled her to qualify for Kona in October, where she went into the race a relative novice on a triathlon bike. Some 9:08hrs after the starter's horn, Welly had ripped up the Hawaii rule book, winning on her first Kona venture and smiling her way through the marathon in 2:59:58 – the second-fastest women's Kona run of all time – to produce arguably Hawaii's biggest upset.

The secret was now out, but Wellington's gold rush continued in 2008. She won Ironman Australia, the Ironman European Championships and returned to Alpe d'Huez to come second only to the men's winner. On her return to Hawaii, she suffered a puncture while leading the field on the bike course and lost 10 minutes to her rivals. After Australia's Rebekah Keat threw her own CO_2 cartridge to the stricken Wellington, the Brit once again picked off the field to take her second Hawaii crown with a 15-minute advantage.

In 2009 she left Team TBB (eventually settling on six-time Hawaii champion Dave Scott as her coach). She won Ironman Australia again, before her strength across all disciplines enabled her to break the women's Iron-distance world record at Challenge Roth with an overall time of 8:31:59. At Hawaii, her 8:54:02 time smashed Newby-Fraser's 1992 course record and got her home 19 minutes ahead of Carfrae.

A second Roth record followed in 2010 before that Kona DNS in October. Showing the resolve of a champion, six weeks later Wellington set the official Ironman world record at Ironman Arizona with 8:36:13 and then beat it at Ironman South Africa in April 2011 with a 8:33:56 finish. Another visit to Roth brought more Iron-distance record-breaking (a still-standing time of 8:18:13) as she came fifth overall and posted the day's second fastest overall marathon of 2:44:35.

Three months later, she produced her Ironman farewell in that unforgettable, stoic triumph of mental fortitude over a far-from-willing body.

△ Chrissie was undefeated in 13 long-distance events, with four of those coming in the Ironman World Champs in Kona

▽ Never one to shirk a challenge, Chrissie takes on 2006's Coast to Coast adventure race in New Zealand

The Triathletes
The Brownlees

▷ The Yorkshire brothers control the pace at the 2012 Olympic Games in London

Highlights

Alistair Brownlee
- Olympic Champion, 2012
- Commonwealth Games Champion, 2014
- ITU World Champion, 2009, 2011
- ETU European Champion, 2010, 2011, 2014

Jonathan Brownlee
- ITU World Champion, 2012
- ITU World Sprint Champion, 2010, 2011
- Olympic Games, bronze, 2012

With 13 ITU World Championships across all levels, five European Championships, and Olympic gold and bronze medals between them, the Brownlee brothers each warrant an entry to themselves in this book. Yet the story of how two young brothers from Yorkshire rose to the top of the triathlon tree to become genuine household names in the UK is just too good not to tell jointly.

Alistair and Jonathan Brownlee were born two years apart, in 1988 and 1990 respectively, in West Yorkshire. The brothers' sporting pedigree was incalculably shaped by their surroundings, with their health-conscious parents (swimmer mum Cath is a GP, runner dad Keith a paediatrician) encouraging the boys and youngest brother Edward to venture into the nearby Yorkshire

Dales for bike rides and off-road runs in their formative years. Alistair was already entering cross-country events at the age of six, with Jonny setting records in the pool at under-10 level.

Multisport was soon to follow, with the duo encouraged into the sport by their triathlete uncle Simon Hearnshaw. At the age of six, Jonny was already competing with Alistair in swimming galas, and by the age of eight he'd followed him into triathlon. Both of them won their categories at a Nottingham children's triathlon in 1997, and their education at the famously sporty Bradford Grammar School (and, crucially, a partnership with triathlon coaches Jack Maitland and Malcolm Brown) hastened their multisport progression.

By the age of 17, Alistair was the 2006 ITU Junior World Champion after beating his future

58 The Triathletes

pro opponent, Russia's Alexander Brukhankov by 13 seconds in Lausanne, Switzerland. The brothers' reputation for being tough as old boots, despite their boyish looks, was also formed early in their career, with Alistair setting a course record at the Helvellyn Triathlon in 2007, and Jonny, although officially too young to appear on the starting list, using the race as a training event and unofficially finishing in sixth after 77km of the hardest kilometres in British triathlon.

Alistair's elite debut came at the Salford ITU World Cup race in 2007; he came 20th in a race won by Javier Gómez. The U23 World title would follow in 2008 before his breakout performance at the 2008 Olympics. The then 20-year-old Leeds University Sports Science student (he had abandoned studying medicine at Cambridge to focus on triathlon) was leading with 3km to go before running out of steam and finishing 12th.

The brave and bold style of racing endeared him to the watching masses, however, and started a purple patch of form with few peers in the sport, winning fifteen out of his next twenty ITU races to take two ITU World Championships and a duo of European Championship titles.

The 21st race in the sequence was the 2012 Olympics, held on home soil in London's Hyde Park on 7 August 2012. On that famous day for British triathlon everything went to plan for the elder Brownlee and he shook off Gómez on the final run lap to become Britain's first Olympic triathlon champion after a 29:07mins 10km run split (it would have been even faster if he hadn't ambled the final 200m with the Union Jack in his hands).

Jonny also experienced a dramatic day in Hyde Park. With an U23 World title and a duo of sprint ITU world titles in the bag, the younger Brownlee went into the Olympics as the third favourite behind Ali and Gómez, midway through an incredible run of consistency that saw the history graduate on the podium at 25 consecutive races from July 2010 until May 2014. After the 1.5km Serpentine swim at the Olympics he mounted his bike a split-second too early and so had to take a 15-second penalty during the run, leaving him

27 seconds adrift of Gómez and all but confirming his third-place bronze position. However, two months later in Auckland Jonny would be crowned with the ITU World Championship title, the biggest crown of his career to date. He ended the year by moving out of the house he shared with Alistair in Bramhope, near Leeds (though he only went 500m down the road). The duo became a walking, talking embodiment of the Olympic legacy, with their beginner-friendly Brownlee Triathlon races drawing in thousands of newcomers to the sport since their launch in 2013 and the brothers making countless mainstream television appearances and releasing a well-received autobiography.

The brave and bold style of racing endeared Alistair to the watching masses, however, and started a purple patch of form with few peers in the sport, winning fifteen out of his next twenty ITU races to take two ITU World Championships and a duo of European Championship titles.

Britain's four-time ITU world champion, Simon Lessing, was just one athlete unanimous in his praise for Alistair after the Commonwealths in Glasgow:

The true mark of a champion is an athlete who can offer consistency, and Alistair has proven that he can do that. I've always said it's easy to go and win one race or major title, it's very, very difficult to do that month after month, year after year.

△ Alistair becomes the first British athlete to take the Olympic Games triathlon gold

▽ Celebrating their 2012 Hyde Park heroics with their GB team-mate and domestique, Stu Hayes

Chris McCormack

△ Macca in his familiar role of being centre stage on the race circuit

Chris McCormack, known as Macca, is famed as a master tactician, triathlon historian, purveyor of pre-race words of warfare more akin to boxing, and one hell of an athletic performer. All these traits and more were evident on 9 October 2010, when the Australian multisport legend won his self-proclaimed masterpiece, the Ironman World Championships, his victory over Andreas Raelert being instantly labelled an Iron War for the twenty-first century.

Everything that has made him a fascinating, fearless and formidable presence on the triathlon circuit for two decades was distilled into that famous victory. But the seeds of success were planted in Hawaii twelve months before, with his disappoiting fourth place in the 2009 event. In his book, *I'm Here to Win*, Macca recalls how he began publicly recruiting strong bikers such as Timo Bracht, Marino Vanhoenacker and Faris Al Sultan to form an alliance with him on the bike leg in a

bid to topple the stronger runners – especially Australia's reigning Ironman world champ Craig Alexander – in the 2010 contest.

The unprecedented plan may have drawn criticism for not being in the spirit of the (individual) sport, yet on that suitably sticky day in Hawaii it came together. After a series of calculated bike surges throughout the 180km course the alliance had dealt with Alexander's chances of victory, creating for Macca a nine-minute advantage out of T2. His chief concern now was the presence of rising German superstar Raelert, two minutes behind him.

Raelert caught Macca with 5km of the run to go. After over seven hours and 221km of racing it would come down to a 5,000m duel between the proven winner and the German new kid on the block, four years Macca's junior. In one of the sport's most iconic moments, Macca turned to Raelert and said,

Highlights

- Ironman World Champion, 2007, 2010
- ITU World Champion, 1997
- Challenge Roth Champion, 2004, 2005, 2006, 2007

'Andreas, best of luck. No matter what happens here, you're a champion. May the best man win.'

A keen historian of the sport, Macca made his first move on the hill where Mark Allen broke Dave Scott in the original Iron War of 1989, but Raelert caught him again on the next crest at Palani. With just 1km to go, Raelert went to take cola at the aid station, and in that moment, Macca produced the decisive break, instantly opening up a 10m advantage.

The race was in the bag by the entrance of Ali'i Drive – what Macca labels the 'Champs-Élysées of triathlon' and a place where the Aussie dreamt of winning in his teenage years – with Macca crossing the line in 8:10:37 to win the greatest Ironman Hawaii race of the twenty-first century. 'A painter or a writer spends his whole career trying to create a masterpiece', writes Macca in *I'm Here to Win*. 'Kona 2010 was my masterpiece.'

Born in April 1973, Chris McCormack grew up in southern Sydney. Surfing was his first love but it was his early displays of running prowess that got him a scholarship at the University of New South Wales. Macca had been intrigued by triathlon when he annually watched the ABC *Wide World of Sports* highlights of Ironman Hawaii, and his interest was heightened when he developed a strong bond with prodigious swimmer Sean Maroney. Like teenage boys before and after him, Macca's first experiences in multisport came in a bid to impress the girls. 'I'd go to triathlons with Sean, and there'd be gorgeous girls in bikinis. The sun was shining, and I thought, this is the sport for me!'

The university running champ's first triathlon came in 1992, when he showed up at the Wollongong Triathlon and beat the nation's best junior athletes by virtue of a 31min 10km run split. More national success followed before the 20-year-old was selected for the Aussie junior squad at the 1993 ITU Worlds in Manchester, where he entered the home straight in second place ... only to be passed by two other competitors while he was reportedly getting girls' phone numbers from the watching crowd!

McCormack graduated with an economics degree in 1995, moved to France, joined the ITU circuit and rarely looked back, winning his first elite race as a wild-card entry at the 1996 ITU World Cup in Drummondville, Canada. The 1997 season would be his finest (and one of the finest ever) in Olympic-distance racing; becoming the only man to win the ITU World Cup series and the ITU World Championship title in the same season, the latter after producing the day's best 10km run split (29:32mins) to beat Hamish Carter, Brad Beven, Greg Welch and Greg Bennett.

He wasn't selected for his home Olympics in 2000 by Triathlon Australia (tragically, his mother passed away from cancer early in the year), yet he bounced back in style on the race course and, fired by his Olympic snub, won 32 races in America – including Alcatraz and Chicago – in an undefeated sequence until 2002. Then he turned his attention to Ironman, winning Ironman Australia on his long-course debut in April 2002: the first of four consecutive victories.

After narrowly losing a classic to Lothar Leder at Challenge Roth in 2003, Macca came back to dominate the German race with four straight victories, three of them under the magical eight-hour mark. Things at Hawaii weren't so easy for him. He arrived on a wave of hype (some of it self-generated) in 2002 and failed to finish; he came 59th in 2003 and failed to finish again in 2004. By chance, the race vehicle that picked Macca up after his 2004 defeat was being driven by one Mark Allen, who suggested to him that he should enter fewer Iron-distance races during the season. After that Macca went on to finish sixth in 2005, then second the following year – behind his new nemesis Normann Stadler (there was evidently no love lost between the two). Finally, he captured the Ironman Hawaii title in 2007 after outpacing Craig Alexander on the run.

Following his 2010 Hawaii victory Macca made an ill-fated attempt to qualify for the 2012 Olympics. Since then he has continued to be a major presence in the sport, keeping his 171,000 Twitter followers engrossed by tempting Lance Armstrong into a race contest, offering outspoken views on the sport, and travelling the world as a Challenge Family ambassador.

△ Ironman and ITU world champ Chris McCormack is one of the sport's true characters

▽ The Aussie hero is an ambassador for Challenge races, with multiple Challenge victories throughout his career

The Triathletes
Craig Alexander

If the 2010 Ironman World Championships were the career high for Chris McCormack, for his compatriot Craig Alexander they marked a rare Hawaiian low. McCormack's tactical masterstroke saw Alexander suffer on the bike and enter the run stage too far in arrears to win his third consecutive Ironman World Championship crown. The man known as Crowie would finish in fourth, hurt by McCormack's alliance and fearing his style of racing had been exposed as one-dimensional.

As one of the most consummate pro athletes ever to grace the sport, Crowie used that stinging defeat to come back stronger. Where lesser athletes might have thought about retirement, the 38-year-old ripped up his existing bike contract to join Specialized and sought added advice from Ironman Hawaii legend Dave Scott, especially in strength and conditioning. Fresh from winning his second Ironman 70.3 world title in September 2011, he returned to Hawaii a stronger all-round athlete in every area.

Eight hours, three minutes and 56 seconds after the starting horn on 8 October 2011 Crowie was leaping across the finish line (in a tribute to Aussie pioneer Greg Welch) as the Ironman World Champion once again. In the process he broke Luc Van Lierde's 15-year Kona course record, become the oldest ever winner of Hawaii and the first man in history to win Ironman and Ironman 70.3 titles in the same year. Key to his success was a bike split of 4:04hrs, one of the fastest ever seen in Hawaii and some 15-minutes faster than his 2010 time.

Craig Alexander was born in Sydney on 22 June 1973, just a couple of months after his future adversary McCormack. But where Macca would be as close to an overnight sensation as triathlon gets, Crowie's was a slower path to stardom. His early love was soccer.

In 1993 a hernia from his part-time labouring job saw Crowie unable to play soccer for six months, so the then physiotherapy student started jogging to keep in shape.

This was around the time that Greg Welch, Michellie Jones and the Australians were doing pretty well at the sport. I watched quite a bit on TV and began to read triathlon magazines. A mate from university said he'd get me started, and I bought a bike from a newspaper called the Trading Post *on the Thursday and I did my first triathlon at Kurnell on the Sunday. I loved it, I was hooked.*

Self-coached, as he still is, Crowie began writing his own training programmes. He was given a pro licence from Triathlon Australia after impressing at a Powerman duathlon in 1995 and raced his first elite event in October 1995 at the Sydney ITU World Cup. He finished eighth, just a second behind Aussie star Greg Bennett.

Even with the world's best athletes ahead of him in the pecking order, Crowie displayed some of his famous positivity during this period. 'I stayed mentally strong and I never became disheartened. I thought it was a massive advantage to be racing against these guys.' A key piece of advice came from Welch, who said that the best triathletes in the world are versatile across all distances; Crowie ran his first middle-distance race at the 1997 National Championships soon after, winning it and enjoying the 113km experience.

He graduated the same year and began to race in the French Grand Prix series, before returning to race in the televized Formula 1 Triathlon Series, back in Australia. Watching the Sydney Olympics in the flesh made Crowie determined to pursue both Commonwealth Games and Olympic places in 2002 and 2004 respectively, but a bad case of chickenpox led him to miss qualifying for the 2002 Games, speeding his move to long-course racing.

A move to America came in 2002, with a schedule of non-drafting and middle-distance races. 'It was the first time I felt like a professional triathlete. I made a lot of friends, trained with Michellie Jones and I never looked back,' says Crowie. His wife Neri had given birth to their daughter Lucy in May 2005, and financial security came quickly, with victory at the big-money Life Time Fitness race in Minnesota in July.

In 2006 Alexander won his first Ironman world title at the inaugural Ironman 70.3 World Championships in Clearwater, Florida. This was his first of three 70.3 World victories (and one of 26 Ironman 70.3 wins), and it automatically qualified him for the Ironman World Championships in Kailua-Kona, Hawaii in 2007.

He came in second on his debut in 2007, just four minutes behind McCormack. Soon, though, he was the King of Kona, with consecutive victories in 2008 and 2009, both won by outpacing his rivals on the run. Then McCormack outmanoeuvred him in 2010, but Crowie came back with his *annus mirabilis* in 2011, as we have seen.

He officially retired from Ironman racing in 2014 but that just marked his entry into triathlon coaching, via his business Sansego (= 'without ego') – the aptest of names for this truly humble, hugely talented and perennially popular triathlete.

◁ The Aussie star with his Specialized Shiv, the bike on which he broke the Ironman Hawaii course record

▽ Crowie is one of the most consummate professionals ever to grace the sport

The Triathletes
Scott Molina

▷ Scott Molina is the Big Four member who dominated short-course racing in the 1980s

▷▷△ Molina was a relentless trainer, which led to his 104 career victories across all distances

▷▷▽ The Californian wins the 1988 Ironman World Championships in Hawaii

Highlights

- Ironman World Champion, 1988

- USA Pro Championship titles, 1983, 1984, 1985, 1986, 1990 and 1994

- 104 career victories

Scott Molina is arguably the least well-known of the Big Four – Mark Allen, Dave Scott and Scott Tinley are the others – the Theodore Roosevelt to Dave Scott's George Washington in the Mount Rushmore of triathlon. All the same he was a fundamental member of that Earth-conquering quartet during the 1980s. His best-known victory may be his Ironman Hawaii title in 1988, but that was just one of his 104 pro career victories between 1982 and 1995; winner's trophies from Powerman Zofingen and Ultraman are also in the bumper trophy collection Molina shares with his fellow world-beater wife, Erin Baker.

Like Scott, Tinley and Allen, Molina was a Californian, born in Pittsburg CA in February 1960. Also like Tinley, he was part of a big family, one of seven siblings in a sporty household in the San Francisco Bay Area. He was already a strong swimmer and runner when attending the 1976 Montreal Olympics as a spectator and seeing Dave Scott winning the 1980 Ironman Hawaii on ABC's *Wide World of Sports* (has a television programme ever done more for a sport?) combined to enhance his professional athlete dreams.

Most of us are happy to just finish our first race without needing a safety canoe on the swim or a Portaloo visit during the run, but in his debut triathlon at Angwin, northern California, in 1980 Molina obliterated the field to win by a huge margin. Then, in his second race later that year, he used his swim/run background to finish third behind early stars Grant Boswell and Dean Harper at the middle-distance toughie Sierra

Nevada Triathlon, hastening his move to becoming a pro triathlete in 1982.

In 1982 Molina soon headed south to the triathlon epicentre of San Diego and hooked up with fellow Team J-David athletes Mark Allen and Scott Tinley. The trio trained together three times a day and became fast friends in Del Mar. If Dave Scott, who trained alone in Davis, near Sacramento, ruled Ironman during this period, Molina would be the dominant force in standard-distance triathlon during the 1980s, winning six USA Pro Championship titles and 50 events in the United States Triathlon Series (UTST), then the nation's premier Olympic-distance series.

Molina's peak came in the mid-eighties especially, with the Chicago Triathlon just one happy hunting ground for the lean and lithe 182cm star, who scored a trio of consecutive wins there from 1983. The *Chicago Tribune* was full of praise for the all-conquering Californian after his 1985 victory.

His friendly, boyish features give him an unassuming appearance. Until the race begins. Although he's not considered the best pure athlete on the US triathlon circuit, he's unequalled in endurance and consistency. His body doesn't quit. There are few bad days. He trains more than any other triathlete, competes every weekend, yet never gets injured and frequently wins. His competitors say he is like a machine.

After the release of Arnold Schwarzenegger's 1984 sci-fi classic this machine-like propensity for victory and ability to rack up the training miles saw Molina become known as 'The Terminator' on the race circuit. 'If I trained as much as he did, I'd be lying dead on the kerb by the side of the road,' said one of his conquests, Charlie Graves, after that dominant 1985 Chicago victory over Mark Allen.

Although he experienced fewer long-course victories than his Big Four brethren, Molina could also do it on the longer stage. He won the now defunct 'World's Toughest Triathlon' title (a 4.8km swim/193km bike/43km run in Lake Tahoe) twice, along with Ironman Hawaii in 1988 (a rare race venture to the Big Island – Molina's huge three-litres-an-hour sweat rate saw him suffer in hot races) and Powerman Zofingen in 1991.

After being beaten by Allen at Nice in 1988 Molina tested positive for nandrolone and was given a one-year ban by the French Federation. After reviewing the testing procedures the US Federation decided not to support the finding and the ban wasn't upheld by any international governing body or other federation.

Two years later, Molina married fellow Kona winner Erin Baker, and the two now live in Baker's native New Zealand with their three children. But Molina is far from done with the sport, coaching pro and age-group athletes and organizing Epic Camp endurance adventures across the world.

Scott Tinley

Scott Tinley has been part of modern triathlon since the mid-seventies. He raced his first triathlon in 1976, his debut Ironman Hawaii in 1981 and scored his first win on the Big Island in 1982. He went on to become reportedly the first man to use aerobars in Hawaii, a Big Four member, and founding father of off-road triathlon. He is also a race organiser, a sports writer (with a long-running column in Triathlete magazine, plus a clutch of acclaimed novels) and a multisport historian. Few, if any, have done more for the sport's development than the blond-haired, Hamlet-quoting academic.

Tinley was born in southern California in October 1956, the first of eight children. The beach communities and warm climate of Fullerton were conducive to outdoor activities, and by his teens he was showing promise in both track and cross-country running at St Paul High School in Santa Fe Springs. His two-decade racing career began in 1976, just two years after the birth of the modern-day version of triathlon in 1974.

The first time he entered Ironman Hawaii was in 1981 on the race's debut in Kona, and a 10:12hr time secured him third place and the first of eight podiums at the event. By February 1982 he was on the top step of the podium after cutting an hour off his previous time and emphatically pushing Dave Scott into second. He also posted what was then the fastest marathon seen at the race (3:03hr), while his brother Jeff came third overall. His feat would have had much more attention but for Julie Moss's finish-line crawl hogging the headlines, two hours later.

When Tinley turned pro in 1983, Dave Scott would take his revenge (and then some) in the next three editions of Hawaii and left him in second place each time; the margin of victory varied from 20 minutes in October 1982 to just 33 seconds after nine hours and 226km of racing in 1983, the closest race in men's Hawaii history. Tinley – now decked-out in aerodynamic booties and an aero helmet and using an innovative wing bar on his track bike – was back on the top step in Hawaii in 1985.

But the field hadn't included Dave Scott, Mark Allen and Scott Molina, who boycotted that race in protest at the lack of prize money given to the pro field. For all that, far from resenting Tinley for crossing the unofficial picket line, Dave Scott rode in the lead vehicle and encouraged him to break the course record (which Scott himself had set). Prefiguring his later and hugely successful coaching career, Scott's selfless gesture pushed Tinley all the way to a record 8:50hr finishing time – maybe the only time a major athlete has willed a rival on to break his own record!

Tinley scored 20 victories out of his 24 races in 1985 at the peak of the Big Four's dominance but he openly admitted he was the least talented of the quartet. He told Ironman.com in 2003:

I feel fortunate to have been part of a unique collection of people who dominated the sport.

But I'm the first to admit that it was my tenacity that allowed me to compete with those guys and that I had to train harder to achieve the results I did.

And what results they were. Tinley won over 100 of the 400 races he entered during his career and was in the Kona top 10 on a dozen occasions up to 1991.

As injuries and the relentless training ethos took their toll on Tinley in the nineties (leading to hip-replacement surgery), he established the world's first off-road triathlon in San Luis Obispo, California – an event still running strong in Lake Lopez Park today. Since hanging up the tri-suit, he has lectured on sport-themed courses at San Diego and California State Universities, written his thoughtful and philosophical column in *Triathlete*, and is the author of a number of well-received books, including *Racing the Sunset*, an exhaustive analysis of athlete retirement. He also co-edits the website Trihistory.com. Oh, and he also co-edits the website Trihistory.com, still giving back to the sport four decades after his love affair with triathlon began.

◁ Scott Tinley was a pioneer in aerodynamic technology and reportedly the first athlete to use aerobars at Ironman Hawaii

◁◁ California's Tinley has been racing triathlon since 1976, securing over 100 career victories along the way

▽ Tinley was victorious twice in Hawaii and finished on the podium a remarkable eight times

The Triathletes
Mirinda Carfrae

Highlights

- Ironman World Champion, 2010, 2013, 2014

- Ironman 70.3 World Champion, 2007

- Challenge Roth Champion, 2014

△ Aussie star Mirinda Carfrae has three Ironman Hawaii titles and one 70.3 world title

Two hours, 50 minutes and 38 seconds. It was a time that sent shockwaves around the Ironman world: Mirinda Carfrae's 42.2km marathon run split at the Ironman World Championships in 2013. Two hours, 50 minutes and 38 seconds: this was a faster time than all but two of the men's and clinched the second of the popular Australian's three Ironman World titles, along with a new Ironman Hawaii course record of 8:52:14.

Mark Allen, a man who owns the men's Hawaii marathon record, was just one onlooker bowled over by the brilliance of the diminutive 161cm Queenslander. 'Her run split was faster than the

men's winner, Frederik Van Lierde, by 40-seconds. I don't know anyone who can match that pacing, skill and domination on the run.'

A year later, Carfrae would be at it again, making up a 14-minute deficit to Switzerland's Daniela Ryf on the run and breaking her own run course record with a 2:50:26 marathon to win title number three. 'She outran the men's winner Sebastian Kienle by four minutes. That's just insane,' continues Allen,

> I don't think Mirinda needs to win six titles to put herself in the same category as Paula Newby-Fraser (eight titles), Natascha Badmann (six titles) and Chrissie Wellington (four titles). . . . she's now won three, and the last two have been done in a way that no one else has ever done before.

Mirinda Carfrae was born on 26 March 1981 in Brisbane. Perhaps surprisingly, given her height, Rinny's first athletic love was playing basketball, before a high school coach noticed her on-court speed and planted the seed of multisport in her mind. Carfrae's first tri came at the age of 19, and she was soon picked for Australia's 2001 junior elite squad. U23 ITU World Championship silver medals came at Cancun in 2002 (a place ahead of future Olympic champ Nicola Spirig) and Queenstown in 2003, and her ITU career peaked with second place behind Michelle Dillon in a stellar field (including Spirig, Leanda Cave and Olympic champ Brigitte McMahon) at Salford's ITU World Cup in 2004.

By this point Carfrae's love affair with long-course racing had begun. She came second and set the first of her many run course records at the middle-distance Lake Tinaroo event in 2002. 'I just remember feeling more comfortable racing the longer distance, and from then I knew I would be racing full Ironman at some point in future,' said Carfrae retrospectively.

A victory at the Nice Long Course Triathlon in 2004 and a silver medal at the 2005 ITU Long Course World Championship were two early successes for Carfrae. At the Ironman 70.3 World Championships she gained first a bronze in 2006 and then victory in Florida in 2007 (the first of her 20 Ironman 70.3 career wins). That win also gave her a qualification spot for the Ironman World Championships in Hawaii. Carfrae raced her first full Ironman at the event in 2009, securing silver behind Chrissie Wellington and posting a course record run of 2:56:51. As Carfrae said in 2014:

> Chrissie changed everybody's perspective. When you're in training and aiming for a certain number, you're only really shooting for whoever's in front. Breaking 9hrs at Kona seemed massive. Then Chrissie came along and blew that out of the water and reset what people thought they were capable of.

Yet Carfrae's own targets were also those of a champion. 'I came into Ironman thinking the three-hour marathon was a bit of a joke. I came in aiming for 2:50hr as it'd be realistic to train to race that fast.' And run close to 2:50hr Carfrae would in 2010, producing a 2:53hr marathon run to take her debut Hawaii title.

Rinny's 2010 victory came in a field without Wellington, who pulled out on race morning due to illness; Chrissie reclaimed her title in a classic in 2011, leaving Carfrae in second place. After a relatively disappointing third at Hawaii in 2012, the hugely popular Aussie came back in 2013 with a different coach (a move back to Siri Lindley), a new bike (the Felt IA) and smaller wheels to chop 14-minutes off her 180km bike leg and break Wellington's course record by two minutes in an overall time of 8:52:14.

Dividing her life between Australia and Boulder, Colorado, Carfrae married the American triathlete

Timothy O'Donnell (fifth at Kona that year) in late 2013 before winning both Challenge Roth and Hawaii in 2014. Ominously for her rivals, the Aussie, who has a knack of staying injury-free, has her sights set on going even faster.' If I can ride around the low 4:50hrs and run in the 2:40hrs, I don't think a record like that would be touched in a while in Kona.'

△ The familiar sight of Carfrae securing Hawaii victory on Ali'i Drive

▽ Carfrae enjoys some Germanic refreshment after her 2014 victory at Challenge Roth

The Triathletes
Nicola Spirig

🏅 **Highlights**

- Olympic Champion, 2012
- Ironman Cozumel Champion, 2014
- ETU European Champion, 2009, 2010, 2012, 2014

△ Switzerland's Nicola Spirig is a major force in both ITU and Ironman racing

Bike course carnage, home-nation heartbreak and the closest sprint finish imaginable. The women's 2012 Olympic Games triathlon had it all and more, as the slippery central London roads and a high-octane pace left just five medal contenders by the midway stage of the 10km run.

With British favourite Helen Jenkins – who'd been nursing an injury in the build-up – dropped at 8km, and American Sarah Groff's hopes extinguished on the approach to the finishing chute, three warriors were left vying for the Olympic title on the blue carpet. Aussie Erin Densham was the first to fall off the pace, and the grandstand spectators rose to their feet as an instant classic unfolded. Upping the speed further was Switzerland's Nicola Spirig, whose combative coach Brett Sutton had sent her to race a 113km Ironman 70.3 event just two weeks before, to quell her urge to train. The 30-year-old soon established daylight between herself and Sweden's Lisa Nordén with 50m to go and held off a late Scandinavian fightback to win the Olympic title in what was instantly dubbed the 'Sprint of the Century'. After 14 years of grit and graft on the ITU circuit, Nicola Spirig was the Olympic champion by a matter of milliseconds.

Like the Brownlees, Scott Tinley, Emma Carney and countless others mentioned in these pages, Nicola Spirig is continued evidence of writer David Epstein's sporting gene theory, with her elder siblings also achieving top-end sporting success. Born in Bülach, northern Switzerland, in February 1982, Spirig started running at the age of seven under the eye of her physical education teacher parents. Cross-country skiing and kayaking were just two activities enjoyed by Spirig in her youth, and her first triathlon came at the age of 10, with a second place finish the start of a formidable career that's witnessed 33 ITU podium finishes alone.

With her father Sepp as coach, Spirig won the junior ETU European Championship title at Funchal in 1999, thanks to a blinding run split, something that was to become familiar on the worldwide circuit over the next few years. The ITU Junior World Championship followed in Edmonton, Canada, in 2001, the 19-year-old producing the day's fastest run split (36:56mins) to beat a field containing future world-beaters Emma Snowsill, Mirinda Carfrae and Britain's Jodie Swallow.

Spirig didn't meet with instant success after her jump to elite status, however. In 2006, after much deliberation, she changed coaches and moved to the Swiss-based squad of arguably triathlon's most famous coach. During his long career Brett Sutton has helped guide Loretta Harrop, Siri Lindley, Jackie Gallagher and Chrissie Wellington to glory, yet he has always attracted controversy with his long-running criticisms of the ITU and the WTC, as well as his very tough training methods. The authoritarian Sutton clashed with Spirig in their early days, but the results soon showed on the race course, with Spirig winning her first ITU World Cup race in Eilat in 2007, placing sixth at the 2008 Beijing Olympics a year later, and winning the first of three European Championship titles in 2009.

After finishing as the ITU World Championship runner-up in 2010, Spirig had a below-par 2011 and fell behind the likes of Jenkins and Nordén in the 2012 Olympic favourite pecking order. Alongside her 2012 Olympic preparations Spirig also found the time to finish a law degree – awarded *magna cum laude* – and won three major races in Eilat, Madrid and Kitzbühel in the run-up to London. As she stood on Hyde Park's Serpentine pontoon on 4 August 2012 Spirig was the bookies' second favourite behind Jenkins (who'd concealed her injury from all but her inner circle), and she was in the mix throughout the contest before posting the day's fastest run split of 33:41mins to become the second Swiss woman to win the Olympic title (after Brigitte McMahon in 2000).

In 2013 Spirig swapped neoprene for nappies after the birth of a son with Swiss triathlete Reto Hug, but then returned with aplomb in 2014, winning every ITU World Cup she entered and

won another European Championship. Showing her versatility and her famed running ability, as well as hinting at the future, she also ran a 2:37hr marathon to come 24th at the European Athletics Championships and won an Ironman on her debut attempt in Cozumel. She then turned her focus to retaining her Olympic title at Rio 2016.

△ Spirig has strength across all three disciplines and is also a strong standalone marathon runner

▽ The sprint of the century with Lisa Nordén at the 2012 Olympic Games

Normann Stadler

- Ironman World Champion, 2004, 2006
- Ironman World Championships, bronze, 2000
- Ironman Australia winner, 2000, 2001

▽ The career of Normann Stadler has been eventful from the get-go

Two Hawaii titles, a bitter rivalry with Chris McCormack and in 2005 triathlon's most famous tantrum. The life and times of Normann Stadler have rarely been dull.

Born near Wertheim in 1973, Stadler showed athletic promise from a young age, and he had the backing of his father, a national-class rower and track and field coach. Although later famous for his bike prowess, Stadler achieved early success in cross-country running before winning several German junior triathlon and duathlon championships.

Olympic-distance triathlon's adoption of draft-legal racing saw Stadler move in 1996 to non-drafting long-course events, where he could unleash his aggressive bike talents without the fear of someone sucking on his wheel. His move to Ironman wasn't instantly successful, and high-profile bonks (vomiting at the roadside at Ironman Switzerland in 1998) and bad luck (colliding with a spectator, suffering hypothermia and being kicked in the stomach during the swim at consecutive Ironman Europe races) punctuated his early 226km career.

Stadler's first Ironman victory came at Ironman Australia in 2000; then in October that year he beat German trail-blazers Thomas Hellriegel and Lothar Leder to take third place at Kona by virtue of a race-best 180km bike leg of 4:35hr. There followed two fourths and a hundredth place at Hawaii (this is a man who doesn't do things by halves), before the man now known as the Normannator – likened to Arnold Schwarzenegger's Terminator due to his machine-

like bike prowess … and probably also his central European accent – shook up Hawaii.

In 2004, when Hawaii was a runner's race, Stadler exploded the myth that the race couldn't be won on the bike by blasting a 4:37hr bike leg (24mins faster than second-place finisher Peter Reid) and holding off the Canadian on the run to win by 10mins. Far from ending the year as a German hero, though, Stadler sparked controversy by publicly criticising his position of ninth in the German Athlete of the Year awards (reportedly making negative comments about the position of para-athlete Wotjek Czyz and the gymnast Fabian Hambüchen). This resulted in his appearance on the front page of the national tabloid *Bild*, a public condemnation by Chancellor Gerhard Schroeder and even death threats.

The next year Stadler again gained infamy for the wrong reasons, this time in Hawaii. Lying third on the bike leg, he suffered a puncture near the Hawi turnaround. Chrissie Wellington and Cat Morrison are just two to suffer flat tyres and win Ironman races, but a bike mechanic had glued the tyre to the wheel so heavily that Stadler was unable to change it. He lost time waiting for a replacement and then suffered another puncture, not to mention a bleeding leg from a nasty bee sting. Sadly for him, the NBC cameras caught his anger, and his shouts of 'Too much gluuuue!' have become a triathlon YouTube classic. His Kuota tri-bike was tossed into the lava fields and a weeping Stadler's race was finished (he regained his composure to congratulate his winning compatriot Faris Al-Sultan at the finish line,

however, and admits that he still loves to watch the footage today).

In 2006, after a bike crash left him in eleventh place at Ironman Germany, that year's Ironman World Championships would be Stadler's greatest race. He exited the swim within sight of the leaders before producing a bike course record of 4:18:23 (an average speed of 42km/h over 180km) to put the race under his control. A 2:55hr marathon run then sufficed to hold off the fast-chasing Chris McCormack by 71secs in one of Hawaii's closest-ever finishes and fastest-ever times. After the race, Stadler made the mistake of criticising McCormack for drafting, leading to a heated debate at the after-party and the creation of one of triathlon's most passionate rivalries (read Macca's *I'm Here to Win* and it becomes clear that the self-confident stars had a genuine dislike for one another). The remarks would fuel McCormack's training for 2007, when the Aussie triumphed in Hawaii . . . and Stadler, suffering from food poisoning, made another very public exit, vomiting at the roadside.

Stadler would never reach those heights at Hawaii again. He became a father in 2009, and his final victory came at Challenge Kraichgau in 2010. In fact that was the last time the world would see the frighteningly fast, always fascinating Normannator on the triathlon course. In 2011 he underwent a successful five-hour heart operation to repair a failing heart valve and an aortic aneurysm, and a month later he announced his retirement from professional triathlon racing,

△ Stadler won two Hawaii titles and dispelled the notion that the race couldn't be won on the bike

▽ Stadler celebrates his 2005 win at Ironman Germany in Frankfurt

Peter Reid

As golden ages in triathlon go, the year 2000 couldn't have gone much better for Canada. In September, Simon Whitfield became the sport's first male Olympic champion, while weeks later in Hawaii, Quebec's Peter Reid topped the Ironman World Championship podium for the second of his three Kona titles. The win confirmed Reid's position as one of the most consistently brilliant athletes of his generation, with his 4th, 4th, 1st, 2nd, 1st, 2nd, 1st, 2nd, 3rd finishing run up there with the greatest ever seen in Hawaii.

Reid was born in Montreal, Quebec, in 1969, and throughout his teenage years was heavily into skiing and cycling. His first triathlon came in 1989, when its demands forced him to resort to breaststroke just 100m into the swim of his debut race.

After graduating with a political science degree, Reid gave himself a year to show clear signs of improvement in tri. Giving early indications of his famous perseverance, he soon came good, winning Japan's 1993 Astroman duathlon in a typhoon. In 1994 he moved to British Columbia to train under coach Roch Frey. The results started to flow, with victory at Wildflower and fourth at his first venture in Hawaii – all in 1996, a year when Reid's education was broadened by weeks spent training with the German powerhouse Thomas Hellriegel.

Another fourth place at Kona followed in 1997 before Reid hooked up as a training partner with the rising American star Tim DeBoom in the summer of 1998 in Boulder, while staying at Paula Newby-Fraser's house.

Whatever advice Newby-Fraser imparted seemed to work. Just months later in 1998 Reid won his first Ironman World Championship victory in 8:24:20hrs after stellar bike and run splits. Canada's Lori Bowden finished second that day, and a year later the roles were reversed when Bowden, now Reid's wife, took gold, and Reid was second behind Luc Van Lierde. In between Reid posted one of the fastest times in long-course history, winning Ironman Austria in a 7:51:56 time.

After being pursued by DeBoom throughout the marathon, Reid would label his 2000 Kona victory the hardest race he ever did. In 2002 they switched positions when DeBoom broke free on the run to secure his second Kona title. Reid's feat in finishing second shouldn't be underestimated, however. He had suffered a mental and physical burn-out earlier in the year and took a break from the sport. Slowly, he found his motivation returning and set about targeting Kona armed with a beginner program written by Mark Allen. His preparations for his 2003 Hawaii victory were also far from ideal after his marriage to Bowden ended a week before Kona race day. Reid, nonetheless, won a decisive victory over Belgium's Rutger Beke.

After two more Kona podium places in 2004 and 2005, Reid announced his retirement from tri to pursue a career as a bush pilot in northern Canada. His triumphs over adversity in Hawaii will forever remain in Ironman folklore, though; few have grafted as hard as Peter the Great for victory in Kona.

▷▷△ Reid wins the 2000 Ironman World Championships, his second of three Kona crowns

▽ Reid was pushed all the way at Hawaii in 2000 by his training partner, Tim DeBoom

Lothar Leder

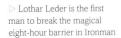

If Dave Scott and Mark Allen are the undisputed Kings of Ironman Hawaii's history, then Chris McCormack and Lothar Leder are Roth's equivalent. Australia's Macca has taken the Bavarian Iron-distance title four times, and Leder of Germany a record five. And, in the equivalent of Scott and Allen's Iron War in 1989, the two of them produced the greatest long-distance battle ever seen in Roth, with their 2003 showdown.

▷ Lothar Leder is the first man to break the magical eight-hour barrier in Ironman

▽ The German is the King of Roth, with five titles to his name

That July, Leder and Macca raced neck-and-neck throughout the 226km of Challenge Roth. After eight hours of racing, and with less than a kilometre to go on the run, Leder made the decisive move and held off his Aussie rival to win his fifth and final Roth title by just three seconds. (His wife Nicole also won on that famous day for the Leders.)

Leder was born in the city of Worms in March 1971, racing his first tri in 1986 and turning pro in 1994. Just two years later, he made history by becoming the first man ever to break the eight-hour barrier in long-distance racing, with a 7:57:02 time in Roth (at that time the event was Ironman-branded). Unlike his German rivals of the time, who dominated the world's bike legs, Leder's major strength was on the run and he finished third at Ironman Hawaii in 1997 behind compatriots Thomas Hellriegel and Jürgen Zäck after posting one of the day's fastest marathons.

Another third at Hawaii followed in 1998 before Leder became Mr Roth with four consecutive wins from 2000 to 2003. A voluntary blood test at Ironman Frankfurt in 2007 saw him accused of blood doping, leading to temporary

bans from Challenge and Ironman races. Leder was never suspended by the German federation, but he never again achieved feats like his Roth wins of 1996 or 2003. But he'll forever be the world's first sub-8hr athlete.

The Triathletes
Yves Cordier

'Sometimes, glorious defeats are more symbolic than easy victories,' said Yves Cordier to xtri.com in 2010. And, the French star is well-versed in glorious defeats, having on several occasions run into the incomparable presence of Mark Allen during the American's ten-year winning streak at the Nice International Triathlon.

The closest Cordier came to victory was in a stone-cold classic in 1992, when the Frenchman was within sight of the Promenade des Anglais finishing tape. 'I ran ahead during the run leg for 31.5km, supported by the crowd who cheered me. I felt I had wings,' he recalls. Just 500m from the line, however, Allen ran through to claim title number nine and leave Cordier once again on a lower step of the podium. Yet Cordier is a lot more than just a gallant loser at Nice: his record five Embrunman crowns between 1987 and 1999, plus the 1989 ETU European Championship title, make him arguably the greatest professional triathlete in French history.

Cordier was born in Nice on 15 July 1964 and was drawn to triathlon by watching the television broadcast of the Nice International Triathlon in 1982. Although a national-level swimmer, he became renowned for his relentless speed on two wheels, dominating the infamous climbs of the long-course Embrunman race to take the classic race's title on a record five occasions (a record he shares with Spain's Marcel Zamora). In 1989 he won the ETU European Championship title, thanks to a 1:04hr 40km bike split – 2mins faster than triathlon heavyweights Rob Barel and Jürgen Zack.

Although Cordier's 19-year pro career wound down in 2002, his presence still looms large over triathlon in the Cote d'Azur. With the Nice International losing some of its shine, Cordier and Triangle Events successfully courted Ironman to take over the branding of the Nice race. From 2005 onwards Ironman France was staged in Nice under Cordier's stewardship, increasing its competitor numbers and attracting some of the world's finest athletes – over thirty years after a French teenager had gazed wide-eyed at the images of Nice being transmitted from his TV screen.

▷ Yves Cordier is arguably France's greatest-ever triathlete

▽ Cordier is now the race director of Ironman France in Nice, the scene of many of his greatest races

Emma Carney

△▷ Emma Carney was part of an Australian women's team that dominated ITU racing in the nineties

▽ The Aussie scored ITU World Cup success in Sydney but failed to qualify for the Sydney Olympics

'When they write the Australian encyclopedia, it's Emma's picture they'll put under the definition of hard,' says Chris McCormack of two-time ITU World Champion Emma Carney. And that's quite some compliment, given that triathletes Brad Beven, Loretta Harrop and Greg Welch, and other sportsmen like Merv Hughes and John Sattler could all vie for the honour.

Emma Carney was born in England in 1971 but moved Down Under to Victoria State at a young age. Like Beven, she would run home from school each day and would soon show promise by beating the boys and setting records in mixed cross-country events in her teens. Although she represented Australia twice at World Cross Country Championships, Carney was unwilling

to wait until her late twenties for her peak middle-distance years and chose to race her first triathlon in 1993 ... and won it despite exiting the 700m swim with a seven-minute deficit to make up! After comparing international times in a tri magazine that night, her Nike rep father reckoned that Emma had what it took to be the best in the world ... if she just learnt how to swim.

Eighteen-months later, and in one of the fastest sporting ascents in history, Carney was the ITU World Champion, holding her own on the swim before producing the race's fastest bike and run splits to take gold in Wellington, New Zealand. In a day to remember for the Carney family, her younger sister Claire won the junior race, and her older sister Jane an age-group title.

And so began one of triathlon's great careers. Carney won 19 of her 22 ITU races from Wellington until Ishigaki in 1998, in the process taking another ITU world title in 1997 (beating Aussie compatriots Jackie Gallagher and Michellie Jones in a classic in Perth) and three consecutive overall ITU World Cup titles in 1995–7. Her record might have been even better had she not been hit by viral infections at the 1995 and 1996 ITU Worlds.

After Ishigaki, Carney's decline was also fairly swift. She won no more ITU races and missed qualification for the Sydney Olympics in 2000. Famed for training at a furiously high intensity she was forced to fully retire from professional triathlon in 2004, joining Greg Welch and Hamish Carter on the list of those experiencing heart problems.

The Triathletes
Pauli Kiuru

Imran Khan, George Weah and Vitali Klitschko may not have much in common with Finland's most famous triathlon son, yet Pauli Kiuru is the latest sporting star to enter the world of politics after hanging up their sports kit for the last time. In 2011 Kiuru plunged into the political pool, having largely conquered the blue waters of triathlon, where just an over-strong carbohydrate drink had apparently prevented him from taking the Ironman World Championship title.

Pauli Antero Kiuru was born on 8 December 1962 in Valkeakoski, 150km north of Helsinki

▽ Triathlete-turned-politician Pauli Kiuru is Finland's most famous triathlon son

in the Finnish Lakeland area. That might have provided ample open-water swimming opportunities in a more southerly country (Kiuru has to be the only major triathlon star to come from north of 60° latitude), but Finland's inhospitable Nordic winters lent themselves more to speed skating. It was a world away from the triathlon heartland of San Diego, yet Kiuru – like his future rival Mark Allen in California – would be drawn to triathlon when he glimpsed Julie Moss crawling over the Ironman Hawaii finish line on television in 1982.

Five years later he came tenth in his debut race in Hawaii. He was tenth again in 1988, but then became a top-five fixture for the next five editions: 5th in 1989, then 3rd, 4th and 3rd, before his brush with Hawaii immortality in 1993.

Consistent across all disciplines and famed for his scientific approach to training and pioneering use of a heart rate monitor, Kiuru out-biked Allen in 1993 and led for much of the run before being struck with cramp in the dying stages, something he later put down to having mixed his carbohydrate drink too thickly. Overtaken by Allen, he comfortably hung on for second, but that was to be his final close encounter with Hawaii gold.

Away from Hawaii, the understated Finn would win seven Ironman titles – four in a row in Australia, two at Ironman Europe and one in New Zealand. And it was in New Zealand in 1990 that he pipped Ken Glah to the finish line by just one second in what's thought to be the closest-ever finish in a 226km Ironman race.

The Triathletes
Luc Van Lierde

△ Van Lierde enters the record books with a 7:50:27 time at Roth in 1997

▷△ The Belgian took two Ironman World titles in the late nineties

Marino Vanhoenacker, Frederik Van Lierde, Rutger Beke ... in the world of men's long-distance triathlon Belgium has long punched well above its weight for a 30,000km² country with an 11m population, outgunning nations 332 times its size (Canada) and six times its population (Great Britain) on the race courses of Hawaii, Roth and Austria. Blazing the trail for Belgian athletes was one Luc Van Lierde, the human bullet from Bruges, who was once the fastest Ironman in the world.

Born in Bruges in April 1969, Van Lierde came into multisport in 1990 after a year's military service in the Belgian army. Already a formidable national-level swimmer, he came ninth on his ITU debut at the European Championships in 1990, a second behind his future adversary, Simon Lessing. Then, after a smattering of top-ten finishes on the Olympic-distance European circuit, he he was hit by a car in 1994. He spent a year in rehab, re-emerging even stronger in late 1995, out-biking and out-running Spencer Smith to take the European Championship silver in Stockholm, and then another silver behind Lessing at the ITU Long Distance Championships in Nice.

Like Mark Allen, Van Lierde could alternate between Olympic and long-distance events, and this was never more apparent than in 1996, when the Belgian won the short-course European Championships before ripping up the rule book in Hawaii. Where Hawaii legends Allen, Chris McCormack and many more have learnt how to achieve success on the Big Island the hard way, Van Lierde only rocked up and won the thing at the

first attempt. He had never even run a marathon before – or raced an Ironman. What's more, he did it in record-breaking fashion too, stunning the onlookers, staying strong as Thomas Hellriegel broke the bike course record and chipping away at the German's lead on the run to pass him at 38km and become the first European man to win Hawaii gold. His time of 8:04:08 smashed Allen's course record and would stand for 15 years; Van Lierde could even have beaten the magical eight-hour barrier at Hawaii if he hadn't had to serve a 3-minute time penalty. Dave Scott, who also won on his Hawaii debut, labelled the result 'frightening'.

And there was more to come from Van Lierde in 1997. In Roth he set an Iron-distance world record of 7:50:27 (including a 44:41mins swim split and 2:36hr marathon run) that lasted for 13 years. But injury saw him skip Hawaii in 1997, and in 1998 he was beaten on the bike by Peter Reid to come second in Kona. The tables were turned in 1999, though, when Van Lierde blew Reid away on the run to win his second Hawaii crown.

Few watching that could guess it would be Van Lierde's final major victory. Just 48hrs before recommencing battle with Reid in 2000, citing personal issues, he sensationally pulled out of the race, despite being free from injury, and took the next plane home to Belgium. Despite wins at Ironman Malaysia in 2003 and 2004, Van Lierde's star would never burn as brightly as it had at those Hawaii highs again, and the athlete is now famous for plotting his unrelated namesake Frederik's successes on the Big Island.

The Triathletes
Conrad Stoltz

Triathletes – indeed people – don't come much tougher than Conrad Stoltz. The South African king of off-road endeavours regularly finishes his races dripping with blood and once broke his back in three places and his wrist in eight ... only to return to racing months later to win the 2007 Xterra World Championship.

There are countless legendary stories about the presence known as the Caveman – from eating roadkill to suffering from gangrene. One favourite concerns the time when he lacked somewhere to swim when training at his family's cattle farm in the province of Mpumalanga. Undeterred, he got a spade, dug himself a 25m long ditch, lined it with sandbags and swam in it.

Stoltz was born in Lydenburg, in the north-east of South Africa, in 1973 and was rarely spotted without his bike from the age of three onwards. Like Aussie racer Brad Beven, a man who swam with crocs in the Australian bush, Stoltz's upbringing in the largely uninhabited 'bundu' in the country's north-eastern reaches instilled a love of all-things outdoors and shaped his tough-guy credentials. So too – as highlighted by Holly Bennett in *Inside Triathlon* magazine in 2011 – did the genes of a father nicknamed Tarzan for his six-pack and bulging chest.

Stoltz's first triathlon came at an IronKids event when he was 14, and he was picking up both African and South African Championship titles in his late teens. A respectable ITU career followed during the 1990s leading to a 20th place at the 2000 Sydney Olympics (having led during the bike leg), before he found his calling in the burgeoning off-road triathlon scene. His 50+ Xterra career wins have included four Xterra World Championships and 10 USA Series Championships, with treacle-like mud, jagged rocks and whatever else has been thrown at him (including a rusty girder that sliced open his foot at Xterra Richmond in 2009) rarely preventing him from securing victory.

Conrad could also have made it as a pro cyclist. He finished third at the 2103 South African Time Trial Championships (40km road bike) in a time of 51:46 at the age of 40, and has long ties with Specialized bikes: the brand even making custom Caveman-proof tyres for the longest-running elite athlete on their books.

Peter Robertson

With Chris McCormack emigrating to long-course triathlon early in the decade, Peter 'Robbo' Robertson gamely filled the gaping void his world-beating predecessor left and became Australia's top male ITU athlete of the twenty-first century. With his trio of ITU World Championship wins Robertson joined the great lineage of Greg Welch, Miles Stewart and McCormack and became the next (and as yet last) Aussie male to achieve that status.

Born in 1976, Robertson grew up in Melbourne, Victoria. He entered his first triathlon in 1992 and swiftly started making his mark on the Australian domestic scene. In April 2000 he won the Sydney Olympic test event, beating off stiff competition to make the 2000 Australian Olympic team.

If Robertson's Olympic Games record is disappointing in terms of results (he finished 34th in Sydney and 24th in Athens), he values his

Sydney qualification highly: 'My dream as a kid was to go to the Olympics, and in 2000, when I won the Sydney ITU World Cup, I achieved my childhood dream, qualifying for the Olympic Games in front of the very people who had helped me achieve this goal.'

After a series of low-ranked ITU performances in 2001, Robertson showed his knack for peaking for the season's climax to produce a win at the ITU World Championships in Edmonton, this time thanks to a race-best bike split. A silver behind Ivan Rana at the 2002 ITU Worlds was followed by a second world title in 2003 in Queenstown, New Zealand, after breaking away from the main pack on the bike and holding off Rana on the run.

Robbo missed the 2004 Worlds to concentrate on Athens, but brought back his fearless and hugely popular style of racing at Gamagori, Japan, in 2005. He broke away from the lead pack early in the 10km run and held on in oppressive heat to win his third men's ITU world title, something only Javier Gómez and Simon Lessing have bettered.

In the latter stages of his career Robertson rarely hit such proud highs as his bronze medal at the 2006 Commonwealth Games on home turf in Melbourne, and he retired in 2010 at the age of just 34. Robbo's post-racing career saw him become a coach on the NTA Young Guns tour in 2010, and it was the energy of this new generation of Australian tri stars that rekindled his own passion for racing. He was soon plotting a path to another world championship, this time in the form of an Ironman title.

△▷ After retiring from tri in 2010, Robertson made a return to the sport to experience Ironman success

▽ Robertson won the Sydney test event before racing on home turf

The Triathletes
Jan Frodeno

'Who is Jan Frodeno?' asked just one magazine cover line in 2008 after a tall, skinny German unknown upset the odds to become the Olympic Games champion a day after his twenty-seventh birthday.

In the muggy heat of Beijing the boy from Cologne stayed with the big hitters of the sport on the swim and bike, but faced a trio of more experienced figures in the dying stages of the run. Standing between the 194cm athlete and gold were Canada's 2000 Olympic Games Champion and wily operator Simon Whitfield, Spain's reigning ITU world champ Javier Gómez and formidable Kiwi sprinter Bevan Docherty. Only the brave and the bold would place their bets on Frodeno.

As the final straight beckoned, Whitfield made what appeared to be the decisive break in his quest for another Olympic title. With Gómez already spent and Docherty unable to repeat his New Plymouth heroics from 2005, Frodeno was the only candidate to stalk the Canadian as the finish tape came into view. Using his long legs and soon-to-be-famous self-belief, Frodeno pushed past Whitfield with 100m to go and produced the biggest men's Olympic upset since the young Whitfield had crossed the line eight years earlier.

Watching that race in 2000 had been the spark that launched Frodeno's triathlon career, and now the man without an ITU victory in his career was the Olympic champion. (A day earlier, Frodeno's future wife Emma Snowsill had won the women's title.)

Frodeno, born in 1981, had started his sporting career as a competitive swimmer in South Africa during his teens. After his 2008 Olympic triumph he finished fourth overall in the ITU World Championships in 2009 and 2010, before coming sixth at the 2012 Olympics in London. By the time he retired from ITU racing in 2013, Frodo had another golden ring and epic journey in his sights: the Ironman World Championships.

He came second at the Ironman 70.3 European Championships in 2013, but Frodeno's long-course career began in earnest in 2014, with a third-place finish and the day's fastest marathon of 2:43hr on his Ironman debut at the European Championships in Frankfurt. The feat was all the more impressive because Frodeno suffered three punctures and lost 10 minutes on the bike leg – but for which he would have leapfrogged the reigning Ironman World Champion Frederik Van Lierde into second place.

Frodeno's Ironman Hawaii debut in October 2014 also provided plenty of drama and athletic feats: he exited the water in second place, but then a couple of punctures and a time penalty for drafting on the bike leg enabled Sebastian Kienle to increase his advantage over his compatriot. Frodeno again dug deep into his reserves of self-belief and his ITU speed work to produce the day's fastest run split of 2:47hrs to finish third behind Kienle and America's Ben Hoffman.

Mark Allen was just one spectator taken by Frodeno's racing ('Frodeno had a great race – he looked like he didn't have a clue what he was doing but he got third place anyway!'). The German was now a major contender to become the first man to take both Olympic Games and Ironman World Championship titles.

▷△ The German produces a huge upset by outsprinting Simon Whitfield to take Olympic gold in 2008

▽ Jan Frodeno was a stalwart of the ITU scene before moving to long-course racing in 2013

The Triathletes
Julie Moss

The Iron War, Paula Newby-Fraser's eighth title, and Simon Whitfield crossing the Sydney Olympic finish line . . . the history of triathlon is full of iconic and key moments in the sport's growth. Yet arguably its most defining and critical moment came in 1982, when a recent college graduate named Julie Moss crawled, stumbled and staggered up the Ironman Hawaii finish line to claim second place in front of the ABC *Wide World of Sports* television cameras.

Those pictures were later beamed to millions of households around the world, and Mark Allen and Pauli Kiuru were just two of the thousands of people who were inspired by Moss's feats to take up the fledgling sport. Far from turning people away from the gruelling swim-bike-and-run format, Moss's heroic efforts vividly captured the essence and attraction of the sport: for the vast majority of triathlon competitors, finishing the journey is far more important than winning.

Julie Moss's main reason for signing up for the 1982 edition of Ironman Hawaii was to gather data for her exercise physiology thesis. The 23-year-old had only begun training in earnest 20 weeks before the race, successfully completing a middle-distance race as part of her training in late 1981.

Cut to race day in February 1982 (two editions of Hawaii were held that year), and Moss exited the 3.8km swim after 1:11hrs with the leaders and continued to hold her own on the bike leg, cycling the 180km in 5:53hrs. When pro cyclist Pat Hines dropped out on the run due to severe leg cramps, Moss inherited the lead but only realized it when she finally noticed the news crews and helicopters trailing her with 15km to go. Her pre-race aim to finish was upgraded to take the Hawaii title, and she became aware of elite athlete Kathleen McCartney reducing the deficit.

As Moss drew closer to the finish line, fatigue began to overwhelm an exhausted body fuelled by just bananas and water since the race's start. She continually dropped to the ground as her legs buckled under her but recovered enough to press on, pushing away the hands of helpers in the process – still mentally aware enough to remember that outside assistance results in disqualification. With only feet to go, Kathleen McCartney shot past Moss and crossed the line first, unaware of her victory and Moss's plight until an organizer told her of the breaking story metres back down the finish line. All a punch-drunk Moss could do was crawl to the tape, crossing the line 29secs after McCartney.

Moss's courageous act would latterly be aired on ABC as the broadcaster labelled it 'one of the most defining moments in sport', with the chief protagonist (and future Mrs Mark Allen) becoming the first triathlete to transcend the sport. Proving that you can lose a race but still be a winner. Nor did she give up after her experience: she raced seven more times at Ironman Hawaii, finishing second in her age-group in 1997 with a time of 10:39:28.

▷ Although world-famous for her 1982 exploits in Hawaii, Moss went on to race in Kona a further seven times

Frederik Van Lierde

△ Frederik followed in the footsteps of his Belgian namesake Luc by winning Ironman World Championships gold

For Frederik Van Lierde (unlike his unrelated namesake and coach Luc Van Lierde) world-beating feats in the Ironman World Championships were not instant. 'I have 17 years of experience in triathlon, so my ability to race in the heat of Hawaii didn't come quickly. I wasn't ready on my first attempts at Hawaii,' he said in 2013. Luc's record at Hawaii reads 1st, 2nd, 1st, 8th, but Frederik's is a slow-burn story of incremental gains and learning curves, resulting in a DNF, 42nd, 14th, DNF and 3rd, before his winning breakthrough on the Big Island in 2013.

Frederik was born in Menen, a Flemish-speaking city on the Franco-Belgian border, in 1979. Like Luc, he first tasted success as a swimmer before entering the sport of triathlon in his late teens. Short-course medals came at the Belgian National Championships and Under 23 European Champs in 2002, but success didn't come until a move to long-distance racing in 2007. Just over an hour's drive along the E17 from his home of Menen, Van Lierde produced the day's best swim and bike times to win the ETU Long Distance European Championships in Brasschaat. Long-course racing had a new star.

The next season saw Van Lierde coming second on his Ironman debut in New Zealand (behind ten-time winner Cameron Brown, of course), and 2011 and 2012 brought success at the Abu Dhabi International Triathlon and Ironman France. His 2013 season was a classic display of the phenomenon of momentum in sport. It began with a win at the megabucks Abu Dhabi event ahead of a stellar field. Another win

▷ The familiar sight of Van Lierde celebrating gold on the worldwide Ironman finish lines

at ExtremeMan Salou followed before the softly-spoken 6ft Belgian grabbed his third successive Ironman France title in sweltering heat, breaking the course record in 8:08:59 in the process.

Van Lierde went into Hawaii looking unstoppable, and so it proved on race day. He dropped some of the sport's best bikers before unleashing a 2:51hr marathon to reel in Australia's Luke McKenzie. Frederik followed his coach Luc's tradition of running the last 16km of the course the week before the race, and it was here that he proved too strong for the Aussie, passing him with 15km to go and holding on to break Australia's grip on the Hawaii crown with a fast time of 8:12hrs.

'I've never worked this hard. I've never had such a feeling,' said the modest star at the finish. 'This is a big reward for my family. We're not in a position where they can travel with me, so there have been a lot of sacrifices.'

Lori Bowden

How's this for consecutive runs at the Ironman World Championships: 8th, 2nd, 2nd, 1st, 2nd, 2nd, 3rd, 1st? Canada's Lori Bowden is up there with the sport's finest for longevity, consistency and determination, regularly producing the women's fastest marathon of the day to haunt Natascha Badmann during Hawaii's run leg.

Born in 1967 in Ontario, Bowden had multisport genes in the family, with both of her parents active triathletes in the sport's early years. In contrast to the Allens, Reids and countless others who had to convince sceptical parents of the merits of pursuing a professional triathlon career, she was apparently talked into it by her elders. After a move to Victoria BC, Lori was soon picking up victories in Canada's Trisports Triathlon Series, until the day she missed out on a spot in the Ontario (Olympic-distance) team after forgetting to wear a bike helmet in a qualification race. To prolong her season, she tried a long-distance race . . . and soon became the queen of Ironman Canada, winning five times in Penticton.

She won famous victories at Ironman Austria (twice) and Australia (thrice), as well as at Powerman Zofingen in 1998, but it's her achievements in Hawaii that see her name etched into Ironman history. After coming eighth on her 1996 debut, Bowden was in the top three for seven years in a row from 1997 (only Paula Newby-Fraser has had more consecutive Hawaii podiums) – and in the process of her 1999 win she became the first woman in Hawaii history to post a sub-3hr marathon time. In 2003 she

bowed out from Hawaii in style: she finally beat Natascha Badmann on the Big Island to take the title on a famous day for Canadian triathlon, with her one-time husband Peter Reid scooping the men's title.

△ Lori Bowden reached the Hawaii podium on a remarkable seven consecutive occasions, winning twice

Thomas Hellriegel

△ Hell on Wheels was the first German winner at Ironman Hawaii in 1997

From the Grip (Mark Allen) to the Man (Dave Scott) and The Normannator (Normann Stadler), the world of long-course racing has thrown up many famous nicknames. None, however, are quite as evocative as Hell on Wheels, a tag that stems from Thomas Hellriegel's incendiary bike prowess. Just imagine being pursued by a man with that nickname for 180km over the lava fields of Kona! Not that Hellriegel pursued anyone for long on the bike.

Hellriegel was born in Bruchsal in 1971. Where most teenagers sneak out of their parents' house to get drunk or go on a date, Hellriegel's athletic ambitions were evident from the age of 19 when he secretly fled the family home to race the 1990 Ironman Europe, where he finished 56th in a quality field.

Before long his ferocious (and soon legendary) ability to rack up thousands of training miles per month on the bike began to reap rewards on the race course when he took silver at the 1993 ETU European Championships. His bike power was more suited to Ironman racing, however, and soon he was pushing Mark Allen all the way at the Ironman World Championships in 1995, having posted a furiously fast 4:29hr bike split (some 17mins faster than Allen, himself no slouch on the bike). 'Hellriegel was 13 years younger than me and hungry for victory,' Allen says. 'I had to make up 30secs per mile during the marathon. But in the end I caught Hellriegel. And it turned out to be the greatest race of my career.'

Another silver behind Luc Van Lierde followed in 1996 in what was then the second-fastest time in Hawaiian history of 8:06hrs (plus the fastest bike ever). Finally, Hellriegel became the first German winner on the Big Island in 1997, blazing a two-wheeled path for Normann Stadler and Faris Al-Sultan to follow.

Rob Barel

While the nickname may have been an obvious one, if there's any triathlete who deserves the title of the Flying Dutchman it's Rob Barel. From the early eighties to the present day he has been one of triathlon's most versatile and consistent performers, winning the European Championships an incredible seven times in the late 1980s and 1990s, the 1994 ITU Long Distance Championship title and scoring a fourth place at Ironman Hawaii in 1990.

Born in Amsterdam in 1957, Barel won his first triathlon at the age of 25 in 1982 before becoming the first-ever ETU European Champion in 1985. ETU European Championships in Olympic-distance (1985, 1986, 1987, 1988) and middle-distance (1986, 1988, 1994) racing would follow during his peak years, with plenty of podium appearances at the Nice Triathlon added to the mix. 'My favourite race first of all is Nice, where I started 13 times and finished mostly second behind Mark Allen,' he recalls.

The nineties would begin with Barel scooping a fourth place at Ironman Hawaii in 1990, before grabbing bronze at the ITU World Championships in 1993 and gold at the ITU Long Distance Championships the following year.

He briefly retired from triathlon after placing 43rd at the Sydney Olympics at the age of 42, but came back in 2007, winning the European men's cross triathlon title in the 50–54 age-group and then stepping up to the elite men's field again in 2008. He won that too, at the age of 50, showing competitors half his age a muddy pair of heels on the off-road run.

◁△ Rob Barel is one of triathlon's most versatile athletes, winning long, short and off-road events

Sebastian Kienle

▷ Sebastian Kienle could be this decade's most dominant long-course triathlon figure

▽ Kienle's speed on the bike led him to the 2014 Ironman world title

Thomas Hellriegel, Lothar Leder, Normann Stadler, Faris Al-Sultan, Andreas Raelert . . . the long and distinguished list of German long-distance powerhouses has enabled the nation to edge Belgium to become the undisputed European heavyweight of men's 226km racing. Added to the roll of honour in October 2014 was one Sebastian Kienle, who followed in the tracks of Stadler and others by proving that Hawaii could be won with an all-out bike leg.

And what a bike leg it was. After exiting the swim 4mins behind the race leaders, Kienle powered to the front of the bike queue by the midway stage at 90km and went on to post a 4:20hr 180km bike split, just two-minutes shy of Stadler's 2006 course record. Then, although he showed signs of discomfort on the run, Kienle's 2:54hr marathon time was enough to hold off the chasers and win him his debut Ironman World Championship title in 8:14hrs.

Unlike many triathletes who come from single-sport backgrounds, Kienle's dream has always been Ironman. Born in 1984, he watched his first race at eight and was racing triathlon events by the age of 12. '[Pro cycling team] T Mobile tried to get him when he was a kid to ride the Tour de France, but all he's ever wanted to do is Ironman Hawaii,' says fellow Kona winner Chris McCormack.

Kienle was soon winning off-road Xterra triathlons in Germany, before moving to long-course racing. In 2009 he won Ironman 70.3 Germany, and a year later he was second behind Rasmus Henning at Challenge Roth. Ironman 70.3 World titles in 2012 and 2013 followed, and his full-distance Ironman Hawaii victory in 2014 at the age of 30 (young for a Kona champ) suggest that the kid from Karlsruhe could dominate long-distance racing for the decade to come.

The Triathletes
Olivier Marceau

Whether racing for France or his adopted Switzerland, Olivier Marceau has been a continual presence on the race circuit for two decades, winning numerous Xterra and French Grand Prix titles, and the ITU World Championships in 2000.

Born on 30 January 1973 in the Parisian suburbs, Marceau tasted junior success before his elite breakthrough on home turf with victory at the Paris ITU World Cup in 1996. The sport's move to draft-legal racing hindered the strong bikers like Marceau, and so, ironically, was a 'turning point' for him, because he had to focus more on developing his run. This new focus then led to an epic triumph in Perth's ITU World Championships in 2000. In a field littered with Antipodean stars

like Craig Walton, Peter Robertson and Hamish Carter, Marceau not only produced the day's fastest bike split of 1:00:18, but was then able to hold off the strong runners on the final leg to become the ITU World Champion.

Five months later, Marceau came seventh at triathlon's Olympic debut in Sydney, the first of three Olympic appearances (he'd race for Switzerland in 2004 and 2008).

A versatile operator in a sport that's become more and more specialised in terms of distances, the 6ft Marceau has won several European Championship victories in the world of Xterra and peaked with third at Ironman France in 2010.

◁△ Marceau is a veteran of the scene, winning titles for both France and Switzerland

▷△ Marceau has also scored success on his off-road ventures

Jackie Fairweather

In November 2014 the world of multisport was rocked by the news that the multiple ITU World Champion, Jackie Fairweather (née Gallagher), had died aged just 46. It was widely reported that she had taken her own life, and her husband, five-time Olympic archer Simon Fairweather, stated that she'd 'lost her battle with depression.' Fairweather's death was a tragic end to a year in which the International Triathlon Union had been celebrating its past, and she was a nominee for its inaugural Hall of Fame.

And what a career hers was, with highs including two ITU World Duathlon titles, one ITU World Championship win and a marathon bronze medal at the 2002 Commonwealth Games.

Jacquilyn Gallagher was born on 10 November 1967 in Perth, Australia. A decent runner in her teens, she moved to triathlon in the early 1990s under the supervision of coach Brett Sutton. She won the elite Australian National Series in 1992, her first season as an elite athlete, before becoming a major presence alongside fellow Australian world-beaters Emma Carney, Loretta Harrop and Michellie Jones throughout the decade.

As well as her three ITU World titles, Gallagher took 29 wins in 51 races in 1995–6 and a trio of World Championship silvers. After missing out on the Sydney Olympics due to overtraining, she won a remarkable bronze at the 2002 Manchester Commonwealth Games in her debut season as a marathon runner.

Throughout this period, Gallagher worked for the Australia Institute of Sport (one of her first

◁ The late Jackie Fairweather (née Gallagher) was a powerful runner who achieved marathon success

▽ Gallagher was part of a formidable Australian women's team in the nineties

recruits was future Olympic champion Emma Snowsill) and the ITU, establishing the junior and Under 23 ITU races during her time to leave a lasting legacy on the sport.

Laurent Vidal

Born just 13 days apart in 1984, French stars David Hauss and Laurent Vidal have been two of the most consistent performers on the ITU circuit during the past decade, peppering the worldwide podiums before finishing fourth and fifth, respectively, behind the Brownlees and Javier Gómez at the 2012 Olympic Games. While the future looks bright for Hauss, whether we'll ever see Vidal's stride on the circuit again is in doubt.

Vidal, from Sète in southern France, is a three-time French national champion, two-time Olympian, and the partner of Kiwi ITU star Andrea Hewitt. He reached the peak of his powers during the build-up to the London Olympics, when he won the ITU race in Mooloolaba, took bronze at the ITU World Series race in Sydney and momentarily topped the ITU rankings.

After another year of top tens aplenty in 2013, Vidal suffered a major heart attack while swimming in 2014 and had to be revived by firefighters. He was placed in an induced coma, and it wasn't until 48hrs later that he tweeted 'Hello world!' At the time of writing the Proust-quoting, electronic music-making Frenchman has yet to return to the race circuit, though he has given a suitably lyrical statement on the question of possible return: 'My building is strong and has resisted many storms. Today it is still too early to say what I can do. It takes time and I will take it.'

▷ Laurent Vidal's career was in the ascendancy before a career-threatening heart attack in 2014

Ai Ueda

◁△ Ai Ueda is a stalwart of the ITU scene, representing Japan at two Olympic Games

▷△ The 155cm star has multiple ITU World Cup victories, including here in Mexico

She comes from a family of kimono-makers, is skilled at creating *anime* pictures and cites a respect for her parents in her 'things to know' section on the International Triathlon Union's website. Could Ai Ueda be more stereotypically Japanese?

Born in Kyoto in central Honshu (Japan's biggest island) in 1983. The diminutive 155cm 'Triathlon Ai' is the superstar of Japanese multisport. Her successes include winning the 2005 and 2008 Asian Triathlon Championships and victories at numerous Asian, Pan American and ITU World Cup races on either side of the Pacific.

Aside from representing her nation at the 2008 and 2012 Olympic Games, Ueda's most noteworthy achievement is winning the 2013 ITU World Duathlon Championships in Cali, Colombia. After the crack French duathlete Sandra Levenez matched her step for step and pedal rotation for pedal rotation on the first run and bike, Ueda used her ITU-competitor's faster leg speed on the final run to open up a minute gap over the chasers to secure her first major championship title.

The following season saw her coming into the peak of her powers, with her last six race placings being 1st, 2nd, 2nd, 1st, 1st, 1st – suggesting there's far more still to come from the Kyoto champ.

The Triathletes
Reinaldo Colucci

'Today you're either a short-distance or a long-distance triathlete.' Clearly no one passed on Mark Allen's words to Reinaldo Colucci, the Brazilian two-time Olympian, resident Ironman 70.3 Pucón winner, Ironman Brazil podium-hopper and one of the world's most versatile athletes.

A popular presence in a worldwide circuit scarcely populated by athletes from his homeland, Colucci hails from Descalvado, a small town in the state of São Paulo. After surprising himself by winning a 200m swim/800m run aquathlon at the age of 13 in 1997, Colucci began entering what triathlon events he could find in the Brazilian provinces, and would soon win his debut triathlon event.

Colucci would make his ITU debut with a fifth position in the 2003 Lausanne European Cup race, and was soon showing his adaptability, winning the ITU Long Distance World Series event in Lorient in 2006 and the Olympic-distance La Paz World Cup race in 2007.

Alternating his time between São Carlos in Brazil and St. Moritz in Switzerland, Colucci would soon become the King of Ironman 70.3 Pucón, winning the event in Chile four-times (taking victory in a thriller in 2013 by 3 seconds) and placing second twice, and taking second on his Ironman debut in Brazil in 2007. His big dream, however, is to pull on the Brazilian tri-suit at the Olympic Games in Rio in 2016.

△ △ Reinaldo Colucci is one of Brazil's foremost triathletes, with short and long-course career successes

Daniel Fontana

▽ After spending his formative years in Argentina, Fontana moved to Italy and was soon racing for his adoptive homeland

△ Fontana is the first athlete representing Italy to win an Ironman event

Throw a stick in Boulder, Stellenbosch or on Australia's Gold Coast at certain times in the season and the chances are you'll hit an international triathlete. Like cyclists, multisport athletes criss-cross the world each year in search of hills, hired help and humidity to produce the best chance of success on the race track. Daniel Monzoro Fontana is a prime example of today's globe-trotting triathlete.

Born in the city of General Roca in central Argentina, in 1975, Fontana began his triathlon career at the age of 19. Soon he was following in the footsteps of Argentina's foremost triathlete Oscar Saul Galíndez and scoring successes on the South American ITU circuit. After representing Argentina at the 2004 Athens Olympics, he relocated to Italy in 2006 and became a naturalized citizen in a successful bid to take his athletic career to another level.

After competing for Italy at the 2008 Beijing Olympics, Fontana made the move to long-distance triathlon and never looked back. His second place behind Michael Raelert at the 2009 Ironman 70.3 World Championships preceded wins at Ironman 70.3s in Pucón and Pescara in 2011. In 2014 he became the first Italian victor of an Ironman, winning the event at Los Cabos, Mexico, in a deeply impressive 8:26hr. Time may not now be on his side to produce many more winning feats in M-Dot racing ... but the racer from Río Negro will always have has first love of fly fishing to fall back on.

Faris Al-Sultan

▽ Seen here at the Abu Dhabi International, Faris Al-Sultan has experienced major long-course success

▷ In his famous Speedos on the worldwide Ironman circuit

An Iraqi father, an Ironman Hawaii win and consistency across all three disciplines … Faris Al-Sultan stands out for many things. Arguably, though, he's best known for wearing the skimpiest Speedos in multisport since Kenny Souza hogged every magazine cover in the late 1980s. Yet Faris's love of racing in budgie-smugglers shouldn't detract from his achievements on the race course; his commanding victory at Hawaii in 2005 was the second-fastest winning time of the decade.

Faris was born on 21 January 1978 in Munich, Germany, to a German mother and an Iraqi father. He started out as a swimmer and quickly showed an aptitude for endurance sport, racing his first marathon at the age of just 16. After watching Thomas Hellriegel racing Ironman Hawaii on television, Al-Sultan competed in his first Ironman at the age of 19 in 1997 (the infamous Lanzarote, no less, as he was too young to enter Challenge Roth), finishing in 10:33hrs.

His Hawaii debut came in 1999 (when he was still only 21) and his first podium there in 2004 with a third-place behind Normann Stadler, a compatriot with whom he soon developed an intense rivalry (there would be even less love lost between Faris and Chris McCormack). A year later, with Stadler sidelined by puncture problems and having a meltdown over them, Al-Sultan stormed to victory after posting two of the day's fastest swim and bike splits in Kona, crossing the line with a 5 minute victory over the Kiwi, Cameron Brown.

He wouldn't scale those heights at Hawaii again, but wins so far at Ironmans Arizona, Malaysia, Regensburg, Austria, Frankfurt and Lanzarote are concrete evidence of the Sultan of Sweat's incredible versatility and strength across every triathlon discipline.

The Triathletes
Tim DeBoom

△ Tim DeBoom has two Ironman World Championship titles to his name

▷△ The popular Iowan is the last American to top the podium in Kona

'The quiet man with a loud name,' is what Mark Allen calls Tim DeBoom, and this quiet American certainly has some incredible feats to shout about. The Boulder-based star's c.v. includes wins at Ironman New Zealand and the Norseman, but it's for his triumphs on Hawaii's Big Island that he will be remembered.

DeBoom was born in Cedar Rapids, Iowa, in 1970. Endurance genes were strong in the family,

with Tim's older brother Tony also a pro triathlete and Ironman winner. Tim finished his exercise physiology studies at university and moved from being a swimmer to a triathlete, winning his age group at the Olympic-distance ITU World Championships.

His Ironman breakthrough came at Ironman New Zealand in 1999, where he beat the much-fancied home hero Cameron Brown to the title. Months later, he made his Ironman World Championship debut in Hawaii, placing third behind Luc Van Lierde and Peter Reid. A year later his firm friend Reid edged him to the title by just 2mins after 8:20hrs of racing, a fact that would motivate DeBoom for the next year's showdown.

By 2001 DeBoom was in the ascendancy. In May he took the Ironman California title ahead of his brother Tony. Then, at the Big Kahuna at Hawaii in October, he took the lead 15km into the run and never relinquished his position. The Ironman world title was his. He was the first American to win since Mark Allen in 1995, and the victory was all the more emotional for coming just a month after the 9/11 terrorist attacks on America.

A year later, DeBoom became the first man since Allen in 1993 to successfully defend the Hawaii title, this time beating Peter Reid with another masterclass in tactical restraint, pacing and consistency (DeBoom's four Hawaii podium times would be 8:25, 8:23, 8:31 and 8:29). Over a decade later, DeBoom is still the last American athlete to stand on the top step in Hawaii.

Lisa Nordén

🇩🇰

▽ Lisa Nordén has scored a host of ITU successes, and was just a second short of Olympic glory

▽ ▽ The Swedish superstar celebrates another title on the Blue Carpet

Sport at the highest level can be cruel, the differences between the winner and the first loser often being a missed tackle, dropped catch or an under-hit putt. In Lisa Nordén's case, that difference was not starting her Olympic Games finish line sprint 0.01 of a second earlier. Thus it was that the Swedish athlete took silver at London 2012, and Swiss athlete Nicola Spirig was handed the ultimate sporting prize with the same official time (1:59.48).

Far from stewing over that photo-finish loss, though, Nordén showed the heart of a champion and went on to end the season taking the ITU World Championship in Yokohama, beating Anne Haug in another photo-finish (both had official times of 1:59:07). But it proved again just how tight the margins of error are in Olympic-distance racing.

Lisa Nordén was born 24 November 1984

in Kristianstad, southern Sweden. Many athletes come from a swim, bike or run background, but Nordén's first sporting love was equestrian. In what has to be a first, the Swede dabbled her toes in triathlon in 2002 because her horse had been injured and she needed to burn off excess energy. Within a year she was coming tenth at the ITU World Junior Champs in New Zealand, by 2007 she was the Under 23 ITU World Champion, and in March 2008 she was standing alongside Emma Snowsill and Vanessa Fernandes on the Mooloolaba ITU World Cup podium, a moment she still ranks as her greatest achievement today.

An ITU sprint world title came in 2010. And now Nordén is eyeing long-course racing under the guidance of her new coach – Craig Alexander – who knows what it takes to make the jump from Olympic to long-course racing?

The Triathletes
Puntous Twins

▷ The Puntous Twins were the first athletes to break the USA's dominance in Hawaii

▽ The duo were often inseparable on both the race track and away from triathlon

Up to 1982 US female athletes had dominated Ironman Hawaii, occupying every podium place in the first five editions of the race. Then, in 1983 and 1984, two identical, inseparable, smiley and cute 23-year-old French Canadian twins showed up and blew away the competition. On both occasions, Sylviane edged her sister Patricia to the title, and in doing so became the first non-US winner in Hawaii and the first woman to score back-to-back victories.

Born in Montreal, the twins were competitive swimmers by the age of eight, before turning to track pursuits in their late teens. In 1981 Patricia developed tendonitis in her heels and was told to cut down on running by her doctor – which led to them racing their first triathlon in Seattle in 1982. In a sign of things to come, they crossed the line together in joint first place.

After their Hawaii successes the twins became triathlon stars, racing around the world and attracting the attention of the media. After skipping Hawaii in 1985, they returned there in 1986 and it was Patricia's turn to cross the line first ... only to be disqualified for drafting (when it was actually Sylviane who was the guilty party). The win was awarded to Paula Newby-Fraser (with Sylviane second), and television cameras captured the twins crying in each other's arms at the finish line.

Sylviane finished second again in 1987 and 1989, but the twins would never jointly reach such Hawaii heights again. They finished fifth and sixth at the first ITU World Championships in 1989 before largely disappearing from multisport, occasionally showing up at running or duathlon events near their home of Montreal in subsequent years.

Bárbara Riveros Díaz

'Something happened that I can't explain. I got this new energy and I got through. It was really magical.' What the 150cm Bárbara Riveros lacks in height she more than makes up for in resilience and determination, and she produced one of ITU triathlon's finest comebacks of the decade to win the ITU Sprint Distance World Championships of 2011. Lying in fourth, behind Australian race leader Emma Jackson, and with 400m to go, the pint-sized star stepped on the gas to reel in Andrea Hewitt and Helen Jenkins before targeting Jackson. Consistently one of the circuit's best runners, Riveros rocketed past the Aussie on the home straight to become the Sprint world champion and secure her nation's debut ITU World Championship.

Born in 1987 in Santiago, Chile, Riveros came up through ITU's Sport Development programme, a project that supports promising young athletes from countries without a well-developed national federation. The ITU's Libby Burrell, the programme's director, was just one coach enamoured of the Chilean's work ethic and determination. 'She's small in stature but big in heart and has a mental ability that's second to none. I've been coaching a long time but her resilience is something I haven't ever seen in my life before.'

That determination to succeed in triathlon saw the hugely popular Riveros uproot from Chile in her teens to train in Australia and Spain before developing into one of the sport's most consistent performers and a regular podium occupant. With two Olympic appearances already in the bag, she now has her sights on the podium at the Games in Brazil in 2016 ... timed perfectly with the peak of her triathlon years.

◁▽ The Chilean star is one of the best runners on the ITU scene and has her sights set on Rio Olympic success in 2016

The Races

Challenge Roth

The mixture: 220,000 raucous spectators, 5,500 athletes doing battle on the world's fastest course, triathlon's most famous hill and 245kg of sausage. Every July, the unremarkable south German town of Roth hosts a four-day triathlon spectacular of endurance power, pilsner and pretzels that's become a genuine contender to Ironman Hawaii as the world's greatest race.

In contrast to the present day's cast of thousands, just one woman and 82 men took part in Roth's inaugural triathlon, the standard-distance Franconian, on Saturday, 22 September 1984

in West Germany. Back when Frankie Goes to Hollywood ruled the radio waves, a few hundred intrigued spectators occupied the side-lines and members of a local family, the Walchshöfers, were involved in the race's organization. Within a year Roth was hosting the Bavarian Championships; within two, the German Championships; and astronomic growth transformed the contest into an Ironman-branded race in 1988.

The nineties saw athletes of the calibre of Paula Newby-Fraser coming to the now-unified Germany to race, and Roth's reputation as the

▷ Athletes exit the water at the Franconian Triathlon, the precursor to the major long-distance events from Ironman and Challenge that were subsequently staged in Roth

▽ The sun rises on the Europakanal, 5,500 athletes prepare for a date with destiny in Deutschland

1984
The first Franconian Triathlon is held on 22 September 1984. Eighty-two men and one woman enter, and Franz Michels of Nuremberg wins the 700m swim/40km bike/10km run event.

1988
The first Ironman race is held in Roth with the classic 226km race distance; 706 participants enter the event. Axel Koenders and Rita Keitmann are the eventual winners.

1994
Zimbabwe's Paula Newby-Fraser sets a long-standing Ironman world record with a time of 8:50:53.

1997
Belgium's Luc Van Lierde set an Ironman world record, his time of 7:50:27 lasting for 14 years.

2001
The Roth organizers end their partnership with Ironman, and in 2002 the first Challenge Roth is held.

2003
A famous duel between Chris McCormack and Lothar Leder ends with the German's final Roth victory and gains widespread media attention.

2007
Herbert Walchshöfer dies on 25 October and is succeeded by his son Felix.

2008
Yvonne van Vlerken breaks Newby-Fraser's 1994 long-distance world record with a time of 8:45:48.

2011
Chrissie Wellington breaks the Roth record for the third year in a row, with a time of 8:18:13. Andreas Raelert also breaks the men's record in 7:45:33.

fastest 226km course on the planet was soon cemented. Newby-Fraser set a 14-year long women's Iron-distance record in 1994, Lothar Leder became the first man in history to go sub-8hr in 1996, and Luc Van Lierde created his own 14-year record in 1997 with a 7:50:27 time.

The dawn of the twenty-first century was dominated by Leder on the race track, yet behind the scenes tension between the World Triathlon Corporation (the owners of Ironman) and the local race team were brewing, with the WTC said to be making 'unacceptable organizational and financial demands' of the organizers.

The agreement with the WTC was torn up in late 2001 and, under the supervision of Herbert Walchshöfer, the Challenge series of long-distance

events was born. After a 'difficult' first edition in 2002, Challenge Roth continued to attract increasingly large crowds and major athletes, with a Leder/Chris McCormack classic in 2003 truly launching Challenge as a race force.

When Herbert passed away in 2007, the race organizer duties passed on to his son Felix, and the family involvement continued through thirty years. As Challenge expanded to destinations in Europe, Asia and beyond, Roth continued to host record-breaking showings from Yvonne van Vlerken, Chrissie Wellington and Andreas Raelert. All were witnessed by crowds exceeding such annual jamborees as the Glastonbury festival.

Local volunteers numbering 5,500 are on hand during the race (roughly one per athlete), with

journalists and athletes encouraged to use local homestays for accommodation (hotels in Roth aren't plentiful) – so guests are often surprised to emerge for a Bavarian breakfast to find they're sharing a table with a Chris McCormack or a Rachel Joyce. Local athletes are also made to wear a yellow sticker on their helmets: a nice touch that sees even more vocal support on the bike leg.

After a couple of days of festivities, including the annual 'meet and greet' where the elite contenders don dirndl dresses and lederhosen, the race starts at 6.30 a.m. with a 3.8km swim leg in the Europakanal, which passes under a huge road bridge thronged with spectators. Europop blasts from the speakers, a compere works his magic on the international crowd, and a handful of hot-air balloons ascend into the early morning sky. As the elite swimmers and fastest age-groupers exit the water, a large portion of the crowd hop on their bikes (the

▽ The Solarer Berg may not be triathlon's toughest climb, but it's arguably the most raucous, with crowds ten-deep lining the ascent

most popular way of following the Roth action) and head to the triathlon's most famous hill.

Located in Hilpoltstein town, the Solarer Berg has entered triathlon folklore and uniformly attracts a crowd of 50,000+ to the slopes. From Helvellyn to Alpe d'Huez and Ironman 70.3 St Croix, there may be more taxing climbs on the worldwide circuit, but nothing comes close to rivalling the wall of sound created at Roth. With the radlers (beer shandies) flowing, the five-deep crowds produce a cacophony of rattles, cowbells and singing. It's an unforgettable experience akin to a Tour de France mountain stage minus the devil chap running around with his giant fork. Mirinda Carfrae is just one athlete who calls it, 'Like nothing I've experienced in triathlon.'

'Bier mile' is the next major draw on the two-lap bike leg, with strategically placed spectator vantage points (or 'hot spots') serving liquid refreshments and pork-based snacks throughout the course. As anyone who's experienced a German football match, music or beer festival will testify, this nation sure knows how to put on a party – and Roth can stand proudly alongside Borussia Dortmund, Rock Am Ring or Oktoberfest as a major international draw.

The flat, rural run course heads out from Roth to Schwand and hugs the Main–Donau Canal before finishing in an increasingly large amphitheatre (by 2014, it's practically become a stadium), where the finishers are treated like returning heroes. A huge fireworks display starts once the final competitor has crossed the 226km finish line (Roth has long been subjected to internet forum debate that the course is a little short), and there's a party for volunteers the next night. Like Ironman Hawaii, Roth proves that, even if you don't have a loved one racing or your interest in the sport is on a once-a-year basis, long-distance racing can be a gripping experience.

But what do the next thirty years hold for Roth? Is a Challenge World Championship in the offing? 'We get asked this question on a daily basis so there's definitely a demand for it,' Zibi Szlufcik, CEO of the Walschöfers' expanded Challenge Family, has said. 'We've been working on a World Finals for the last two and half years. When the time is right, expect something spectacular!'

Szlufcik or the Roth team have been coy about whether Roth would be the destination of a Challenge World Final but watching the world's best long-distance athletes go head-to-head for a major long-distance world tri title would be a huge draw for European triathlon fans. If you thought an eight-hour spectacle couldn't be a spectator sport, clearly no one has told the residents and organizers of Roth that!

△ A stadium finish awaits the athletes, with the mother of all fireworks displays taking place once the final finisher comes home

Wildflower

'It's a classic race with roots in the heart of triathlon. It helped create the Half Ironman distance around the world. If Hawaii is the Tour de France, then Wildflower is the Tour of Flanders. Hard and relentless. I'm very proud to have won a title on that brutal course.' So says the 2003 Wildflower winner Tim DeBoom on the influence of the Californian classic on the history of triathlon.

While beautiful, scenic and resplendent are adjectives commonly associated with the triathlon lexicon, cool rarely enters the

▷ Wildflower has been a classic on the American calendar since the mid-eighties, drawing some of the world's finest athletes and thousands of age-groupers to remotest California each year

▽ Thousands of athletes run down Harris Ramp for the start of Wildflower in 2010

multisport vernacular, thanks largely to the neon clothing and European techno music booming out. Wildflower more than any other race, however, can lay claim to being hip, with the five-time Wildflower winner Paula Newby-Fraser famously labelling it the 'Woodstock of Triathlon' and Greg Welch echoing the statement before simply saying, 'Phew, what a race!'

Wildflower began its colourful journey in 1983, two years after Escape from Alcatraz was first held 300km up the Pacific coast. In a scene familiar to anyone who's witnessed *Parks and Recreation*, the acclaimed NBC sitcom, the Monterey County Parks and Recreation department threw some ideas at a flip chart and what stuck was a bluegrass music festival with arts and crafts, wildflower exhibits, a 10km run and a 100km triathlon, held on inland Monterey County parkland along the shores of Lake San Antonio. Won by Dean 'The Machine' Harper (a man still aiming for Hawaii age-group podiums today), the event drew just 86 triathletes, who were greeted with bad weather and chilly waters on the lake swim.

Despite the mixed reviews, the race, nonetheless, would grace the first-ever issue of *Triathlete* magazine in 1983, and the Monterey County Parks department (led by Terry Davis, the future CEO of race organizer Tri-California, who also host events in Pacific Grove and San Francisco and Scott Tinley's Triathlon) would persevere to create a world-famous race that would lure tens of thousands of competitors and the world's greatest athletes to campsites in the middle of nowhere in Monterey County over its 32 editions to date.

The line-up of winners reads like a Who's Who of the sport, with ITU and/or Ironman World Champions who have won at Wildflower including Scott Molina, Paula Newby-Fraser, Peter Reid, Heather Fuhr, Natascha Badmann, Simon Lessing, Chris McCormack, Tim DeBoom and Leanda

◁ Wildflower regularly attracts a number of top elite racers to Monterey County each May

▷ South Africa's off-road King Conrad Stoltz takes on the 88km Wildflower bike leg in 2010

△ Over a thousand student volunteers man the aid stations at Wildflower, helping to create the unique atmosphere

Grade' and the 1,000ft climb of 'Heart Rate Hill', and 60% of the run taking place on trails.

Top British off-road triathlete Lesley Paterson, never one to shirk a challenge, is just one of those to suffer at the hands of the Long Course race. 'That is one tough race,' says the Xterra World Championship-winning Scot. 'I haven't had a race like that for a while where I genuinely wanted to quit and I had to muster up all my mental energy just to finish the darn thing. I don't think I'll be back any time soon!'

Far from being a solitary venture in the wilds akin to the Norseman, the race throws up plenty of quirks to keep competitors amused. The excitement generated at the swim start has only a handful of contenders worldwide, with the compere and crowd increasing in volume as the countdown begins. The local college San Luis Obispo also supply 1,200 student volunteers in bikinis and swimming trunks to man the aid stations throughout the 550 acres of Californian countryside (the infamous nude aid station at 7km of the run is now a thing of the past). The student population is also well represented behind the race barriers, with fancy dress, cowbells, live music and runners being sprayed with garden hoses adding to the sense of fun.

While the qualification slots for the Ironman 70.3 World Championships have long been taken away, for age-groupers who break the tape the achievement has become a badge of honour, with USA Triathlon making the Long Course race a qualifier for the age-group ITU World Championships and the event also hosting the Wildflower Collegiate Championships.

As the triathlons at Wildflower have continued to grow, the bluegrass festival now plays second fiddle to the athletic endeavours. Lake San Antonio's future Wildflower presence is also under threat, with the water levels becoming so low that the 2014 race was held 3km south-east in the Harris Creek area. But while there's triathlon, there'll always be a Wildflower, sticking to its roots and resisting mass commercialization like a grizzled veteran of the music festival that provides the alternative moniker for this classic triathlon.

Cave. The list of those who have come and not graced the podium's top step is arguably even greater, with Dave Scott, Mark Allen, Scott Tinley, Mike Pigg and Greg Welch all clipping into their cleats (and possibly camping) in one of California's remotest spots.

Tri-California's twenty-first-century incarnation of Wildflower hasn't strayed far from its roots, yet regularly attracts 30,000 athletes, supporters and spectators over the weekend. Up to 8,000 competitors sign up for either a mountain bike sprint race, an Olympic-distance event or the weekend's premier attraction, Saturday's 1.9km swim/88.5km bike/21.1km run 'Long Course' race: what McCormack labels the 'unofficial World Championship of half-Iron-distance racing'.

Away from the festival fun and campfires (given its proximity to the middle of nowhere, camping or hiring an RV is easier than finding an hotel), the course is Wildflower's major draw, with rugged bike routes that weave their way through woodland and the Lake San Antonio waterfront. Scenic it may be, but Wildflower is unquestionably a hot, hilly and hard task to negotiate, with the bike course featuring legendary climbs 'Nasty

WILDFLOWER
TRIATHLONS

4:27.54
chronomix cc3000

ND ONLY

MAY 1 - 2, 2010

◁ Top British athlete and coach Julie Dibens takes the 2010 Wildflower title

The Races

Windsor Triathlon

Since its inception in 1991 the Windsor Triathlon has played a fundamental role in the development of swim, bike and run in Britain and beyond, hosting classic elite showdowns and providing the backdrop to thousands of age-grouper experiences.

The race started life in 1991 as part of the 220 Triathlon Series, a series of races organized by five stalwarts of the UK triathlon scene – Trevor Gunning, Robin Brew, Graham Matthews, 220's founder John Lilley and John Lunt, who took the reins of the Windsor Triathlon.

Lunt raced his first triathlon in 1984 in Dorking on the UK's low-key race scene and in 1985 took on the first London Triathlon (which he would later direct). Human Race, which stemmed from his work managing leisure centres, was set up in October 1990, and Windsor followed in the summer of 1990 with the help of Jasmine Flatters. Lunt organized the race until 2013. 'I'd got to know the top British athletes by training with the likes of Spencer Smith, Stuart Hayes and Tim Don at the Thames Turbo Tri Club,' he says today. '220 Triathlon magazine had also played a major part in the start of the Windsor Triathlon. The editor, John Lilley, was starting a five-series race and encouraged me to be part of it. Without John's emotional and financial input, the sport wouldn't be where it is today.'

Via phone, fax and postal entries, the debut race in 1991 attracted 250 athletes to the Windsor Leisure Centre, including rising British star Spencer Smith. In contrast to the slick operation of Windsor's later years, the event suffered some teething troubles, with 20 of the elite field not ready when the gun went (causing athletes – who were later awarded time penalties – to run along the river bank of the Thames and dive into the water) and a poorly signposted course sending them on a variety of routes around Windsor. Undeterred, Smith posted a 33min, 10km time, finishing 1:45mins ahead of the chasing Glenn Cook in the first of his many Windsor triumphs.

Smith won gold again in 1992 before Colin Dixon (a man still placing high at Windsor today) and Steve Burton took the next overall titles. Smith hadn't raced in Britain since taking the 1993 ITU World title in Salford but returned to Windsor in 1995 to win a landmark event, fighting off a group of drafters on the bike to blitz the field by over three minutes. Top British pro Loretta Sollars would take the women's title, and it was all televised on the BBC's *Grandstand*, at a time when Smith and Simon Lessing (who's never raced Windsor) were taking the sport to new levels.

'Being on *Grandstand* gave me the opportunity to go to the council to say that we need to move the race into the centre of Windsor and next to the castle,' continues Lunt. 'There was initial opposition but, in a quirk of fate, the castle had just started charging visitors to enter, leading to a massive drop in tourist numbers. So the council needed the promotion that a run leg past the castle would provide.'

Sian Brice took the first of her four titles in 1996, and Smith won three consecutive titles from 1997 to 1999 to take his Windsor tally to a

▽ The Windsor Triathlon has been a classic on the UK circuit for 25 years

▷ The race starts with a notoriously early swim in the River Thames

△ Along with the elite race, Windsor has a huge age-group field of all abilities

◁ Supporters line the roads of Windsor's town centre outside of the huge transition area

record six wins. In 2000 the event was a Sydney Olympic Games qualifier, with Tim Don and Brice taking the honours and NFL star Darryl 'The Fridge' Haley also on the start line. (Three-time winner Don, incidentally, used to stuff race packs for Human Race in return for free entries to races when he first started out.) In 2001 another King of Windsor, Andrew Johns, edged Spencer Smith by 1sec on the Barry Avenue finishing chute to win the battle of the double European Champions and the first of his three Windsor titles.

In 2003 almost the entire elite field wrongly turned early at the sprint-distance buoy in the swim, apart from three athletes who completed the correct course. After the race, officials disqualified virtually all the elite entrants, resulting in the biggest win of his career for Malta's Dermot Galea, whose 2:12:25 was the slowest winning time ever at Windsor. Another eventful year was 2012; the event turned into a duathlon after a deluge of rain rendered the Thames too dangerous for swimming.

The noughties saw British luminaries Liz Blatchford, Julie Dibens, Helen Jenkins and Jodie

Stimpson all taking the title. The event also scooped plenty of gongs, including the *220 Triathlon* Race of the Year title and the British Triathlon 'Event of the Year' on seven separate occasions. While the pro fields of the present decade rarely rival the depth of the 1990s starting line ups, the race's major draw has unquestionably become the 2,500 age-group athletes who do battle in the shadow of Windsor Castle.

The notoriously early start to an out-and-back swim in the River Thames leads on to the pretty, gently undulating Windsor Great Park bike route, and finally one of UK triathlon's greatest-run legs. Backed by deep crowds, Olympic-distance athletes negotiate a circuit that takes them into Eton's High Street before returning to face the infamous short, sharp hill on the approach to the castle – and there are three laps, so they have it all to do on three separate occasions. Like the climb, the memorable finish on Barry Avenue has become an iconic rite of passage for British triathletes, ever since that day in June 1991 when John Lunt's Windsor adventure began.

▽ Rising Brit star Emma Pallant takes the 2014 Windsor title to join a winner's list that includes Julie Dibens, Helen Jenkins and Jodie Stimpson

▷ 'This is England!' says six-time winner Spencer Smith on the Windsor experience

The Races

Escape from Alcatraz

From the starting point of infamous former prison island Alcatraz to the Clint Eastwood connection and the boulevards named after John F. Kennedy and Martin Luther King, the Escape from Alcatraz Triathlon draws on American history and mythology to produce an experience unlike any other in triathlon.

Held in the shadow of the 'Rock' and Golden Gate Bridge, the race has also over its 34-year history become an essential component of the triathlon story, with previous winners including past and present royalty such as Mike Pigg, Greg Welch, Paula Newby-Fraser, Simon Lessing, Chris McCormack, Leanda Cave and Javier Gómez. In 2006 the race was ranked as the number one triathlon in the world by *Inside Triathlon* magazine, with *220 Triathlon* in 2009 naming it the second-best event (behind Kona) of the magazine's then 20-year lifetime.

The conception for Escape from Alcatraz came to Joe Oakes soon after he returned from participating at the second Ironman Hawaii race in 1979. A two-year development period followed before his idea bore fruit in the summer of 1981, when the first Escape from Alcatraz race was held as a private club event for Oakes' Dolphin Club.

▽ Athletes leap from the San Francisco Belle steamboat into the 12°C waters of San Francisco Bay for triathlon's most iconic start

The inaugural event started with a swim in San Francisco Bay from Alcatraz Island, where the notorious federal prison was situated from 1933 to 1963, to San Francisco city, then a bike ride over the Golden Gate Bridge to the mountain biking stronghold of Marin County, before a run course over Mount Tamalpais to Stinson Beach and back. The race was split in 1983, with a separate commercial event open to the public, now an aquathlon held on a course entirely within San Francisco.

The course has also altered on a number of occasions, with those of the early nineties taking in the Great Highway, multiple trails in the Presidio of San Francisco and across Rodeo Beach before climbing an 850-foot ascent up Wolf Ridge. This 1990–93 course was won three-times by hard-core Ironman racer Mike Pigg and Paula-Newby Fraser, with fellow M-Dot legend Greg Welch breaking the course record in 2:54hrs in 1992.

'Alcatraz has one of the most eerie starts in the whole world' Welch says today. 'There's a reason why no one ever escaped from Alcatraz. When I raced, I was guided over the wrong side of the Golden Gate and had to lob my bike over the rail to run across eight lanes of traffic with cars screeching to a halt. That, incidentally, was the last time the race went over the bridge so I blame that volunteer! The race is also where I created a magnificent friendship with Robin Williams.'

The current incarnation of Escape from Alcatraz is organized by IMG, the team behind the London Triathlon and Abu Dhabi International, and takes place annually in June. Aptly for a race that begins at what the Native Americans referred to as 'Evil island', the course design certainly has a sadistic air, with a chilly and choppy sea crossing and the infamous 'sand ladder' on the run leg awaiting triathletes on their 44.1km voyage. (Despite being Escape from Alcatraz's third-highest search engine ranking, sharks aren't a danger at the event, with organizers claiming the small ones that inhabit San Francisco Bay 'have no interest in triathletes'.)

In a similar vein to the Norseman, the event kicks off with a leap of faith from a boat, in this instance an old steamboat named the San Francisco Belle with a 2,000-athlete capacity, into the bracing 12°C waters of San Francisco Bay, off Alcatraz Island. Fresh from singing the

△▽ Choppy seas and strong currents greet the athletes in the Bay during the 2.4km crossing to the mainland. A one-hour cut-off is strictly enforced

'Star-Spangled Banner', all the 2,000 athletes are dispatched from the boat in just 8mins, before facing choppy seas and swift currents – with alternate sideways breaths bringing the Golden Gate Bridge into view – to make the 2.4km crossing to shore at the Marina Green Beach.

'That was probably the most afraid I've been before a swim,' says Hawaii champ Karen Smyers, who raced in 2002. 'You don't get to practise jumping out of a boat very often. Being a rookie, I didn't stand near the doors so I was held up and just had to jump out into the water without looking. Hitting that freezing-cold water sees the adrenaline rise!'

Before athletes can clip in their bike shoes, a 400m run follows from the bay to the transition zone at Marina Green. The 28.9km bike leg is up next, taking athletes through the Presidio to Camino del Mar before heading south on the Great Highway to Golden Gate Park. Competitors are given the chance to race on Martin Luther King Jr. and John F. Kennedy Drives next before heading back to the Great Highway

and Marina Green for the transition to the run.

Rivalling the swim leg in the infamy stakes, the 12.8km run is one of the most iconic in triathlon, proving that it's not just the former inmates of Alcatraz who signed up for punishment in San Francisco Bay. Beginning at Fort Point within touching distance of the Golden Gate Bridge, athletes battle the Presidio Headlands up and under the Golden Gate Bridge through the tunnel and onto the sandy trails of the Golden Gate Recreation Area. At 8km, they are faced with the formidable Sand Ladder – 400 nigh-on vertical, uneven log steps (thankfully, there's a hand cable) up a cliff face from Baker Beach, back up to the road. Such is the draw of the Sand Ladder, it even has its own column on the results page (Javier Gómez did it in 1:50min in 2013).

Runners will follow their path back under the Golden Gate Bridge, pass Crissy Field and finish in the grass at Marina Green amongst thousands of cheering fans. 'Ah, the finish!' says veteran Ironman and coach Mark Kleanthous. 'Overlooked by the

△ Athletes land ashore at Marina Green Beach at Escape from Alcatraz in 2003 before a 400m run to transition

▷ The iconic Cliff House is just one of the tourist draws on the 28km bike leg through the west of San Francisco

million-dollar houses on the cliffs of the South Bay and greeted by thousands of excited American spectators . . . San Francisco will love you forever.'

The list of winners who have been adored by San Francisco include eight-time winner Michellie Jones, four-time winners Mike Pigg, Chris McCormack and Leanda Cave, Simon Lessing and Paula Newby-Fraser (three-time champs) and Greg Welch, who won twice. Javier Gómez and Heather Jackson took the titles in 2013, with the most recent edition of Escape from Alcatraz in 2014 witnessing American über-swimmer and Escape from Alcatraz veteran Andy Potts earning his sixth win on the course by virtue of his swim split, while new mum Sarah Haskins claimed the victory on her first attempt at escaping from Alcatraz.

Sadly, due to the San Francisco Belle's limited capacity and strict time limits placed on the organizers, entry for the Escape from Alcatraz is almost as tough as the race itself. The majority of the slots are chosen by a lottery process, with the remainder through qualification via a decent rank in the previous Escape from Alcatraz event or in qualification races held during the preceding year.

◁ British pro racer Leanda Cave races along Baker Beach to the infamous Sand Ladder on the final leg of the Escape from Alcatraz Triathlon

△ 'San Francisco will love you forever,' says finisher Mark Kleanthous on completing the epic Escape from Alcatraz experience

Ironman France

Ironman France, the Nice Triathlon, the Nice Long-Distance Triathlon, whatever you call it, this is a race that's drenched in triathlon history. From the early years, when Mark Allen made it his own, to the latter days of 80,000 spectators lining the course of what Allen calls 'the best outside of the granddaddy itself in Kona,' the Cote d'Azur event has played a major part in the evolution of triathlon in Europe.

Given that many, including Scott Tinley, believe that triathlon began life in 1920s France, it's apt that modern triathlon's development should also be tied to the country, with Nice hosting what many believe is the first major modern-day triathlon in Europe. Details about the debut race are scarce, but the overriding consensus is that early Ironman athlete Scott Tinley had been commissioned to devise a race for Barry Frank, the powerful vice president of IMG's television sports programming, in Monaco. Tinley's Tri-Country Triathlon would find athletes leaping from a boat in Monte Carlo, riding to Italy and finishing back on the Cote d'Azur.

△ The Promenade des Anglais is the setting for the multi-lap marathon run of Ironman France

At a time when Ironman Hawaii offered no race winnings, a $50,000 prize purse was touted and television exposure promised. The Tinley/Frank Tri-Country dream ended when the Princess of Monaco, otherwise known as American actress Grace Kelly, died in a car accident on the Corniche in September 1982, and sporting events were cancelled as the Principality mourned.

An adapted event moved along the coast to Nice and was first held on a chilly November morning in 1982 with the unique 4km swim, 120km bike and 30km run distance (compared to the Ironman distance of 3.8km/180km/42.2km), with a healthy British contingent drawing inspiration from the event to launch the UK's debut triathlon at Reading in 1983.

The event was still to be televized in Europe. Yves Cordier, France's fledgling star of triathlon and the future Ironman France race director, was just one athlete lured to race in southern France. Mark Allen, another athlete drawn to the French Riviera, embarked on a winning streak that would see him take 10 consecutive titles at a time when

▽ Ironman France takes over Nice for one weekend every June, with the transition area located on the famous Promenade des Anglais

the Nice Triathlon, along with Hawaii and Powerman Zofingen, was one of the big three to win – a feat Allen rates as highly as his Hawaii achievements.

'I raced the event 10 times. I won it 10 times. In many ways that's more amazing to me than winning six times in Hawaii,' says Allen. 'I had some really tough races there. The most difficult was my penultimate victory in 1992 when Yves Cordier was over 7mins ahead at T2. By the turn around of the run I'd only made up about 2mins. It wasn't happening. Yves was going to win. So I just told myself that if I continued to run like a triathlete I would lose, but if I tried running like a runner I might have a chance. So what I did was to just surge for as long as I could take it, as if I was going 1km repeats on the track. It took

me until the sign that said 400m to the finish before I was able to get close to him. Then I passed him with just metres to go.'

Fellow Hawaii immortal Paula Newby-Fraser would be the other victor in 1992, winning the event just four weeks after taking another of the Big Three titles, Powerman Zofingen. Allen would take his final title in 1993, beating the British ITU World Champion Simon Lessing in an event the Brit cherishes highly. 'I still have fond memories racing Mark Allen in Nice in 1993,' Lessing told Slowtwitch's Timothy Carlson in 2008. 'I was 22 and I ran side by side with Mark as he was chasing his 10th straight win. There were 25 or so spectators and journalists on bikes chasing and shouting for Mark or for me. Mark pulled away with 5km to go but the atmosphere was unbelievably fantastic.'

◁ Top Irish middle- and long-distance Eimear Mullan races the 180km bike route north of Nice in June 2014

▷ Heat and humidity is a major factor to contend with in Nice, with temperatures regularly reaching into the 30s

The ITU would hold the first of its ITU Long Distance World Championships at Nice in 1994 (won by Rob Barel and Isabelle Mouthon-Michellys), with Lessing returning in 1995 to take the title ahead of Luc Van Lierde and Peter Reid. The ITU would host its Long-Distance showpiece in Nice on three more occasions in 1997, 2000 and 2002, but the race had lost a little of its lustre. Over a five-year period, race organizer Georg Hochegger of Triangle Events and Yves Cordier started to chase the Ironman route. After extending the ITU distances (the ITU still use the original Nice Triathlon distances for its Long-Distance World Championships), the switch to an Ironman branded event took place in 2005, with Ironman France being moved south from its previous location of Gerardmer.

Once the event was given the M-Dot stamp, Spain's Marcel Zamora quickly became the present-day Mark Allen, winning on five consecutive occasions from 2006 to 2010. Belgium's Frederik Van Lierde is another who's reaped the rewards on the Riviera, taking the title in 2011, 2012 and 2013 on his march to the Ironman World title in Hawaii. (Lance Armstrong was just days from making his Ironman debut at Nice in 2012 when the U.S. Anti-Doping Agency came calling.)

While the course may not serve up any sub-8hr action (Van Lierde's course record is 8:21:51), the lure of the event to pro athletes and age-groupers is clear to see. Triathlon truly takes over the Promenade des Anglais during Ironman France weekend, with M-Dot-tattooed triathletes and their support crews outnumbering the tanned European holiday-makers on Nice's sweeping pebble beaches and in the warm, azure waters of France's fifth biggest city.

Much of the acclaim and demand for entry spots at the event is down to the unparalleled 180km bike course. Following much of the original Nice Triathlon route, the course passes through villages and features 5,000ft of climbing in the hills of the Alpes Maritimes, complete with panoramic views of the glistening Mediterranean below. While the views are unforgettable – if athletes are able to catch a breath to admire the scenery – the event is far from a sight-seeing tour of the Rivera: heat and humidity play a part in making the course one of Ironman's toughest days in the sun.

The marathon run provides a counterbalance to the vertical ascents of the bike, with four flat and fast loops along Nice's promenade in front of 80,000 spectators providing the finale to one of triathlon's truly iconic events.

▽ Thousands line the Nice promenade for the four-loop marathon run of Ironman France

Abu Dhabi International Triathlon

A helicopter buzzing over a beach in the Persian Gulf and a legion of lean soldiers ready to do battle. All it needs is Wagner's 'The Ride of the Valkyries' and the scene is more *Apocalypse Now* than your average triathlon. But average the Abu Dhabi International Triathlon certainly ain't, with a mega-bucks prize pot, unconventional and controversial race distances and a belter of a pro field instantly lifting the race into triathlon's big leagues.

When race organizers IMG and the Abu Dhabi Tourism Authority launched the Abu Dhabi International Triathlon to much fanfare in November 2009, the facts and figures involved instantly sent an army of off-season triathletes to either a) the online forums or b) the travel agent. Eye-watering prize fund? Check. Closed highways and a Formula 1 race circuit? Check. A format that ripped up the traditional distances of tri? Oh yes!

Catching the eye was that $250,000 prize purse – with a healthy $20,000 for age-groupers – that saw the race join the Hy-Vee ITU Elite Cup and Ironman Hawaii as one of triathlon's biggest paydays. But another set of figures was grabbing plenty of attention too. The skewed distance splits saw a 3km swim followed by a 200km bike before finishing with a 20km run – compared to the official Ironman distances of 3.8km swim, 180km

▽ The swim start of the Abu Dhabi International Tri takes place at dawn in front of the opulent $6-billion Emirates Palace

bike, 42.2km run. The tri purists were quick to point out that the oversized bike leg contradicted John Collins' original aim of discovering the best all-round athlete.

Triathlon's best riders couldn't care less, however, with Brit pro Phil Graves swiftly signing up and Björn Andersson claiming, 'I've been waiting my whole career for a race like this with a short run!' Raynard Tissink, meanwhile, mused, 'I look at it as a bike race with a little bit of a swim and a run. Whoever can run after 200km is going to do pretty well.'

Once the dust settled, the truth is that the Abu Dhabi International Triathlon has regularly drawn the best field outside Kona, in its first year alone luring Eneko Llanos, Frederik Van Lierde (who has won it twice), Rachel Joyce, Leanda Cave, Julie Dibens and Caroline Steffen. Later racers of the event have included Chris McCormack, Marino Vanhoenacker and Craig Alexander, with the Brownlee brothers proving victorious at the 'Short Course' (1.5km swim, 100km bike and 10km run) event together in 2014, their longest triathlon to date at 3:12hrs.

Lost in the hype surrounding the race was the fact that the emirate had hosted a sprint-distance event in the late nineties, with Welsh athlete Marc Jenkins the victor in 1998 and Simon Lessing winning in 1999. Jenkins recalls, 'It was hot as hell and really good fun. The organizers had bought hundreds of bikes for the kids to use.'

Up to and including 2014 (the event had joined the ITU World Series from 2015 and moved to the Abu Dhabi Sailing & Yacht Club), the race kicked off in the salty, buoyant lagoon in front of the ostentatious, $6-billion Emirates Palace's private beach (the second most expensive hotel in history, with some eye-watering buffet prices to boot), where the pond-like conditions were unlikely to pose much of a problem for the elites, and only that helicopter caused any sort of waves.

◁ The unique 200km bike course was hosted on closed roads and headed east out of the city towards Yas Island

◁ Pro and age-group long-course athletes alike race on the Abu Dhabi Formula One Grand Prix circuit

▷ Two-time winner Frederik Van Lierde battles the sweltering heat on the run in Abu Dhabi.

The 2015 bike and run leg routes had not yet been announced at the time of writing, but seemed likely to involve some of the previous courses. Thankfully, given the reputation of Abu Dhabi's drivers, the bike course has hitherto taken place on completely closed roads. It wove through central Abu Dhabi heading east and passing over Saadiyat Island before reaching a major draw for elites and age-groupers alike – Yas Island, the home of Ferrari World, the Yas Waterworld and the Abu Dhabi Formula One Grand Prix circuit – then headed into the desert before returning to the seafront for transition to a flat, lapped run course in the unforgiving mid-30s Gulf heat.

In addition to some pre-season racing, another reason for the huge take-up of age-group athlete places at this event is the chance to rub shoulders on the same course and at the same time with the world's greatest long-distance pro racers: something few, if any, other sports in the world allow. Over 2,400 athletes from 68 countries entered the sold-out 2014 event, with Algeria, China, Ethiopia, Peru, Trinidad & Tobago, Ukraine and Vietnam all represented on the UAE start line.

The Abu Dhabi International Triathlon has helped promote the sport in the Middle East, and also paved the way for the launch of Challenge Bahrain, which saw a prize pot totalling $500,000 again luring the world's best racers to the Persian Gulf in December 2014.

The Races

Laguna Phuket Triathlon

It's fair to say that the Laguna Phuket Triathlon is a race like no other. The multisport festival takes place over a full week in late November, with proceedings kicking off with an Olympic(ish)-distance race consisting of a 1.8km swim, 55km bike and 12km run, before a week of social and sporting shindigs build up to a middle-distance event on the following weekend.

The Asian event has been a triathlon-lovers' paradise for over twenty years and is known as

▽ Athletes at the 2010 Laguna Phuket prepare for a non-wetsuit swim in the blue waters of the Laguna Beach Resort

Asia's first-ever triathlon, attracting scores of athletes to one of the most cherished spots in Thailand for a final triathlon fling before the season's end. Legends of the sport, including Mark Allen, Greg Welch, Craig Alexander, Paul Newby-Fraser, Chris McCormack, Michellie Jones and Chrissie Wellington (with 26 Ironman World Championship titles between them) have ventured to south-east Asia to race, unsurprisingly drawn to the tropical scenery of Thailand's largest island. The giant shrimp Tom Yum soup is worth the trip alone!

The race began with a bang in 1994, Mike Pigg edging Mark Allen in the men's event and Karen Smyers overcoming Paula Newby-Fraser in the women's race – a dress rehearsal of 1995's Ironman Hawaii race (minus Newby-Fraser bonking 200m before the finish). Smyers still holds Phuket in high regard today:

Laguna Phuket falls a few weeks after Hawaii, so all I had to do was recover from Kona and rise to the occasion on race day. Our hotel had the best water slide; we had a slew of pro athletes just goofing around. I almost broke my nose on one ride down with Mike Pigg! The race itself was unique. The swim in the ocean was followed by a run across the sand to dive into a lagoon – a great way to wash off the salt water but one helluva challenge. The bike was hilly and hot, and you couldn't take it lightly. And the run was challenging as well, and we saw crazy things like water buffalo wandering across the course.

A year later Pigg overcame Greg Welch, and Michellie Jones beat both Smyers and Newby-Fraser to take the honours, with the 1996 edition

△ Multiple-Laguna Phuket champ and Swiss Olympian Ruedi Wild on the bike course in 2013

featuring one of the strongest top-five fields you
could ever hope to see: Simon Lessing standing on
top of the podium ahead of Mark Allen, Andrew
Johns, Brad Beven and Spencer Smith in an
Olympic-distance showdown.

As well as the Hawaii legends already
mentioned, athletes of the calibre of Lori Bowden,
Peter Reid, Tim DeBoom, Normann Stadler
and Leanda Cave also made their imprint on
Phuket's white sands in later years. Ironman
even briefly hosted its Ironman 70.3 Asia Pacific
Championships at the event from 2010 to 2012
(Chris McCormack and Caroline Steffen were two
of the winners) before curtailing its partnership,
citing the race's small scale and inability to grow.

Challenge took up the reins in 2013 and
launched the Laguna Phuket Tri Fest, hosting
a middle-distance race, the Challenge Laguna
Phuket event, a week after the classic Laguna
Phuket Triathlon, with Melissa Hauschildt and
Rasmus Petreus its first winners. Challenge
ambassador Chris McCormack was happy to
promote the race's multisport legacy: 'Challenge
Roth is the oldest race in Europe, Challenge
Penticton the oldest in North America, and now
we have Challenge Laguna Phuket, the oldest race
in Asia – that speaks volumes to me about the
importance Challenge Family places on the legacy
of our sport.'

Like the format, the races are unconventional as
well. What's become known as the Race of Legends
begins from the beach tops of the Andaman
Sea before plunging into the azure waters of the
Laguna Beach Resort for a 1.8km swim. Two-thirds
of the way through the swim, the athletes then
have to jump out of the ocean and sprint 100m to
enter the lagoon before the final swim leg.

The bike leg takes in the northern part of
Phuket, encompassing the steep challenging
sections of the Naithon Hills. 2010's runner-up
and British pro Emma Ruth Smith says:

*On the bike, I relied on my mountain bike skills
to negotiate Phuket's steep, lung-busting hills.
Rest assured, they're short-lived and, for the
most part, you'll have flat, stunning rainforest
scenery to enjoy before a two-lap loop around
the beautifully well-maintained Laguna Resort.
The weather is as hot and humid as a steam
room, however. But you don't have to overexert
yourself; it's the end of season, after all.*

Another quirk finds athletes dismounting from
their bikes to cross a bridge and remount towards
the finale of the bike leg.

The classic distance run is flat and leads
runners north through the Laguna Phuket resort
complex before looping back past the Wedding
Chapel and through the Canal Shopping Village.
The race weekend culminates at the Laguna
Grove, with the after-party said to be up with the
Xterra World Champs in Maui for its feel-good
factor and free-flowing cocktails.

Slateman

▽ The Slateman commences
with one of UK triathlon's most
beautiful swims in the waters
of Llyn Padarn

swim ringed by the mountains of Snowdonia. A bike course teleported from the Tour de France. A trail run past a power station and up a disused quarry. In just four years, the organizers of the Slateman have created an experience with a genuine claim to be the UK's best and craziest Olympic(ish)-distance triathlon.

Set in the pleasant tourist town of Llanberis in North Wales' Snowdonia National Park, the Slateman started with 450 competitors in 2011 but has already expanded to 1,700 triathletes competing over the Slateman Full and Half courses. For the Full athletes, the 63km Snowdonian adventure kicks off with a 1km swim in the 14°C waters of Llyn Padarn with the foreboding mountains of Snowdonia, soon to be tackled on the bike course, looming above.

After T1 the relentless, leg-sapping Llanberis Pass takes you up to the 360m-high Pen-y-Pass, where the most welcome aid station is located. After that an exhilarating 60km/h (faster, if you have more nerve than us) descent to Capel Curig follows, with the waters of Lynnau Mymbyr adding

△ The Snowdon Sherpa races age-grouper Andrew Noble to the top of the 360m high Pen-y-Pass

to the epic scenery. If the bike route fails to scale these highs again (and what highs they are), the support is relentless, with enthusiastic cries from passing cars and families offering refreshments, and plenty of flag-waving, from outside their houses.

After the 51km route takes athletes back into transition via the western side of Llanberis, the incomparable, frankly bonkers 11km run/ power walk begins. The first kilometre passes the entrance to the Dinorwig Power Station and follows a circular bridge, but the real 'fun' starts with the ascent into the Dinorwig Slate Quarries. Comically steep climbs lurk after each corner, with athletes choosing to succumb to the challenge and walk, or to power up the slopes with a view to taking the Quarryman title awarded for the fastest time up the infamous zig-zags of Dinorwig quarry.

After 330m of climbing, the course enters the Coed Dinorwig woodland for some classic single-track trail running of leaping logs and sliding on stones. A spell-binding view of the finish line some 300m below precedes a 2km descent to the finishing arch. Like the crowds and cowbells

▷ The relentless, quad-burning Llanberis Pass faces athletes straight out of T1

throughout the course, the race's final throes are accompanied by a raucous atmosphere, akin to another Welsh wonder, Ironman Wales, with deep throngs lining the chute until the final athlete comes home after about five-and-a-half hours. It's a far cry from the muted support triathletes receive in certain areas of the UK.

The organizers, Always Aim High, donate 50% of their profits to local community projects and charities, and the love is definitely returned. 'We work very closely with the local communities,' says race director Tim Lloyd. 'We employ a community liaison officer, and our policy is to support community projects and local charities. In 2013 over 50% of our company profits were spent in this way. This takes a massive amount of work and commitment from our side, but the benefits speak for themselves; the 2014 Slateman will generate over £1 million for the local economy. This is especially satisfying for me as I'm a local man, born and raised in Llanberis.'

As for evidence of the race's tough credentials, a quick scan of the results list shows even the top athletes don't have it easy at the Slateman,

with the Full distance winner home in 2:20hrs, with plenty of DNFs littered around the Welsh mountains (this author added an hour to his usual Olympic-distance time).

For 2015 and beyond, the organizers are coy on where any expansion plans would come. 'There's definitely further growth potential for the event,' continues Lloyd. 'But we won't allow the event to grow too quickly, and we've deliberately capped the entry numbers in order that the event experience for the competitors isn't compromised.' A new addition for 2015 is the Slateman Savage, which entices competitors with the lure of a special T-shirt to complete the Slateman Sprint on the Saturday and the Full race on the Sunday.

▷ The former Dinorwic Slate Quarry provides the unique backdrop for the 11km run

▷ The Slateman has quadrupled in numbers since its birth in 2011, with the incomparable run a major draw

Hever Castle Triathlon

Like the Slateman, the Hever Castle Triathlon has swiftly established itself as an essential fixture on the UK multisport circuit. In just six years it has become the biggest children's triathlon in the world (with 2,000 junior racers), a contender for the title of the UK's second largest event (with Blenheim) and the finale of the five-date Pan European Castle Triathlon Series, held at fortress locations in Ireland, England and France. And, like the Slateman's power stations and quarries, the location has plenty of quirks for athletes and supporters, from searching for the ghost of Anne Boleyn to spotting filming locations used in the fantasy classic *The Princess Bride*.

Launched by former Marines helicopter pilot Brian Adcock (and stewarded with precision by a host of his former military colleagues), the Hever Castle Triathlon was established in 2009. Around 1,000 athletes headed to Kent in the south-east of England for that inaugural event, and the numbers have rapidly increased to 7,000 for 13 different race distances at the 2014 Castle Series showcase,

▷ Age-group athletes attentively listen to race director Brian Adcock's pre-race briefing on the castle's Loggia

▽ Hever now hosts the biggest children's triathlon in the world with 2,000 junior racers

(including a 226km long-distance Bastion race held at Hever in July).

Key to that growth has been the focus on children's triathlon, with numbers almost doubling each year, from 400 youth athletes in 2011 to 700 in 2012, 1,300 in 2013 and nearly 2,000 in 2014 (overtaking the Chicago Triathlon as the world's largest children's triathlon). Kid-friendly touches include allowing parents into transition to help with wetsuit removal and changing, a completely off-road children's course and race distances starting with a manageable 100m swim before a 4km bike and a 1.3km run. Away from the race itself, the organizers have created a triathlon scheme to be assimilated into the National Curriculum in the hope of schools adding triathlon to their sporting schedule.

The organizers haven't been shy of attracting mainstream media attention either, with Sky Sports, Eurosport and Channel 4 cameras all in evidence, radio stations interviewing participants and plenty of national print coverage. The elite

▽ The 38-acre Hever lake is the host of the swim leg, with a Japanese Tea House just one of the visual attractions

races attract a smattering of pro athletes, too; top Scot Fraser Cartmell, England's rising Ironman star Lucy Gossage and a number of the British Triathlon squad have all been recent racers. The 2014 Olympic-distance race was won by Calum Johnson and India Lee, with a host of French athletes also doing battle in the Team France versus Team GB challenge.

The choice of female-only starting waves has also helped women athletes account for one third of the starting list, and the beginner-heavy quota for the whole race is exemplified by the number of mountain bikes, shopper bikes and even the sight of a basket or two in transition. Additionally,

the organizers host open-water acclimatization sessions in the months before the event.

The races themselves begin with an early-morning open-water swim in the misty and murky 38-acre Hever Castle Lake. After T1, the bike leg is deceptively tough, with barely a flat section on the route that takes athletes on a circuit through the quiet roads of the High Weald of Kent and, quite cruelly, past some of the county's finest-looking beer gardens.

The largely off-road light trail run circum-navigates the estate and leafy castle grounds, before making the dash to the tree-lined finishing chute beside the lake and adjacent to the castle.

△ Hybrids, mountain bikes, state-of-the-art tri-bikes are all in abundance on Hever's bike course

▽ A huge number of fans and free cake greet competitors at the tree-lined finish line

▷ The thirteenth-century castle is looped by athletes on the run route

A man dressed as Henry VIII and plenty of cake await participants at the finish, and the festival fun includes live bands, an archery event and, naturally, bouncy castles.

Another draw is the chance to experience Hever Castle itself, which dates back to 1270 and in the early 1500s was the childhood home of Henry VIII's second wife Anne Boleyn, who met a grisly end at his orders and whose ghost is said to appear on the River Eden bridge at Hever. In 1903 William Waldorf Astor restored Hever Castle, creating the gardens and Hever Castle Lake (where the swim section of the triathlon is held), which it took 800 men two years to dig out by hand.

The castle itself houses tapestries and two prayer books inscribed by Anne Boleyn, and the various race distances are given Hever- and castle-related titles, including the Anne Boleyn, Henry VIII and the middle-distance Gauntlet. Film buffs, meanwhile, will note that Hever Castle provides the backdrop to the 1987 fairy-tale comedy classic *The Princess Bride*, starring Cary Elwes and Robin Wright, and 2008's *Inkheart*, with Brendan Fraser.

Ironman South Africa

With 75 qualifying slots for Ironman Hawaii, a prize purse of $150,000 and the Ironman African Championship on the line, Ironman South Africa is a major long-course attraction.

The 226km event is held in Nelson Mandela Bay, in the city of Port Elizabeth on South Africa's southern coast. Hobie Beach is the setting for the one-lap swim, then a bike course that takes competitors along the coastline and through nature reserves before a three-lap run in front of 70,000 spectators on Marine Drive.

Natascha Badmann is a multiple South Africa champion, and four-time Ironman World Champ Chrissie Wellington also set the women's Ironman record on the course in 2011, with the staggering time of 8:33hr. Who better then to talk us through the attraction of racing in the Rainbow Nation?

There aren't many races in the world where you can stand on a clear white beach, watching the sun rise over the ocean, and see a pod of dolphins playing in the waves. Ironman South Africa is a phenomenal race. I'm glad I listened to my gut instinct to enter.

The crowds on Marine Drive were huge, noisy and uplifting. They'd been lined up, five or six deep, since the crack of dawn, cheering, shouting, eating, drinking and creating the most amazing tunnel of energy ... not to mention the delicious aroma from the traditional South African braai (barbecue). The finish chute is one of the best in the world. I ran down the red carpet, a rainbow of confetti raining down and a beaming smile on my face.

△ Tens of thousands of spectators surround Nelson Mandela Bay for one of Ironman's most epic race starts

▷▽ The quiet, undulating roads of Port Elizabeth's nature reserves are negotiated on the bike before an electric atmosphere on Marine Drive awaits on the run

Indian Ocean Triathlon

◁ There are worse ways to make an end-of-season flourish than the Indian Ocean Triathlon in Mauritius

Turning down a free press trip to the Indian Ocean Triathlon in Mauritius was one of this author's most painful days, for here is the perfect season-ending race/wind-down after spending a summer navigating the chilly, choppy waters of Western Europe.

It begins with a 1.8km swim in the turquoise 25°C waters of south Mauritius before a 55km bike course into the honeymoon island's interior and a three-lap 7.5km run through the shade of the mangroves at the foot of Le Morne Mountain to finish on the fine sand of Le Morne. That's not to say the race is a breeze, with the bike course offering 14% climbs and the southern hemisphere summer heat to contend with.

The 2000 ITU World Champion, Olivier Marceau, one of the many French athletes to experience the event, has won the title on three occasions. 'The Indian Ocean Triathlon is one of the most beautiful races I've ever done,' the 2000 Olympian says.

The swim takes place in the crystal-clear water in the warm lagoon, the bike course is quite challenging, but the roads are mostly smooth; you start with a 3km climb with a magnificent view, then it's mainly flat and fast. With the heat it's not easy and, once the bike is over, you're happy to start running along the sea. Some parts are on the road and some on the beach. . . . it's very hard but also quite funny!

▷ Competitors don't have it all their own way, however, with heat, a hilly bike course and leg-sapping beach run

The Races

Israman

'With the wind, hills, deserted landscape and superb organization, this race has a Kona-cum-Lanzarote feel to it.' So says German legend Normann Stadler of Israel's Israman, and with two Ironman Hawaii titles the 'Norminator' is a man who should know.

Israman began life in 1999 and remains the only long-distance triathlon on the country's small but dedicated multisport scene. Hosting both 113km middle- and 226km long-course races, the Israman attracts 1,600 athletes and starts in the southern Israeli holiday resort of Eilat, nestling between the mountainous terrain of Jordan to the east and Egypt to the west.

After a swim in the salty Red Sea the race heads north for the unforgiving hands of the Negev desert, starting with a 12km climb straight out of transition up to 600m. The plateau dominates the rest of the bike course, with athletes getting to within touching distance of the immense fence that separates Israel and Egypt.

While rain is unlikely (Eilat receives just 31mm of rainfall a year), throughout Israman's history athletes have been subjected to 60mph sandstorms and temperatures both close to zero and in the thirties, with crosswinds also a factor on the 4,000m of climbing in the 180km bike course (hence some of the Kona/Lanza references).

Age-group athlete and journalist Tim Heming suggests, 'If you're forever dreaming of Hawaii but have little hope of ever being able to swim, bike, run well enough to reach the Big Island, then sate that need by getting your ill-prepared backside over to Israel.'

▷ Israman has been attracting triathletes to the Red Sea and Negev desert of southern Israel since 1999

Ironman Cozumel

As the Mexican state after which Dan Empfield named his triathlon brand, Quintana Roo has plenty of multisport resonance, and it also hosts one of the most picturesque races on the M-Dot circuit. The divers' paradise of the Yucatan Peninsula on the eastern coast is the setting for Ironman Cozumel each November, with athletes sharing their one-lap sea swim leg with shoals of tropical fish in the protected waters of Cozumel National Park.

Mexican character abounds on the fast and flat three-lap bike course, with the local population turning out in force and pockets of sombrero-wearing musicians playing mariachi classics. The route takes athletes along the coastline and into 30mph headwinds before weaving through the town of San Miguel de Cozumel.

Competitors are subjected to rising temperatures on the run, and the finish line adds a Latino festival atmosphere in the city hall square. Age-grouper Blair Glencorse raced Cozumel in 2012. 'The entire population seems to be out and doing their best to encourage us. The post-race massage from a blind Chihuahuan called Toni was the best of my life and remains an unbelievably good end to an unbelievably well-organized, well-supported and beautiful event.'

The race offers 40 qualifying slots for the following year's Ironman World Championships and also draws a strong pro field for a last Ironman blast of the season; recent winners include Ivan Rana and Mary-Beth Ellis.

◁ Athletes exit the water at the end of the one-lap 3.8km sea swim in the protected waters of Cozumel National Park

▷ Age-grouper Blair Glencorse, seen here on the bike route in 2012, calls Cozumel 'an unbelievably beautiful event.'

The Races

Outlaw

▷ The 180km bike course is set amidst scenic Nottinghamshire countryside in the Midlands of England

▽ A 3.8km swim in the National Water Sports Centre is in store for competitors at the Nottinghamshire Outlaw event

Drawing on the mythology of Robin Hood, Nottingham's Outlaw Triathlon has firmly established itself as an essential fixture on the UK's long-distance calendar since its launch in 2010, scooping plenty of awards along the way and selling out in a handful of days.

The race is the first long-distance triathlon from established race organizers One Step Beyond (led by Iain Hamilton, who once battled Spencer Smith on the Outlaw's Holme Pierrepont course), and has since expanded to include the Outlaw Half a month earlier, offering athletes the chance to become an Outlaw twice in the same season.

With the sun rising over Holme Pierrepont, the race regularly starts under an orange sky with a 3.8km swim in the National Water Sports Centre lake. The bike leg takes in some pretty Nottinghamshire countryside before the run finds the 1,450 athletes cheered on by locals lining the River Trent path.

While the pro field is small, the event has provided plenty of memorable victories, from Paul Hawkins leading for the duration in 2010 to local dentist Eugene Grant taking 2013's heatwave edition. Perhaps the most impressive is Harry Wiltshire's surprise win in July 2012, where the British pro athlete, after failing to source any relay team members, led throughout to take the title despite, 'only putting my trainers on in T2 so I could jog back to the car.'

TriAthlone

▷ TriAthlone is one of Ireland's most famous races and hosted the ETU European Championships in 2010

▽◁ After exiting the River Shannon swim, athletes head to transition in Athlone's old town

'Athlone looks like a great place. Plenty of character and loads of pubs!' was Alistair Brownlee's unique take on the news that Athlone had been named as the host of the 2010 ETU European Championships. A few months later, Brownlee dominated the field to take the European title, and Athlone hosted the largest European champs in history, attracting 4,500 athletes to the County Westmeath town in central Ireland.

Hosting the Euros was just reward for TriAthlone, along with TriAthy and Hell of the West, for playing a fundamental role in Ireland's burgeoning triathlon scene. The race has seen plenty of Ireland's top athletes on the podium, with Aileen Morrison (née Reid), Bryan Keane and Gavin Noble all keen to promote the event. Three-time winner Noble believes the race has 'the best race atmospheres in all of Europe, with multiple races and distances all on offer. And all on a flat, fast and championship route to boot. The race takes over the town from first light to last orders.'

The event kicks off with an up- and downstream swim in the River Shannon, before the bike leg takes place on closed roads in the surrounding countryside. The last leg is a run through the narrow streets of old Athlone's west bank. In 2014 the organizers successfully added the middle- and long-distance Shadowman to Athlone's race CV, taking place a month after TriAthlone in August.

The Races

Ironman Australia

Ironman Australia celebrates its thirtieth birthday in 2015 with 50 spots for the Ironman World Championships and, no doubt, a finish-line party up there with the best of them.

The event began life in Forster-Tuncurry in 1985 and has established itself as one of M-Dot's most historic events. In 2006 it moved 110km further up the New South Wales coast to Port Macquarie, almost equidistant between Sydney and Brisbane.

After a low-key start to its new residency, the event stepped up a gear this decade to build upon the tradition that started nearly 30 years ago with a new finish line area that the First off the Bike website labels as 'the best in Australia'. The event itself starts with a sea swim between the mainland and Pelican Island, boasts a bike course that hugs the Pacific coastline and culminates with a run that takes in Macquarie's famous 'rock wall' and the historic town centre.

Pete Jacobs, the 2011 Port Macquarie winner and 2012 Ironman World Champion, holds the race in high regard.

The course is incredible and shows the best of the New South Wales coastal landscape. Although not a fast bike course, it's my favourite, and I'm sure the undulations will appeal to those who train in the UK. The location is quintessentially Australian, with headlands between beaches and breakwalls between beaches and rivers. Not forgetting the finish line and pubs along the river, which are great for a post-race feed and celebratory glass of beer.

△ Port Macquarie is the host of Ironman Australia and sees a 3.8km sea swim between the mainland and Pelican Island

▷△ 2011 Ironman Australia winner Pete Jacobs adorns the aero-tuck on the 180km bike route

▷▽ Jacobs takes the Ironman Australia title in 2011. He would win the Ironman World title a year later in Hawaii

Ironman Hawaii

▽ Since 1982, the 3.8km swim of the Ironman World Championships has taken place in Kailua Bay, Kona

The granddaddy of the sport. Long-distance triathlon's spiritual home. The Wembley, Wimbledon and Lords of multisport all rolled into one. The impact that the Ironman World Championships in Hawaii have had on the sport of triathlon cannot be overestimated.

For nearly forty years, the annual events in Kailua-Kona on Hawaii's Big Island have gripped triathlon fans worldwide, via ABC's highlights programme, word of mouth from returning athletes, magazine reports or the Internet, and now via social media and live-streaming of the event. And what events they've been on the lava fields of Kona, with the sport's most iconic bonks (Julie Moss, the Sian Welch and Wendy Ingraham crawl-off), the greatest-ever race (Mark Allen and Dave Scott's Iron War), the most famous and heart-rending triumphs over adversity (Team Hoyt) and the biggest stars (Scott, Allen, Paula Newby-Fraser, Natascha Badmann, Chris McCormack, Craig Alexander and Chrissie Wellington) becoming icons of the triathlon world and the wider world as well. The yearly drama could fill a book, and indeed has: Bob Babbitt's *30 Years of the Ironman: Triathlon World Championship*?

As mentioned in the introductory pages, Ironman Hawaii has played a fundamental role in the development and growth of triathlon; without it the sport would be very different. And for that we have to thank a US naval commander by the name of John Collins and the battling egos of swimmers and runners. At an awards ceremony for the Oahu Perimeter running event in 1977 Collins and 14 of his friends began having a regular discussion about who the fittest: runners or swimmers were. Collins suggested an event that combined Hawaii's three biggest endurance races – the Waikiki Roughwater Swim (3.8km), the Around-Oahu Cycle Race (185km) and the Honolulu Marathon (42.2km) – before delivering the immortal line, 'Whoever finishes first, we'll call him the Ironman.'

The first Ironman Hawaii was staged on 18 February 1978 in Honolulu. A field of 15 athletes started, with 12 crossing the finish line, each rewarded with a trophy handmade by Collins

out of copper pipe. Gordon Haller was the first Ironman champion, with a time of 11:46:58. A year later Lyn Lemaire became the first woman to win the event in a time of 12:55:38, placing fifth in a field of 15. Tom Warren's winning feats in that 1979 edition were covered by Barry McDermott in a major *Sports Illustrated* magazine article, and as a result Collins was soon inundated with entries (Dave Scott was just one athlete to sign up for the next event).

Californian swim coach Scott would win the first of his six titles in 1980, the year US

▽ OVERLEAF The inhospitable lava fields of Kona host the bike and run legs, with heat and crosswinds battering competitors on their 226km voyage

 Ironman Hawaii Timeline

1978
The first Ironman Hawaii takes place with 15 competitors paying $5 to be on the start line. Just 12 would finish, with Gordon Haller the first Ironman champion.

1980
American cable channel ABC record their first *Wide World of Sports* programme at the event. A 26-year-old Dave Scott takes his first of six titles.

1981
Valerie Silk takes the event from John Collins and it moves from Waikiki to Kona. Walt Stack finishes the event in 26:20hrs, the longest-ever time to finish an Ironman. A 17hr cut-off is soon implemented.

1982
College student Julie Moss collapses due to dehydration on the finishing straight after leading throughout. Moss crawls to the line to produce the race's most iconic image.

1989
Mark Allen and Dave Scott battle for over 8hrs before Allen triumphs in a course record of 8:09:15. *Competitor* magazine's Bob Babbitt christens it the 'Iron War'. Paula Newby-Fraser takes her third of a record eight titles.

1990
Dr. James P. Gills purchases the Ironman Brand for $3 million from Silk. The World Triathlon Corporation is formed a year later.

1997
The Crawl 2.0. The depleted Wendy Ingraham and Sian Welch stagger, crab-walk and crawl up the finishing straight to finish fourth and fifth and produce a video classic for the ages.

2010
Chris McCormack and Andreas Raelert embark on Iron War 2.0, with McCormack dropping his German rival with less than 2km to go to win his second Ironman World Championship title.

2011
Chrissie Wellington takes her fourth and final title, despite suffering a serious bike crash in training two weeks before the event. Craig Alexander smashes the men's course record to win his third title.

2013
Australia's Mirinda Carfrae breaks Wellington's female course record with a time of 8:52:14. Her 2:50hr marathon is the fastest of the day bar all but two men.

broadcaster ABC brought the race into American living rooms for the very first time. When the Navy posted him to Washington, DC, Collins handed over the reins of the race to local gym owner Valerie Silk in 1981. The next year Silk moved the course to the quieter Kailua-Kona on the Big Island, yet the iconic moments of Hawaii have continued to come thick and fast on an annual basis.

The race was held twice in 1982, with the first race in February changing the sport forever. Just when the ABC *Wide World of Sports* producer was struggling for a story to fill the highlights programme, college student Julie Moss collapsed twenty yards from the finish line after leading throughout. As a punch-drunk Moss staggered and crawled to the line, Kathleen McCartney passed her for victory under the watch of the ABC cameras. The story was soon projected into millions of American households, and Moss and McCartney became overnight stars. By 1985 the event was holding qualification races worldwide; in 1989 Mark Allen and Dave Scott battled neck-and-neck for eight hours in the sport's greatest ever showdown, and in 1991 NBC began televising the race annually.

We have covered the feats of winners Scott, Allen, Newby-Fraser, Wellington *et al.* in the individual athlete entries, but the HI 96740 zip-code of Ali'i Drive in Kailua-Kona has also witnessed some unforgettable achievements from the non-professionals. The most famous examples include Dick Hoyt towing and pushing his physically impaired son Rick along the 226km course in 1988, the late Jim MacLaren completing the race with one leg in 10:42hrs in 1989 and John MacLean becoming the first wheelchair athlete to tame the 'Big One' in 1995 (while he was wheeling himself backwards up one hill, his best friend Johnno Young famously said to him: 'The pain won't last forever, but the memories will.')

Apart from the pro and para events, Ironman Hawaii also fulfils another role: it is the Holy Grail for the world's finest age-group long-course triathletes. Imagine sharing a pitch with Lionel Messi, a court with Rafa Nadal or a wicket with Sachin Tendulkar? That's exactly what happens in Kona each October. The age-group fields start

◁ The hugely popular Natascha Badmann wins her sixth and final Ironman World Championship title in 2005

30mins after Kienle, Carfrae and Co., and are soon sharing the swim, bike and run course with the international stars of Ironman throughout. Not that star-spotting will be on the agenda of age-groupers who, having most likely spent years trying to qualify, are now undergoing some of triathlon's toughest conditions in a bid to ride high in their ultra-competitive age-group categories.

'If you manage to bag yourself a starting place, the whole Kona experience is one to savour,' says age-grouper Andy Blow, 255th at Ironman Hawaii 2004. And the race itself?

◁ The Queen Ka'ahumanu Highway is triathlon's most iconic stretch of concrete, taking the world's best pro and age-group athletes from Kailua-Kona to the turnaround in Hawaii

It's suitably brutal and unforgiving, with howling headwinds and searing heat to contend with. But the feeling of running down that famous finish line on Ali'i Drive to be told 'You are an Ironman' will put goose pimples on the back of your neck. Not only then but for the years to come as you recall the experience.

As Collins would have it, 'Swim 2.4 miles, ride 112, run 26.2. Then brag for the rest of your life.'

Chicago Triathlon

△ The swim leg of the Chicago Triathlon takes place in Monroe Harbor in the heart of the city

1993 would deliver over 120 events in 30 different US cities, host 100,000 entrants and pay out more than $1,000,000 in prize money (Quintana Roo founder Dan Empfield and athlete Scott Tinley are just two to highlight how the series helped establish Olympic-distance racing).

Big Four member Scott Molina would be the first winner of the Chicago Triathlon in 1983, and by 1984 the event had Bud Lite as the first of its many sponsors and Mark Allen, Scott Tinley and the Puntous twins all riding high on the finishers' list. The number of competitors quickly reached 1,460 to make the race the world's biggest triathlon in terms of participation, an honour it held for over two decades. Although the USTS quickly became a major standard-distance (1.5km swim/40km bike/10km run) series and played a role in triathlon's Olympic acceptance, the Chicago Triathlon would leave the series in 1987 to join the Tri-America Series.

That year's debut race in the new series drew 3,500 age-group triathletes, and Kirsten Hanssen and Mark Allen were the victors. In 1988 the *Chicago Sun-Times* became the sponsor, Mike Pigg took the men's title, and Erin Baker had the first of her three consecutive Chicago wins. Heavyweight winners came thick and fast in the following years, with Allen, Pigg, Michellie Jones (seven times), Brad Beven, Carol Montgomery, and the British duo of Simon Lessing and Spencer Smith all topping the podium.

By the time of Lessing's win in 1994 the race was hosting the 'International Distance Triathlon ProTour Championships', and its long-term

If the London Triathlon has recently taken away its World's Biggest Race mantle, in terms of history and location the Chicago Triathlon still has the edge over its Transatlantic rival, plus an honours board full of triathlon greats and the city's downtown skyscrapers looking over the Lake Michigan swim.

Back when the Police's 'Every Breath You Take' was immovably topping the *Billboard* charts, the Chicago Triathlon began life in August 1983 after its founders Jim Curl and Jan Caillé finally obtained the necessary road closure permits from Chicago City Hall. The race would form part of Carl Thomas and Curl's year-old US Triathlon Series (USTS), which from 1982 to

△ Beginners and hardened triathletes rub shoulders on the race course over the weekend of racing

headline sponsor was Mrs T's Pierogies (stuffed dumplings of Polish origin, if you were wondering). Multiple national championships were held at the race throughout the nineties and noughties, and the pro winners continued to be Ironman and Olympic greats such as Chris McCormack, Greg Welch, Hamish Carter, Craig Alexander, Greg Bennett and Emma Snowsill. The event joined the mega-money Life Time Fitness Series in 2006 and entered the Guinness World Records as officially the world's biggest triathlon the same year.

The Chicago Triathlon course is in the heart of Chicago, beginning at Monroe Harbor, with pro racers heading south along the sea wall. 'The swim is simply amazing,' says 2008 winner and British Olympian Stuart Hayes. 'The water is crystal clear and you can see the skyscrapers looming over you, which is a one-of-a-kind experience. Onto

the bike and Chicago is nicknamed the Windy City for a reason, so have a deep-section rear wheel as a substitute for a disc wheel in case of adverse weather conditions. My other advice would be to wear compression wear if you're flying to the event, as I ended up in hospital with a swollen knee the night before the race. Somehow it had settled down by race start and actually made me more relaxed, so that I ended up winning quite comfortably!'

The bike course also takes in the city landmarks, with elite athletes having a unique chance to ride underneath the city on the closed-roads of Intermediate Wacker Drive. The next unparalleled experience sees athletes racing on the exclusive Lower Randolph Busway, the gated $43m road (labelled the Bat Cave or Magic Road) that's closed to the public.

◁ American athlete Hunter Kemper enjoys the closed roads of the Windy City

The run course begins just south of Randolph and heads south to the lake front path, taking in Waldron Drive, McCormick Place and the Shedd Aquarium, ending with the famous finish line on Columbus Drive, an unforgettable experience for today's 10,000 sprint and Olympic-distance athletes.

◁ The race is a rite of passage for many American athletes, with bumper support pushing them to the finish line

△ The race annually witnesses 10,000 athletes entering the Columbus Drive finishing straight

Noosa Triathlon

Created in 1983, the Noosa Triathlon is intimately linked with the history and growth of triathlon in Australia. The lineage of Australian greats can be charted by reviewing its winners; Stephen Foster, Brad Beven, Miles Stewart, Emma Carney, Loretta Harrop, Craig Walton, Emma Snowsill, Chris McCormack, Courtney Atkinson and Emma Moffatt have all topped the podium at the Sunshine Coast event in Queensland.

▽ Noosa has graced the Australian tri calendar since 1983, with the current day event attracting nearly 10,000 triathletes to the Sunshine Coast

Today 10,000 people come to the Noosa Triathlon weekend jamboree — thought to be the fourth largest Olympic-distance triathlon in the world, behind London, Chicago and Hamburg. But Australia's oldest and foremost triathlon began life as a 150-competitor community fundraiser, back in the days when premier Bob Hawke occupied The Lodge and Austen Tayshus's 'Australiana' topped the Aussie pop charts.

That 1983 event was won by Michael Harris

△ An athlete tackles the cycling portion of the course at Noosa

and Liz Hepple, and New Zealand's future Ironman World Champion Erin Baker was the first non-Australian winner in 1984. The lure of the race would soon expand, with rising superstars like Stephen Foster and Brad Beven entering early incarnations of Noosa and taking the title in 1987 and 1988 respectively, at a time when Australian triathletes were starting to challenge America's multisport hegemony.

Miles Stewart, one of Australia's racers to experience major ITU success, won Noosa in blisteringly fast course record times in 1990 (1:52:17) and 1994 (1:46:58), before the British bulldog Spencer Smith became the first non-Australian male winner in 1995. Twenty years later the significance of a Pom winning on Aussie soil was still not lost on the patriotic Londoner:

△ The age-group experience is a strong one in Noosa, with grandstands erected to house the tens of thousands of spectators

◁ The flat and fast run is held on closed roads around Noosa Heads

I won my first car at Noosa, now that's some winner's prize. It's a race that I absolutely love. The course at the time was perfect for my strengths: a good honest swim, a challenging bike and a lightning fast run, which had the added motivation of shiny new cars at each of the two turnarounds. Best of all, though, was beating the Aussies on home soil . . . priceless!

The following year marked the start of the ITU's relationship with Noosa; ITU World Cup races held there in 1996, 1998 and 1999 drew a host of international athletes. Canada's Carol Montgomery, Venezuela's Gilberto Gonzalez, Kiwi Shane Reed and Britain's Michelle Dillon, who grew up in Australia, all took the Noosa title in this period.

In 1997 Craig Walton – who was to have an iron grip on Noosa in the noughties –set a still-standing men's course record of 1:44:13. Emma Carney did the same in the women's race, her time of 1:54:22 yet unbeaten (Emma Snowsill came closest in 2004, with a 1:54:55 finish). Walton won in Noosa five more times over the next decade, and his one-time fiancée Emma Snowsill (an athlete he also coached) also took five Noosa crowns in this period.

The race went on attracting star athletes Chris McCormack, Craig Alexander, Courtney Atkinson and Emma Moffatt to the Sunshine Coast during this period and beyond, and USM Events (owned by Ironman) expanded the event into a five-day multisport festival barely recognizable from its 1983 incarnation.

Generally taking place during the last week of October, the current Noosa Triathlon Multi Sport Festival (the largest of its type in the southern hemisphere) begins on a Wednesday with children and adult aquathlon races taking place on the pristine sands of Noosa's main beach. Charity golf events, organized bike rides around the Shire of Noosa and family fun runs keep things active until the Friday afternoon, when the 1,000m Ocean Swim sees them get competitive between the triathlete community and their namesakes/rivals, the Ironman surf lifesaving athletes. Then Saturday brings the SuperKids children's race and

△ Home favourite Aaron Royle wins the 2014 edition of the Noosa Triathlon

▷ Versatile Swiss star Caroline Steffen soaks up the applause on her way to finishing third in 2014

▽ Ashleigh Gentle secures her second Noosa title in 2014 ahead of a crack field of ITU athletes

the Noosa Special Triathlon for athletes with a disability, before a women's and men's cycling criterium, a 5km run and the Legends Triathlon (complete with pro athletes and celebrities) take place in front of a crowd of 20,000 spectators.

The blue-riband Olympic-distance Noosa Triathlon is held on the Sunday, and 2015 saw the pro field and 8,500 age-group athletes lining up at 6.15 a.m. on Noosa's main beach for the first time (up to 2014 the swim was held in the warm, calm Noosa canal). 'It's one of the world's best beaches,' Ironman Asia-Pacific chief executive Geoff Meyer explained. 'For us to move that swim across to the beach is fantastic for the athletes, fantastic for the spectators and the global audience, and it keeps allowing us to grow the event as well.'

The 40km closed-road bike course sets out from Noosa Heads and runs up to Noosa Sound on smooth, fast and flat roads, with some testing ascents and tricky descents to negotiate throughout, before heading back to Noosa Heads. The 10km run, also on closed roads, is fast and flat, with huge stands full of spectators welcoming home the athletes at the finish line.

Then comes the fun finale to the festival. Noosa, with its backdrop of sun, sand and sea, certainly knows how to have fun, and the Surf Club kicks off the celebrations before the Reef Hotel throws what's been described as the best after-party in all of triathlon.

Xterra World Championships

The Xterra Worlds on the island of Maui are the off-roading world's Ironman World Championships. And, like its Big Island neighbour, Maui is volcano country. Unlike the Ironman World Champs, though, 800 of the world's best dirt-lovers actually have to bike and run over it to complete the Xterra challenge.

The first-ever Xterra was born on Maui in 1996, yet the origins of the brand are rooted in the late 1980s, when Tom Kiely, the founder of Xterra organizer Team Unlimited, was asked to create publicity for the Waikiki Oahu Visitors Association. Kiely came up with the Hawaiian International Ocean Challenge lifeguard skills competition. In 1990 the Ocean Challenge was broadcast on ESPN, and millions of viewers were exposed to the sun, sand and crystal-clear waters of Waikiki.

The event's success snowballed, with Team Unlimited producing three more shows for ESPN in 1991, seven in 1992 and 12 shows by 1995. The mid-nineties saw arguably the peak of mountain biking's popularity, and Team Unlimited produced the Hawaiian Mountain Tour, in which many future Xterra greats (Ned Overend, Melanie McQuaid, Steve Larsen) appeared. After the race the mountain bikers reportedly rode down to the beach and jumped into the Pacific – which sparked an idea … why not have a mountain bike triathlon?

Soon after, one of the Aston hotels on Maui was searching for an idea for their grand opening, and the Maui Visitors Bureau was looking for a new event that could sell Maui's south shore. Kiely called Aston and the MVB, and the first Xterra event was a go. 'There really wasn't an off-road tri scene in '96, and no international races that we knew of. Scott Tinley put on an off-road tri in San Diego, and there was another smaller race by Paris Lake, but that was the extent of it that we knew,' says Xterra vice president Trey Garman.

The first race in Maui was originally called 'AquaTerra', but the name was trademarked by a South Carolina kayak company. Instead of dishing out the cash, Kiely came up with Xterra and trademarked it. 'The X is a numerical term which means "unknown" and Terra is Latin for land/ territory, thus … Unknown territory,' says Kiely. Then the car manufacturer Nissan – after a million dollars worth of market research on a model name for their new SUV – decided on Xterra and called Kiely up to secure the rights. Nissan got a licence to the name in exchange for a sponsorship deal that lasted nine years.

For Xterra World Tour managing director Dave 'Big Kahuna' Nicholas that debut event is still the most memorable.

We'd designed the race distances so that the triathlete/swimmer would get an early lead, the mountain biker would have time to catch up, and the triathlete/runner could use their

◁ The world's best off-road triathletes enter the waters of Honokahua Bay in search of Xterra glory

leg speed to make it a race. That first race played out exactly like that in both the men's and women's races. Take Ned Overend, who couldn't swim at all and was nearly dead last out of the water but then passed almost the entire field to move to the front of the pack by the end of the bike. Then the foot speed of Jimmy Riccitello took over on the run. Michellie Jones did the same thing in the women's race, where she was in front in the swim, got passed on the bike by world cup mountain biker Shari Kain, then re-took the lead on the run.

The world-beating Jones and future Ironman cycling official Riccitello took those first Xterra World titles, and Fox Sports Net broadcast the race to mainland America. 'That race was magical, and the reaction by everyone – our staff, the competitors, the hotel, the Maui Visitors Bureau, the people that watched on TV, was that we had truly uncovered something special,' says Kiely.

The Xterra Series expanded rapidly, with worldwide events launched in 2000, 50 races organized in 2003 and a full-blown European Tour by 2004. The Xterra trail running series followed in 2005, and today Team Unlimited produce 300 Xterra events in 25 countries across the globe. The heartbeat of Xterra will always be Maui, however, with the event holding its 20th race in November 2015 and inviting all its winners back to compete.

And what winners there have been, with some of the world's best road triathletes (Mike Pigg, Eneko Llanos, Hamish Carter, Julie Dibens and Javier Gómez) topping the podium, and the race creating off-road triathlon stars of its own, including Overend, Melanie McQuaid, Conrad Stoltz, Nicolas Lebrun and Ruben Ruzafa.

Today's race sees 800 competitors take to the Pacific waters of Honokahua Bay in the north-west

◁ Josiah Middaugh finished in fourth place in 2013 – the highest placed American

◁ Conrad 'The Caveman' Stoltz is a legend of Xterra, winning four world titles in Maui

▽ Spain's Ruben Ruzafa wins the 2013 Xterra World Championship, his second of three titles in Maui

of Maui, outside the Ritz-Carlton, for a mass start (pros and age-groupers at the same time) to a non-wetsuit sea swim in water temperatures of around 25°C. After that comes a one-loop 32km off-road bike leg, which top British Xterra pro Sam Gardner likens to 'riding on marbles the size of your fist,' that goes up and down the lower slopes of the West Maui Mountains more than a dozen times and includes over 1,000m of elevation gain.

If there's anyone left for the 10km run – there's a high DNF rate in Maui, due to dehydration, crashes, punctures and the heat – they then have to pick a very cautious path inland from the Ritz-Carlton over lava rock and more. As Dave Nicholas explains:

Obstacles are everywhere, including a technical, steep downhill into a gully where racers will have to jump over and duck under fallen trees, navigate a rocky dry creek, head through thick elephant grass, up a short rope-assisted scramble and along a narrow single-track trail with switchbacks that drop all the way down to the beach. The final test of skill and endurance is a calf-busting 250-metre sandy beach run.

French off-roader Nico Lebrun demonstrated just how lethal the run can be, and also what this race actually means to an athlete, when in 2006 he tripped and broke his arm, but still crossed the line as a champion. Camaraderie reigns supreme in Maui, with athletes from more than twenty countries and forty US states putting the day's rivalry behind them at one of triathlon's greatest after-parties.

Norseman

If an Ironman race forces athletes to find out what they're really made of, this one-day 226.3-km challenge peels back the layers to reveal their very soul.

Every August, 250 of the world's toughest athletes descend upon Eidfjord, a small village nestled in the dramatic terrain of Norway's west fjordland region to take on Norseman, a raw, no-frills Iron-distance event. A freezing swim in a Norwegian fjord, enormous climbs to conquer on the bike and a mountain top finish for the run – all in treacherous weather conditions – make this a defining event in extreme triathlon.

In 2000, Paal Hårek Stranheim had a vision to create an event so unique, so spectacular and so unforgiving that it would lure triathletes and thrill-seekers from around the world to the daunting landscape of western Norway. The event was designed to focus on the journey rather than clocking a swift finishing time and would tell more about an athlete's grit and determination than any other endurance triathlon on the planet.

Twenty-one men took part in the inaugural event, on 19 July 2003. Christian Houge-Thiis was the first athlete over the line in 12 hours 48 minutes, but the digits on the clock mattered little – it was the frisson of fear, the course's enormity and the extreme environment along the way that created an instant classic.

More than ten years on, the race remains deliberately small, with race entry being decided by a lottery a year before each edition. In that time, the race's mystique and dark glamour has only increased. In 2005 and 2007, strong winds

and heavy snow disrupted the race so badly that it couldn't continue, while in 2011 the water was so cold that the swim was moved – adding an extra 20km to the bike leg.

It's not just age-group athletes who see the value in conquering this unique race, 2011 saw two-time Ironman World Champion Tim DeBoom place first. His finishing time of 11:18:52 was nearly three hours longer than his winning Ironman World Championship times in Hawaii -- a course considered extremely tough in its own right.

As tough as it is on the body, the event is equally challenging for the mind. The mental games begin at 4 a.m. on race morning as the Norseman's 250 wetsuit-clad victims tread through the village in the pitch-dark and up the gangplank of the ferry that will cast off into the Hardangerfjord. Engines thumping, water churning around the ferry, there's almost an hour's agonizing limbo for the competitors as they are driven inexorably to the start. Many stare silently into the distance, a trance of thought about what's to come. The ramp on the rear of the ferry is lowered and all that's left is a 15-foot plunge into the dark, icy waters and 226.3km to the finish line.

Pouring lemming-like off the back of the boat, the field of hardy souls are dunked under the surface before their buoyant wetsuits pop them back up on top of the water, where they ready themselves, with fearful anticipation, for the loud burst of the ferry's horn and the start of the world's hardest triathlon.

There's 3.8km of freezing water between the athletes and their bikes and it's soon frothing into

white spray with the thrashing of hands and feet crashing into the surface of the fjord.

Tide and currents can play a huge role in the outcome of the swim, throwing competitors off-course in the gloom and forcing them to expend more energy if the 400m-deep Hardangerfjord is draining against them. The wind can whip the surface of the water into a frenzy of rising waves, only adding to the challenge of the swim to shore. Nevertheless, this is the flattest the terrain will be all day.

The athletes have to force themselves out of the cold water on slippy seaweed, knowing that the worst – and best – is still to come.

Next comes the achingly tough, but astonishingly beautiful bike course, allowing those with the energy to revel in the glorious landscape around them.

The 180km point-to-point route begins with a 40km climb that scales 1,250m up to the Hardangervidda mountain plateau and the village of Dyranut. The first 20km of the ascent

△ Athletes rise from the Norseman's cold, treacherous swim in 2012 with over 222km of biking and running ahead

△ The Norseman begins with a leap of faith into the chilly water of the Hardangerfjord for a 3.8km swim to the shore

follows the 'old road', a tourist route closed to cars – leaving only the sound of rolling tyres, clicking gears and hard breathing to echo through the tunnels cut into the dark rock of the ancient mountains. The otherworldly surroundings are bisected by a ribbon of tarmac that takes athletes on a rollercoaster of emotional highs and lows as they soak up the majesty of western Norway.

Finally, up onto the plateau, dramatic vistas open up as the road levels alongside snow-dusted escarpments, rushing mountain rivers and mirror-like glacial pools, offering the legs some respite. It's time to take on some energy, but with no aid stations on the Norseman's bike course, competitors must each have a support crew to provide them with the drink, food and kit necessary to keep them fuelled enough to grind their way to the finish.

Crossing the Hardangervidda can certainly be a battle against the elements with the wide-open space and desolate landscape making cyclists easy prey for the gusting, bitterly cold crosswinds. Rain can also join the tumult, battering down and colluding with the wind to drop the temperature and stiffen muscles.

With three more peaks and troughs to conquer before the final climb, the unrelenting course continues to ask more of its charges' wills and bodies. If the clouds hang low, descending on the winding, switchback bedevilled route can quickly become treacherous.

The last ascent on the bike asks competitors to scale Imminfjell to the Telemark Plateau, over 500m elevation gain with a steep and gruelling 6km section with numerous zig-zagging corners before 10km of false crests to sap morale before the road finally reaches its highpoint. Here, there's deep relief that it's all downhill to transition in the village of Austbygde.

Finally off two wheels, athletes can be buoyed with the satisfaction that they've completed one of the most challenging bike courses on the planet.

Compared to what's been faced so far, the 42.2km run begins on relatively gentle terrain, an undulating road skirting Lake Tinnsjø, which borders the village. Here, it's usually heat rather than cold that beats down upon competitors as they push bravely on.

Around 18km into the run, athletes get their first sight of the towering, 1,800m summit of

Gaustatoppen, the highest peak in the Telemark region and the eventual finishing point for the quickest athletes. Competitors have time to dwell on its enormity as the road meanders around the foot of the mountain before a switchback signals the course's turn skywards onto its steep lower slopes.

This incredibly tough section is an upwards slog covering 900m of height at a dizzying 10 per cent gradient. Named Zombie Hill after the stricken faces and limping forms of the competitors striving to conquer it, the pain of the day's toil bites harder than ever here, yet every step takes each runner closer to their goal. For a select few, there's a bigger objective at stake than simply completing the world's toughest triathlon.

They put themselves through this extra anguish in the hope of securing nothing more exotic than a black T-shirt. This exclusive finisher's garb is gifted only to the first 160 athletes who reach 32.5km before 2.30 p.m. and go on to summit Gaustatoppen. Those who don't make it in time climb to 1,000m before being diverted over a 10km track to the Gaustablikk Mountain Hotel, the post-race rest of all finishers, and the promise of a white T-shirt.

Black T-shirt contenders continue along the road before collecting their mandatory backpacks, which contain survival essentials, should they become stranded on the mountain. Here, they are joined by a member of their support team, who must accompany them over the final push to the summit, the most challenging section of the marathon.

The last 5km trudge is up a steep, narrow path pointing up the mountain. Signs along the route helpfully remind athletes of the agony, measured in metres, still to go.

At this point Norseman turns into nothing more than a personal battle waged by each athlete against the mountain. The rocky landscape becomes more lunar-like as each competitor strides, heaves or crawls towards the finish.

There's no grandstand, no finisher's chute and little in the way of fanfare to welcome them to the finish, but as they take the final few steps, bodies wracked with pain and on the very brink of collapse, their journey is complete. Elation and incredible satisfaction relieves aching muscles and tired minds – they've measured their bodies and souls against the biggest challenge in triathlon and found themselves equal to the adventure of a lifetime.

▽ The beautiful and tough bike course of the Norseman Xtreme Triathlon literally takes the breath away

The last 5km trudge is up a steep, narrow path pointing up the mountain. The littering of loose rocks makes finding firm footing tiresome work for race-weary athletes

The Races

Challenge Wanaka

From the Cote d'Azur to Mauritius, Hawaii and the beaches of Thailand, there is no lack of picture-postcard settings for triathletes' multisport adventures. But all these and other far-flung locations are arguably outshone by New Zealand's Challenge Wanaka: the long-course race set in the most beautiful region of possibly the world's most beautiful country.

Instead of picking up an existing triathlon, the Challenge venture started from scratch with just 200 competitors in its debut year of 2007. Significantly, the race was the first Challenge Family event outside Roth.

Wanaka (pop. 7,320), in the Otago Region of New Zealand's South Island, is the gateway to Mount Aspiring National Park in the Southern Alps. The town nestles at the southern end of turquoise-blue Lake Wanaka, ringed by snow-topped mountains, with the Crown Range to the south and the Haast Pass to the north.

The event starts at Roy's Bay, with the athletes diving into crisp Lake Wanaka for an L-shaped 3.8km swim loop in water so clean you can drink it. A two-lap, gently undulating 180km bike route (total climbing of 1,684m) follows, with the course taking in both Lake Wanaka and Lake Hawea before returning to Wanaka for the marathon run leg. Unusually for long-distance races, three-quarters of the 42.2km foot race takes place on off-road trails, with athletes doing two laps of a course that heads east to Albert Town and back.

The beauty of the scenery belies the challenge of the event, however, with athletes occasionally facing choppy and chilly waters in Lake Wanaka

▽ Unusually for a long-distance triathlon, three quarters of Challenge Wanaka's 42.2km marathon run is on off-road trails

▷ The undulating bike route features 1,684m of ascent in the Otago region of New Zealand's South Island

Chilly and choppy waters plus some of the world's greatest scenery greet competitors at Challenge Wanaka

(the warmest lake in the Southern Island, yet thick neoprene swim hats are a common sight here), severe crosswinds on the bike course and uneven trails on the run.

'I underestimated the event. You have to fight for every metre in Wanaka,' said Chris McCormack after placing third at the race in 2013. Other pro athletes to have taken the Wanaka challenge and topped the podium include Canada's Luke Dragstra and Belinda Granger of Australia, who won the inaugural 2007 event to take the $15,000 first-prize cheque. Later years have seen Kiwi stars top the honours board: Richard Ussher, Dylan McNeice (twice) and Gina Crawford (four times); McNeice had planned to retire from the sport until he won in 2013 and went on to carve out a strong long-course career.

The UK's Jo Carritt, who placed fourth in 2011, is just one pro athlete smitten with the charms of Wanaka:

Many people regard Challenge Wanaka as boasting the most spectacular scenery of any race in the world. With snow-topped mountains surrounding the crisp lakes, it's certainly the most beautiful race scenery that I've experienced. But it's also an appropriate backdrop for one of the most challenging races on the circuit.

Being surrounded by mountains and glaciers, Lake Wanaka can be very cold, *even in the height of the Kiwi summer, so be prepared for brain freeze. The bike course is full of steeply undulating roads and shocking crosswinds: two features that contribute to the relatively slow times. The support from the locals and competitors makes for the most enjoyable marathon run possible. It really is a wonderful experience: beautiful, intimate and superbly organized.*

The Aussie long-course veteran Belinda Granger rates the run course as one of the best in the world. Yet it's not just the pros who are enamoured. From 200 competitors in 2007, the race now features 2,200 mostly age-group athletes over the weekend, with a half-distance race, relays, junior races, a charity fun run and standalone swim event all taking place in addition to the flagship 226km long-distance challenge.

In 2015 the race moved from its early January billing to late February. 'By moving the race to February we can give athletes a more relaxed Christmas and take advantage of probably the best weather month in the Southern Alps,' says race director Victoria Murray-Orr.

▽ Wanaka was Challenge's first international race after Roth, with both races proving memorable finish line experiences

▷ New Zealand's Simon Maier in January 2014 finishing the Challenge Wanaka

Alpe d'Huez Triathlon

A 700m-high swim in a mountain reservoir opened once a year; a bike course that's played a central role in the Tour de France; the world's highest transition area; and a run that takes place at 2,000m above sea level. In less than a decade, the Alpe d'Huez Triathlon has joined the select list of truly iconic triathlons, rubbing shoulders with Hawaii, Roth, Alcatraz and Lanzarote as one of the most unforgettable days in multisport.

Organized by the 2002 ITU Long Distance World Champion, Cyrille Neveu, the race in south-east France started in 2006 and was ambitious in scope from the outset. The split transition means that before the race competitors have to rack their bike and run gear some 15km apart (they are encouraged to cycle from Transition Two down to the swim start some 1,300m lower down). Surrounded by lush mountain scenery, the swim leg takes place in the crystal-clear, if decidedly chilly, 16°C waters of the Lac du Verney (700m above sea level), opened once a year by event partner and energy giant EDF just for the event.

▷▽ The Alpe d'Huez Triathlon only started life in 2006, yet it has already acquired legendary status due to its Alpine setting

▽ The 2.2km 'Long Distance' swim is flanked by wooded mountain tops

▽▽ The 700m above sea level Lac du Verney is only opened once a year to swimmers by energy giants EDF

The race then sends long-course athletes off on a 115km venture along roads etched in Tour de France history by riders like Fausto Coppi and Bernard Hinault, and Lance Armstrong's famous glare at Jan Ullrich in 2001. As legendary Tour de France journalist Jacques Augendre put it: 'From the first edition, shown on live television, the Alpe d'Huez definitively transformed the way the Grande Boucle ran. No other stage has had such drama. With its 21 bends, its gradient and the number of spectators, it is a climb in the style of Hollywood.'

The triathlon bike route takes athletes via smooth French roads over three steep mountain passes, beginning with the Alpe du Grand Serre (1,375m above sea level) before heading to the 1,371m high Col d'Ornon and the *pièce de résistance*, the 21 hairpin bends on the ascent up the Alpe d'Huez. While recreational cyclists venture onto the summit each day, the Alpe d'Huez Triathlon gives athletes the opportunity to do so in a race format, with buoyant crowds and the feeling of following in the recent tyre tracks of the world's finest cyclists enrapturing triathletes year after year.

The race is far more than just a Tour de France tribute act, however, with all the mountain passes of the Écrins National Park and their varying altitudes throwing a further key obstacle into the triathletes' path. With the last of the 21 hairpins on the Alpe d'Huez ticked off, athletes head to a AstroTurf bike-to-run transition area overlooked by cable cars that sits 2,000m above sea level, a world record for multisport. The 22km long-course run leg is a three-lap affair that takes place on a mixture of mountain paths and asphalted roads within the majestic setting of the resort of Alpe d'Huez.

▷ The 115km bike leg follows in the tread marks of the Tour de France's greatest riders and over three mountain passes

△ A duathlon is also held over the multisport festival weekend, with duathletes sent up Alpe d'Huez on the bike leg

▷△ Mountain paths and asphalt roads form the terrain of the 22km run leg

▷▽ The four-day event boasts a family-friendly festival atmosphere for the 2,500 entrants

Since its inception, the Alpe d'Huez Triathlon has drawn athletes of the calibre of Brazil's finest Reinaldo Colucci, Frédéric Belaubre and Tim Don to the short-course event, with long-course winners including Nicola Spirig in 2009, top tri couple James Cunnama and Jodie Swallow in 2010 and Cat Morrison in 2011.

Chrissie Wellington's feats in 2007 and 2008, meanwhile, have gone down in Alpe d'Huez legend. In 2007, at the behest of her coach Brett Sutton, she entered the race as her first 'long-course' event … ending up crashing through a race barrier and receiving a puncture but still winning the women's race. A year later, the future four-time Ironman World Champion beat all but one of the men (Brazil's Marcus Ornellas) and obliterated the women's field by 25mins with a time of 6:18:25, just 90 seconds away from taking the overall title. In 2013 Wellington said to *Triathlete* magazine,

I've never competed in a race as beautiful as Alpe d'Huez Triathlon. The location is simply amazing: a swimming area in crystal-clear water, a wonderful bike round with the legendary Alpe d'Huez climb and a running section with unbelievable landscapes. The atmosphere was also very festive. I will never forget this race.

Apart from the short- and long-course events, there are also a sprint-distance race, a children's event and a duathlon (consisting of a 5km run in Bourg d'Oisans, a 15km bike course that goes straight up Alpe d'Huez and a 2.5km run around the ski resort), and the four-day carnival boasts a decent race village and plenty of entertainment for the 2,500-plus entrants and their support crews.

The Races

Ironman 70.3 St Croix

Ironman 70.3 St Croix – or Beauty and the Beast, to give an alternative title – offers quintessential Caribbean splendour of turquoise waters, golden sands and sub-tropical rainforests … plus a legendary 1.28km climb that comes as a sinister sucker punch for anyone who forgets this is one of the toughest middle-distance races on the planet. Ask anyone who has raced St Croix over the past 27 years and the most common response will focus on 'The Beast'. At just over a kilometre long, its length pales in comparison to climbs like the Big Savage Mountain at the

Savageman and Alpe d'Huez, but it still packs a meaty punch, testing athletes with gradients ranging from 15 to 22 per cent.

St Croix and the Beast have been tested by the finest triathletes in history since 1988, with those who came and conquered essentially reading like a who's who of the sport. 'It's an old race with a lot of history and prestige. All the best triathletes in the history of our sport have raced and won there,' says four-time St Croix champion Craig Alexander. That cast list has included Mark Allen, Scott Tinley, Dave Scott, Scott Molina, Mike Pigg, Paula Newby-Fraser, Erin Baker, Karen Smyers, Greg Welch, Michellie Jones, Natascha Badmann, Luc Van Lierde, Mirinda Carfrae and Spencer Smith.

Mike Pigg was long believed to have recorded the fastest time up the Beast, but his informal record is said by Devashish Paul on the influential tri website xtri.com to have been beaten by

three-time Ironman World Champion Alexander in a time of 5:20mins – over 2mins faster than the top age-groupers would hope to take. Like the Westernport Wall, again at the Savageman – which also claims a place in triathlon's rogues gallery of most infamous climbs – 'The Beast' marks the true start of the race's hardships: the gateway to a gruelling world of pain that consists of winds, rolling hills and oppressive heat set against a backdrop of paradise.

St Croix, the largest of the 50-odd islands and islets of the US Virgin Islands, has been testing triathletes since 1988 when Pigg won the first edition of the race, his first of four titles on the island. 'Winning St Croix was one of my biggest highs in the sport,' he said later. 'Big money, car, TV, and the best athletes in the world to go against'. Following him home in that maiden 3km swim/95km bike/20km run were Mark Allen,

▽ The blue waters of St Croix provide some calm before one of the toughest 70.3 bike courses

Scott Tinley and Dave Scott, while the women's top five included Paula Newby-Fraser and the Puntous twins; a very young Lance Armstrong also competed in the event. Allen had his revenge in 1989 in his unbeaten build-up to finally taking the Ironman Hawaii title.

The 1991 edition of the St Croix event moved to a 2km/55km/12km format and entered the record books as the first-ever ITU World Cup event; Carol Montgomery took the women's title and a rampant Pigg pushed Greg Welch and Mark Allen into the lower podium spots. Long-term race director Tom Gutherie joined the event in 1992, and the race carried on drawing the world's biggest pro racers, with Welch, Smyers, Jones, Smith and Jimmy Riccitello all taking the title before the century ended.

The race joined the Ironman 70.3 series in 2002, with the distances now involving a 1.9km loop swim in Christiansted Harbour, a 90km bike around the island and a two-loop run affair. Ironman 70.3 winners have included Mirinda Carfrae (twice), who is quick to point out the island's famous friendliness. 'It's one of my top three races in the world. What's not to love about it? There's humid heat, a swim in the beautiful warm waters of the Caribbean Ocean, but, mostly, I love the people of the island.' Scottish athlete Cat Morrison, who beat Carfrae to the title in 2011, is another convert to the combination of hospitality and striking scenery. 'The St Croix 70.3 is more than just a race. For over twenty years the island has embraced local, national and international athletes in a weekend of triathlon activity. I felt truly blessed to ride around the island, swim in the Caribbean and run through the island's trails.'

▷ The race has attracted plenty of the world's best triathletes since its inception in 1988

▽ Wetsuits aren't required at this Caribbean classic on the tri calendar

FINISH

◁ Despite the backdrop of paradise, the bike course provides a whole world of pain for athletes

▷ The run finishes at the pretty beach town of Christiansted on the north of the island

1015

Powerman Zofingen

Powerman Zofingen is duathlon's equivalent of the Ironman World Championships in Hawaii, the mythologized home of a sport where quads burn, lungs bust and legends are born. While the days of sitting in the 'Big Three' of multisport events with Ironman Hawaii and the Nice Triathlon are a distant memory, the fundamental role it has played in the growth of duathlon, plus the cast of Mark Allen, Paula Newby-Fraser, the Vansteelant brothers, Karin

△ Athletes enjoy some respite from the climbs that populate Zofingen's famous bike course

Thurig, Erika Csomor and Olivier Bernhard make it one of multisport's landmark events. Mark Allen has called it the 'greatest race in the world,' and who are we to argue against one of the greatest-ever multisport athletes?

The event's history began in 1988, when the 'Run&Bike Zofingen' organizing committee first met in the provincial town (pop. 11,000) in northern Switzerland. Six months later, on 4 June 1989, the starting horn blared for the first Zofingen race: an opening 25km run followed by a 150km bike and a 30km run. The first winners were Hermine Haas of Switzerland and Dr Andreas Rudolph of Germany (Rudolph still acts as the main announcer for Powerman races).

That debut event – back when duathlon was still commonly referred to as biathlon – also saw a young Natascha Badmann enter her first multisport event, taking sixth place at a race she would later come to dominate.

From 1990 to 1996, the distances would be 7.5km/150km/30km and, like the Nice Triathlon, the event would quickly become a major draw for the dominant American athletes. Kenny Souza, the neon Speedo-wearing rock star of the sport, took the Zofingen title in early 1990, and Big Four member Scott Molina broke the tape the following year, with another Ironman World Champion, Paula Newby-Fraser, coming home not far behind him.

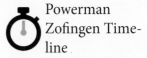

Powerman Zofingen Time-line

1988
The first meeting of the 'Run&Bike Zofingen' organizing committee is held in the Swiss town.

1989
The inaugural duathlon is held in Zofingen. Hermine Haas of Switzerland and Dr Andreas Rudolph of Germany are the winners.

1991
Ironman World Champions Scott Molina and Paula Newby-Fraser take the titles in the first year the Bodenburg climb is added to the route.

1993
Reigning Ironman Hawaii champion Mark Allen takes his only Zofingen title.

1994
Oliver Bernhard starts a decade-long winning run for Switzerland's men.

1997
The Swiss women join the party as Natascha Badmann gains the first of her three full Zofingen titles.

2003
Financial issues and staff shortages bring the event close to folding.

2004
Erika Csomor takes the first of her six Zofingen titles.

2007
Days after dropping out at Zofingen, two-time winner Benny Vansteelant is hit by a car and dies of his injuries.

2009
Benny's younger brother Joerie wins the event at the first attempt as the race celebrates its twentieth birthday.

◁ Gaël Le Bellec and Yannick Cadalen made it a French one-two at Zofingen in 2014

And 1991 was the first year the famous Bodenburg ascent was included in the bike course. Ranking alongside The Beast at St Croix, in the roll of multisport infamy, the Bodenburg consists of a 4km climb with a plethora of gradients up to 16%. Competitors are subjected to this not once but three times over the three-lap course. Souza was just one athlete to succumb to the challenge and fail to finish ... albeit in a snowstorm and while wearing his trademark briefs and a tank top.

The early nineties were the high point for Zofingen, drawing major athletes to Switzerland: two-time Ironman World Champion Erin Baker won the women's race in 1992 and 1994; Mark Allen finished fourth in 1992 and took the title (and a $40,000 winner's cheque) a year later. A period of Swiss dominance followed – Olivier Bernhard, Urs Dellsperger and Stefan Riesen hogging the top step of the men's podium up to, and including, 2004. In the women's race Natascha Badmann and Karin Thürig confirmed the nation's duathlon dominance, with six-time Hawaii champ Badmann winning the title in 1996, 1997 and 2000 and Thürig winning in 2001 and 2002.

Stellar cyclist Thürig would soon be focusing on racing the individual time-trial at the Athens 2004 Olympics, while triathlon's debut at the Sydney Olympics in 2000 led multisport athletes to chase Olympic dreams instead of Zofingen glory. 'It [triathlon's inclusion in the Olympic programme] wasn't viewed as a negative development for Powerman Zofingen initially, but more and more endurance athletes started focusing on the more lucrative sport of triathlon, which resulted in a continuous loss of participants,' says Powerman Zofingen media officer Raphael Galliker.

In 1997 the swim leg had been doubled in length to 13km, before being cut again in 2000. In 2002 the Zofingen event was moved to September, and there was more Swiss success, with Olivier Bernhard (6:25:37) and Karin Thürig (7:04:08) taking the titles. Then in 2003 the event came close to folding, due to staff shortages and financial woes, before Swiss banker, Stefan Ruf, resuscitated it and put a new board together. Ruf was helped by events on the course, with Stefan Riesen beating Belgium's Benny Vansteelant in a

nail-biting encounter later that year. Hungary's Erika Csomor came second that year, before starting a run of six consecutive Zofingen titles from 2004.

Going into the 2005 race Benny Vansteelant was the unrivalled superstar of twenty-first-century duathlon. He had already notched up four standard-distance ITU World Championships, three of his four ITU Long Distance Duathlon world titles and four of his five European Duathlon gold medals. Spearheading a huge Belgian invasion of the 2005 event, he achieved a race best 3:57.18 bike split and went on to break the tape in 6:31:01 ahead of another Belgian, Maris Koen. The following year another formidable bike leg was the foundation of his second Zofingen win.

Few could have predicted it would be his last. Ten days after dropping out of the 2007 event with stomach problems on the run, Benny Vansteelant was hit by a car during a training bike ride in Belgium. He suffered a broken leg, facial injuries, a torn spleen and damage to lungs and heart. Initially he showed signs of recovery and was close to leaving the intensive care when he suffered a cardiac arrest. Despite receiving CPR in time, he died of a pulmonary embolism. Duathlon had lost its leading light.

Two years later – as the race celebrated its twentieth birthday – Benny's younger brother Joerie won the Zofingen event at his first attempt, producing a 6:11:35 course record to secure an emotional victory for all involved in the sport. That year there were over 1,000 entrants, the most since the start of the decade, and *220 Triathlon* magazine listed the race as one of the top five of its 20-year lifetime.

By the time of its 25th anniversary in 2014 Zofingen was annually hosting the ITU Long Distance Duathlon World Championships, and Powerman had a worldwide series of over ten races: proof that even with triathlon's stratospheric growth, Zofingen and duathlon will remain perennially popular with multisport aficionados.

▷ Britain's former cycling superstar Emma Pooley obliterated the women's field by over 30mins to win the 2014 title

Embrunman

Proof that St Croix doesn't have the exclusive right to call a bike climb 'The Beast' is Embrunman, a race that positively drips with French triathlon history and is infamous for its unforgiving climbs on both the bike and run courses. The course records alone highlight the gruelling nature of the challenge, with the times posted by the French duo Hervé Faure (9:34:10) and Jeanne Collonge (10:56:43) a long way short of Andreas Raelert's and Chrissie Wellington's long-distance world records at Challenge Roth (7:41:33 and 8:18:13).

The inaugural Embrunman was held in Embrun, in the Hautes-Alpes near the France/Italy border,
on 19 August 1984, two years after the first Nice Triathlon was held 200km further south. That event consisted of a 750m swim, 30km bike and 10km race walk, but already present in the bike section was the Cote de Chalvet climb, which is still tormenting triathletes today.

Just a year later the race became the standard-distance championships of France, with the rare

▽ The 6 a.m. start of this French classic takes place in near-darkness, with the canoes with lights guiding athletes through the waters

▷ Tunnel vision: The long-distance bike course is one of the toughest in tri, forcing athletes up, down and through the Hautes-Alpes

Open highways and hairpins
are just two features of the
186km bike course

race distances of 1.5km swim/70km bike/21km run attracting 280 athletes and some 20,000 spectators to the small south-eastern commune (pop. 6,000). The event would go long in 1986, with a format of 4km swim in the sheltered lake, a 131.5km bike and a hilly 42.1km run punctuated with ferocious climbs introduced by the organizers with the claim that it would be tougher than Ironman Hawaii.

In 1987, seemingly possessing a misanthropic streak, the course architects added another 1km onto the swim and made the bike 180km, only to have the swim reduced to the Ironman distance of 3.8km in 1989 by the French Triathlon Federation (FFTRI). By this time the event was starting to attract major athletes, French superstar Yves Cordier recording his first two of five titles in 1987 and 1988.

In 1990 the route was changed for a final time with the introduction of the ascent of the Col d'Izoard on the bike course. The new 186km route came with increased difficulty, contributing to a total of 3,600m of climbing on the course: over 1,000m more than the infamous Ironman Lanzarote. Big Four star Scott Molina won the 1991 race in a time of 10:19hrs (nearly two hours slower than his 1988 Ironman Hawaii winning time), then for the rest of the decade the podium's top step was dominated by the French athletes Cordier and Philippe Lie.

In the twenty-first century French domination switched to the women's race, with eight of the winners wearing le Tricolore tri-suits. Bella Bayliss would be the British thorn in the French side during this period, taking a record three titles and smashing the course record in a time of 11:02hrs.

Over in the men's race, Spain's Félix Rubio Martínez won four titles at the start of the decade and was the first athlete to go under 10hrs at the race. Marcel Zamora bookended the decade with more Spanish gold, equalling Cordier's record of five Embrunman titles. The course records are currently French, however, with Hervé Faure (9:34hrs) and Jeanne Collonge (10:56) the holders of the honour.

Away from the long-distance event, in 1988 the organizers added an Olympic-distance triathlon to the schedule that would attract 520 competitors. The race hosted a quartet of ITU World Cup events throughout the nineties, drawing nearly 100,000 spectators to the 1991 edition, won by Mark Allen. Simon Lessing took the title a year later, and in 1993 a record 1,500 athletes would take on the various formats of the Embrunman, again in front of a crowd numbering 100,000 people.

Like the Alpe d'Huez Triathlon, the present incarnation of Embrunman is a multi-day affair, with a duathlon held over the weekend, and events for youth and beginner athletes. The event, however, will most likely remain infamous for its challenging slopes on the bike and run (not to mention the chance of extreme heat) that put it very near the top of the list of the world's toughest triathlons.

◁ Yves Cordier, Mark Allen and Simon Lessing are just some of the names to have graced Embrunman's course, with the race still attracting huge numbers of pro and age-groupers

△ The run course keeps the hills a coming, with course times at Embrunman noticeably slower than other long-course events

◁◁ Locals of Embrun greet the finishers of one of triathlon's toughest days in the sun

Ironman Lanzarote

On paper and in the flesh, Ironman Lanzarote is world-renowned as quite possibly the hardest Ironman event in the world. The 226km journey, with over 2,500m of climbing on the bike alone, is reason enough for it to nestle at the top of the toughest Ironman bike courses. Then throw in a choppy sea swim, blistering heat and skin-burning winds and you'll see why this one annually chews up athletes and spits them back out again just for the fun of it. But it's a classic of triathlon, presenting onslaught after onslaught under a punishing sun, with many a competitor having to hook up to an IV drip on finishing.

'What makes Ironman Lanzarote so fearsome?' asks 13hr finisher and author Martyn Brunt.

Is it the heat of over 30°C? Or the 40mph winds? Or is it the 2,551m of climbing with the masses of Timanfaya, Haria and Mirador Del Rio evenly interspersed between a load of other hills? Actually, it's all three, which combine to turn the island into a lumpy, windswept furnace of Hell and the last place you'd expect anyone to do 226km armed only with a wetsuit, trainers and a piece of carbon.

Ironman Lanzarote takes place on the island of Lanzarote, the fourth-largest of the Canary Islands off the west coast of Africa. The event was created in 1992 by Kenneth Gasque (reportedly the first Dane to enter Ironman Hawaii in 1985) and hosted at his ever-popular triathlon training venue, Club la Santa. The Netherlands' Ben van Zelst and America's Janine Daley were the first male and female athletes home out of the 148 entrants. A year later the race moved to its current home of Puerto del Carmen, with the May schedule luring Ironman Hawaii legends to race (three-time Lanza winner Paula Newby-Fraser, Thomas Hellriegel and Peter Reid all tasted success on both these volcanic islands), and Eneko Llanos, Rachel Joyce, Bella Bayliss and Ain-Alar Juhanson are amongst the long-distance heavyweights to win the Lanzarote title.

Germany's Timo Bracht broke the men's course record in 2011 with a 8:30:34 time, but he had a warning for future competitors about the winds.

You need to know the wind is the main factor on the island. Because there are no trees or flags on the majority of the bike course, you don't ever see it, but you definitely feel it. And when you're riding, you really hear it. But the Ironman here in Lanzarote is a special race in a special place, and one of the most memorable events of my career.

◁ Nerves jangle as competitors prepare for arguably Ironman's toughest 226km of racing

▽ The sheltered 3.8km swim soon gives way to a ferocious bike leg of hills, heat and headwinds

Some of the world's toughest triathletes navigate the clear Playa Grande waters before embarking on one of Ironman's truly iconic bike legs

Although far from touching Newby-Fraser's course record of 9:24:39, Scotland's Cat Morrison produced one of the greatest comebacks in multisport history in 2010. At 80km of the 180km bike leg, the multiple world duathlon champion had a lead of over 8mins before her chain broke and she was forced to watch helplessly from the sidelines for 45mins as her rivals passed her by. By the time the chain was fixed, the deficit was 37mins on new race leader Tara Norton.

Onto the run, and, with Morrison seemingly out of the picture, Nottingham age-grouper Lou Collins (in her maiden Ironman race) took the lead with less than 10km to go. Collins' lead continued until 3km from the finish line when Morrison passed her to produce a marathon of 3:04hrs, crossing the line in 10:03:52.

Morrison, who admitted she'll forever carry a chain tool during races, added, 'My race was over, but I thought I could still have a good training day. It wasn't until the last 5km that I thought there was a chance I was going to win!'

Ironman Lanzarote starts at Playa Grande on the south side of the island, with a two-lap swim in the sheltered Atlantic waters. The bike course is a one-loop tour of the island, with barely a flat straight; competitors face two mountain climbs and plenty of hills in between, as well as the El Jable desert for good measure. The three-lap marathon run is mercifully flat, yet entrants are still subjected to the island's ever-present winds and the searing sun.

Thankfully for age-group athletes, the sun-fuelled crowd keeps the party going until the very last competitor runs/crawls across the finishing line, regardless of loss of daylight and sleep deprivation. And there to greet them is the legendary race organizer Gasque ('the world's coolest man,' according to Martin Brunt), who shakes every finisher's hand.

▷ The crowd keep the atmosphere alive throughout the day and up to the 17-hour cut-off and beyond

The Races

SavageMan

The Westernport Wall, the Big Savage Mountain and the Killer Miller. In less than a decade, the ultra-tough SavageMan has entered triathlon folklore for its satanic ascents and hair-raising descents. So much so that *Triathlete* magazine named it the hardest race on Planet Earth, and six-time Ironman World Champion Dave Scott was even forced to unclip his bike shoes on its most notorious stretch.

The brainchild of its founder and course architect Kyle Yost, the middle-distance SavageMan began life in 2006 and is held in the heart of the Allegheny Mountains, in Garrett County, western Maryland, USA. Its name alludes to the Savage River State Forest (named after an eighteenth-century surveyor) through which the course runs, as well as the terrifying terrain.

The 1.9km swim takes place in the crystal-clear waters of Deep Creek Lake before the fun and games begin with 2,000m of elevation gain on the 90km bike route. After a taste of things to come on the short, 16% gradient 'Toothpick' just 1km out of transition, the route features a long, fast descent to reach the Westernport Wall

▽ The blue waters of Deep Creek Lake are the home of the SavageMan swim

in Allegany County at 28km. At just four street blocks long, the Wall is far from the longest climb in triathlon but it's reportedly the steepest, with an average gradient of 25% building up to a maximum incline of 31% on the final stretch – a stretch deemed so steep it's long been closed to cars. If the climb isn't diabolical enough, the road surface is decidedly dicey, with potholes galore, and the organizers also throw in a posse of officials dressed as pitchfork-wielding devils to line the route.

The Westernport Wall has claimed plenty of scalps over its short lifespan, with falls aplenty, and Ironman legend Dave Scott is just one man forced to unclip and walk to the top. Anyone who does conquer the climb receives a brick engraved with their name laid into the Wall itself. Never mind giving athletes a respite after Westernport, the climbing continues with the 10km Big Savage Mountain ascent, which has 600m of elevation gain and extended sections

in excess of 20%. Here, if riders have the energy to look up, the panoramic vista of the Allegheny Mountains is a sight to behold ... before a swift, technical descent snaps athletes out of their comfort zone once more.

The final stretch of infamy is the short, sharp Killer Miller at 64km, the culmination of quite possibly the toughest 40km passage of cycling in all multisport and yet another ascent involving gradients of over 20%. The route then returns to T2 in Deep Creek Lake State Park before the 21.1km half-marathon run course takes in three more significant climbs as it heads towards the Appalachian Mountains.

If that hasn't put you off entering, the SavageMan middle-distance race takes place every September with entry capped at around 500 competitors (an Olympic-distance version is also available), with the non-profit event giving all proceeds to the Joanna M. Nicolay Melanoma Foundation.

△ The event began life in 2006 and quickly became a sell-out edition to the US tri calendar

▽ Savage shake: The bike course is famous across the globe for its climbs and characters

▷ The Westernport Wall has an average gradient of 25%, with legendary status awaiting anyone who conquers it

The Races

Elbaman

A swim in the turquoise Tyrrhenian Sea, a rolling bike in the Tuscan Archipelago and a marathon run through the Italian resort of Marina di Campo. Small wonder this event is sold out months in advance! It is Elbaman, Italy's most famous triathlon and greatest (and, admittedly, only) long-distance event, held since 2005.

Its setting is Elba, Italy's third-largest Island (after Sicily and Sardinia), which lies 20km south-west of the mainland town of Piombino in the province of Livorno. With a 7 a.m. start, the swim features two 1.9km laps in the warm 20°C-plus waters of Marina di Campo Bay, on the south side of the island, with athletes exiting onto the bay's golden sands and into T1 before three 60km loops around the island's western end.

If the waters are almost always calm, the bike course makes a lumpy contrast; it has 2,500m of elevation gain and barely a flat section anywhere in its 180km. Mediterranean scrub, pine forests and views of the Corsican coast about 50km further west provide the eye candy, along with the gorgeous nineteenth-century fishing village

▽ Athletes prepare to embark on a two-lap long-course swim in Marina di Campo Bay

△ A rare flat straight on the hilly 180km bike leg that traverses the Italian island

▷ Numbers at the Elbaman long-course race are restricted to just 280 to ensure a day of clear racing for triathletes

of Marciana Marina on the north coast, which is traversed three times.

The 42.2km marathon run is split into three 14km laps, taking athletes north of the Marina di Campo resort made popular in the fifties and back to a coastline finish. While fast, flat and with plenty of support en route, athletes face the rising September heat here on the run leg, with temperatures hitting the upper twenties and the three-loop format proving mentally exhausting.

Since its beginning in 2005, the race's organizers (led by experienced long-course athlete Marco Scotti) have developed a reputation for athlete care, with numbers restricted to just 280 for the long-distance showpiece (a middle-distance event attracting 430 racers is held alongside the full Elbaman) to ensure clear road racing and a manageable mass swim start.

While the world's top pro elites are absent, the start list has a huge international flavour, with athletes from over 20 nations regularly racing. And every November spaces sell out almost as fast as the brilliantly-named Alessandri Allessandro's 9:39hr course record, with athletes drawn to the late September sun and low-key tourism.

Mark Kleanthous, coach and author of *The Complete Book of Triathlon Training*, has 465 triathlons under his belt, Elbaman included. Here's his take:

The famous Italian passion is shown by every enthusiastic spectator and volunteer at Elbaman cheering you on as if you were a close relation. Many athletes travel to Elba because of the fine weather and the technical road routes.

The race day experience sees a sea full of inquisitive fish and amazing mountain views along the bike course, which can distract you from the enormity and the toughness of the course. I think Elbaman should be on every triathlete's bucket list of events to do before they retire.

▽ The race boasts an international feel, with athletes drawn from over 20 nations

Helvellyn Triathlon

Martin Cain, the Helvellyn course record holder and a man with a healthy shout to be called the UK's hardest triathlete, has this to say on the Cumbrian classic:

Looking for a challenge? Then the Helvellyn Triathlon is it. I've raced it four times and, despite the blisters, blood and the fact that I walk around like John Wayne for days afterwards, I'll keep going back for more. The swim is beautiful ... but freezing; the bike is superb ... as long as you enjoy 1:4 hills; and the run scenery is outstanding ... if you can lift your head to look at it.

A skull-crushingly cold swim, brutal climbs and hair-raising descents have forged the Helvellyn Triathlon's reputation as the UK's toughest multisport event. Since its inception in 2004 (it is, in fact, a reinvention of the original Slateman Triathlon, a police-only race that ran from 1993 to 1998), snowballing word of mouth has seen 600 of the UK's hardiest triathletes come to Cumbria each August/September armed with the mandatory survival blanket, map, compass and whistle.

In the stunning setting of England's Lake District, the course features a 1.6km swim in the bitter-cold waters of mountain-ringed Ullswater.

▽ Helvellyn has carved itself a reputation as one of the UK's toughest races, kicking off with a bitingly cold swim in Ullswater

The 61.2km bike route is legendary for The Struggle climb over the Kirkstone Pass at 44km. Rising 400m in 5km, it's an absolute brute, loaded with 20% ascents that will force even the most experienced athletes to push their steeds skyward. Then, far from offering a relaxing route home, the descent from Kirkstone Pass is highly technical, with exposed upper slopes, tight turns that need to be negotiated at speed and drystone walls lurking ominously at the side of the roads.

TriHard Event's 14.5km run route continues piling on the punishment, sending athletes to within touching distance of the 949m summit of Helvellyn, the third-highest peak in England (only 22m less than the highest). 'Accept that you won't be able to run all the way to the top of Helvellyn. On the really steep sections it's both faster and more energy-efficient to power walk, with the final stretch up Swirral Edge a rock scramble,' says 2013 winner Richard Anderson.

The descent, again, is no picnic either and will test athletes' downhill running skills to the max. Cain labels it 'hair-raising and brutal ... and I almost always fall,' and the race organizers

△ The Helvellyn Triathlon annually attracts 600 of the UK's hardiest triathletes to the Lake District in late summer

recommend all athletes cut their toenails, because they won't have any left by the finish line.

Although mid-pack competitors will take 2:30hrs just to finish the 14.5km route, one athlete to complete the run in 1:22hr was a 19-year-old Alistair Brownlee in 2007, setting a four-year course record of 3:28:14 in the process (until Cain went 24secs better in 2011). Although Jonny Brownlee was too young to take part, his father was happy for him to go around with a timing chip as a training run, completing it in 3:45:47 and slotting in between the fifth and sixth finishers to become the event's youngest-ever finisher.

◁ The 14.5km run sees athletes scale the heights of Helvellyn, the third-highest peak in England

△ Walking is a common sight on the run leg, with even experienced athletes taking 2:30hrs to complete the 14.5km to the finish

The Races

ÖtillÖ

▽ ÖtillÖ started life in 2006 with just 11 competitors, yet has swiftly grown to become most famous swim/run experiences in multisport

T he Stockholm Archipelago is one of Europe's great tourist experiences, a cluster of some 30,000 islands, skerries and rocks sprinkled over the blue Baltic Sea. Seals and skärgården ferries line the calm waters throughout the year, but each September they're joined by 120 teams of two paired together some even via a rope, who will swim and run 75km across 26 of the Archipelago's islands in a bid to take the ÖtillÖ title.

After starting with just 11 pairs of athletes in 2006 (and only two of those would make the cut-off), organizers Michael Lemmel and Mats Skott's aquathlon – now labelled the SwimRun World Championship – has increasingly gained international appeal, with 23 nationalities entering

▷△▽ Athletes will swim and run a total of 75km across 26 of the islands in the Stockholm Archipelago

the 2014 edition. 'The ÖtillÖ is probably the most challenging and enjoyable endurance-adventure race I've ever done, and all across beautiful countryside. I'd strongly recommend it to other competent swimmers-trail runners,' says two-time ÖtillÖ entrant and UK age-grouper Roland Kelly, who finished in 11:15hrs with his race partner Francois-Xavier Li in 2014.

Beyond the bucolic late summer Swedish landscape, the logistics and statistics of the race tell their own story, with each pair of athletes embarking on 64.5km of trail running and 9.5km of open-water swimming, with 52, yes, 52, transitions between each discipline. And all of this in 10–15°C Baltic Sea waters at the same latitude as the Orkney Isles.

Starting at 6 a.m., the race begins at the Seglarhotel in Sandön Island. The route is broken into five sections, with strict cut-off times enforced at the Runmarö, Nämdö, Morto-Bunso,

Kymmendo and Ornö checkpoints (where athletes can top up on cinnamon buns, hot dogs and Jelly Babies) before the event culminates at the Utö Värdshus on lovely Utö.

Athletes must carry their swim and run kit plus nutrition with them at all times, along with trail shoes for negotiating the slippery rocks and forest trails, and shorty wetsuits that can be used to run in. Mandatory race kit includes a first aid pressure bandage, waterproofs, wetsuits suitable for a water temperature of 10°C, a compass, a waterproof map holder, two whistles and a way to carry the mandatory equipment.

With team work an added dimension of the event, the race has been hailed as one of the toughest one-day races in the world, with 2014's Swedish winners Daniel Hansson and Lelle Moberg completing in 8:16hrs and the final competitors to cross the Utö finish line in 14:05hrs. Such is the rising popularity of ÖtillÖ, the organizers now host a qualifying race every July in Switzerland, the 54km Engadin Swimrun, in Alpine scenery that may even top ÖtillÖ Archipelago experience.

▽▷ Competitors carry all of their race supplies throughout and are also tasked with plotting a route around the aquatic wonderland

London Triathlon

A biggy. And by biggy we mean over 13,000 triathletes competing across super sprint, sprint, Olympic and Olympic Plus distances – plus a myriad of relay options – over two days at the ExCeL Centre in London's East End. So big, in fact, that the race has now superseded the Chicago Triathlon as the world's largest in terms of participation. And, with around a third of the annual influx of over 13,000 athletes being beginners to the sport, the IMG-organized London Triathlon has played host to thousands of debut triathlon races, becoming an important rite of passage for age-group athletes across the British Isles.

Admittedly, the East London docklands setting poses no challenge to events like Challenge Wanaka, the Norseman or Ironman France in terms of beauty, but for sheer scale the event is undeniably impressive. The vast army of marshals, medics and technical officials – the invaluable and mostly voluntary supporting cast without whom triathlon would barely exist – take a major share of the credit for the mammoth logistics of the operation, over the course of two days shepherding each wave of athletes in and out of the world's largest transition area before the next wave arrives. No mean feat when there are so many competitors.

A first London Triathlon was held at the Docklands for three years from 1985 to 1987, before the major redevelopment of the area took place. The race was relaunched with the help of Human Race's John Lunt in 1997 and 1998, being in 2001 to SBI before ending up in the hands of Escape from Alcatraz organizer IMG.

The event has now been held in London's Docklands for 18 consecutive years. The swim begins with a deep-water start in front of the ExCeL Centre, before proceeding with an out-and-back route in the occasionally choppy yet current-free waters of the Royal Victoria Dock. Then (if you can remember where to find your bike in the cavernous indoor transition area) the flat bike route takes place on closed roads – a rarity in London – with the sub 2:30hr athletes using a course that takes in Big Ben, Westminster and Embankment before returning to the ExCel via Canary Wharf.

◁◁ The world's biggest transition area hosts 13,000 triathletes over the weekend of the London Triathlon

▽ Canary Wharf is the backdrop for the Royal Victoria Dock swim leg

Fast, flat and perfect for a personal best (Internet forums have long speculated that the 10km run route is a little short), the multi-lap run route heads through the venue to Royal Albert Dock and returns to the indoor finish line gantry. With 13,500 athletes bringing their support crews, the route is lined with cheering spectators and intrigued locals. Celebrity spotting also adds another element of fun, with *Baywatch* star David Hasselhoff, racing driver Jenson Button and Virgin founder Richard Branson the recent pick of famous participants, alongside a host of reality television stars and retired pop performers.

The event also offers the chance for spectators to see age-group athletes race on the same course as some of the world's top triathletes like Daniela Ryf, Jodie Stimpson, Courtney Atkinson and Helen Jenkins, to name some recent winners.

◁ Cycling on closed London roads is a major draw for the hordes of age-group athletes

△ GB athletes Emma Pallant and India Lee celebrate their podium success in 2014

Hy-Vee Triathlon

◁▽ Des Moines has attracted the world's biggest Olympic-distance athletes since 2007

◁ ITU stars Simon Whitfield, Javier Gomez, and Greg and Laura Bennett are all past winners in Iowa

An employee-owned supermarket chain based in Iowa, may seem a strange cog in the mechanism of triathlon's evolution, but that's what happened in Des Moines. Following the precedent of Bahram Akradi's Life Time Fitness Series, the Hy-Vee Triathlon was launched by Ric Jurgens, CEO of the Iowan grocer, in 2007 with the aim of promoting healthy living and raising money for children's charity Variety.

While Hy-Vee undoubtedly gained international exposure as the title-sponsor of the event, and the local economy reportedly benefited to the tune of $2million, the race took triathlon to another level with an unrivalled $1million prize pot. The event became a rare chance for the world-hopping pro racers to earn money on a par with golf and tennis (this being a sport where age-group amateurs at the back, often with lucrative day jobs, are probably earning more than the ill-paid pros near the front).

After the first event in 2007 drew more than 2,000 athletes and 10,000 spectators to Des Moines, the Hy-Vee Triathlon became part of the ITU World Cup series for four seasons, with winners including Laura Bennett, Emma Snowsill and Simon Whitfield, who won a classic for the ages (and a giant $200,000 cheque) in 2009.

In 2011 the race became part of the World Triathlon Corporation's short-course 5150 Series, with Greg Bennett, Lisa Nordén and Javier Gómez a trio of famous winners. Hy-Vee departed as a sponsor in early 2015 but the race was swiftly revived with a race targeted at age-group athletes.

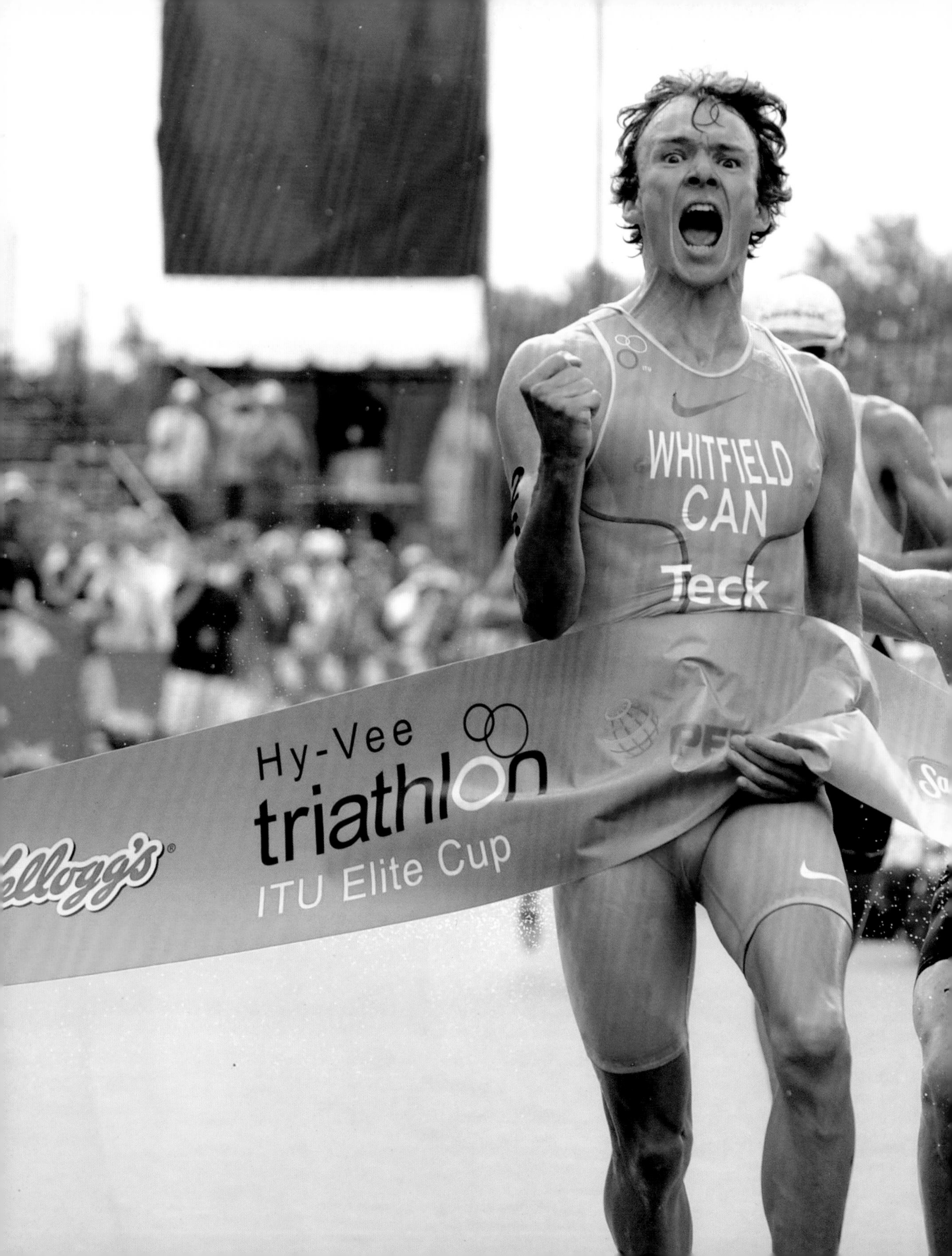
WHITFIELD
CAN
Teck
Hy-Vee
triathlon
ITU Elite Cup
Kellogg's

Ironman Austria

While Lanzarote may be undeniably tougher, Frankfurt has the pick of the pro racers and France the fabled history, Ironman Austria has quietly established itself as one of, if not *the*, most popular Ironman race on the European continent in its 17-year-history. Every June, the race sees 40,000 hotel rooms booked in Klagenfurt am Wörthersee for the race, 100,000 spectators descend on the beautiful Lake Wörthersee and 3,000 athletes from 60 countries taking on the 226km state of Carinthia challenge. And yet those age-group numbers could be even higher …

'The popularity of Ironman Austria is such that most people take longer to remove their wetsuits than it takes for the online entries to be sold out,' says veteran age-grouper Mark Kleanthous, a man who's raced Ironman Austria and coached many athletes to the finish line. 'Every time I hear the word Austria I instantly think of Klagenfurt. Without doubt it's one of the top five Ironman races in the world for its organization and beautiful scenery.' High praise indeed from a man with 37 worldwide Ironman finishes to his name.

And what scenery it is. The swim takes place in the 22°C waters of Lake Wörthersee in Austria's deep south, ringed by forested hills and snow-capped Alpine mountains standing majestically in the background. After 3.8km in the turquoise, transparent waters, athletes embark

▷ Since 1998, Ironman Austria has lured scores of athletes to Klagenfurt in the nation's south

▽ Ironman Austria's Lake Wörthersee is arguably the most beautiful swim setting on the Ironman circuit

on a two-loop course, which was co-designed by one Mark Allen, into the Alpine foothills around Carinthia for one of Ironman's fastest bike routes. While mostly flat (and on what Kleanthous calls 'some of the smoothest roads in the world,'), the two steep gradients on each lap are crammed with spectators lining the route ten-deep, producing a motivational din up there with Roth in the decibel stakes.

After a hero's welcome back in Klagenfurt, athletes embark on a largely flat and shady 42.1km run around the lake's shoreline before heading into Klagenfurt for one of Ironman's greatest finishes. 'When you run along the Magic Carpet to the finish line in Klagenfurt, you cannot fail to be overcome with emotion,' continues Kleanthous. 'There are even louder cheering spectators, with some of the biggest crowds lining up just before midnight to see the last competitors finish.'

Long-course racing in Klagenfurt began in 1998 when triathletes and Triangle Events creators Georg Hochegger, Helge Lorenz and Stefan Petschnig launched the TriMania event (Triangle would go on to host Ironman South Africa and France). Some 124 competitors would take part that day, and the race would become Ironman Austria the following season, with 800 athletes taking on the Mark Allen-designed course.

Peter Reid would smash the magical eight-hour barrier that day with a 7:51:56 time, creating the course's reputation as the fastest on the Ironman circuit. Other notable winners would include Wendy Ingraham, Lori Bowden, Kate Allen, Erika Csomor and, most famously, six-time champ Marino Vanhoenacker. The Belgian would smash Luc Van Lierde's 14-year Ironman record in 2011 with a time of 7:45:58 … only to have Andreas Raelert go 25secs faster seven days later at Challenge Roth.

Hochegger, Lorenz and Petschnig were inducted into the Ironman Hall of Fame in October 2014, with the race's present-day numbers including 40 million worldwide television viewers on 200 TV stations (the race is also shown live on Austrian domestic television) in 50 countries.

◁ Designed with the help of one Mark Allen, the 180km bike course is one of Ironman's fastest

Byron Bay Triathlon

Fast nearing its twentieth birthday, the Byron Bay Triathlon is a classic of the Australian triathlon calendar. Held on the second weekend in May, at the very end of the southern-hemisphere season, the event has long acted as the annual season-closer for athletes in Queensland and New South Wales, traditionally hosting a memorable after-party on the Saturday night. And the setting isn't bad either.

The tourist-friendly location 165km south of Brisbane leads plenty of competitors to plan their holidays around the Olympic-distance race, which attracts athletes from all over Australia and beyond. Each year around 1,300 athletes take to the waters of Byron Bay for a 1.5km swim in the clear, if occasionally wave-heavy, south Pacific waters before the 40km bike leg heads south to Lennox Head and back, traversing cane fields, coastal bush land, rainforest and the rolling countryside of northern New South Wales. The denouement features four 2.5km laps around the streets of Byron Bay, overlooked by the Cape Byron Lighthouse. Australian world-beaters Emma Carney, Jackie Gallagher, Chris McCormack, Pete Jacobs and Luke McKenzie are just a handful of Aussie greats who have claimed honours at the race.

Steve Wilson, editor of *220 Triathlon Australia*, is just one convert: 'The Byron Bay Triathlon is an insanely popular race for good reason. It's very athlete-friendly, offering plenty of fun in a beautiful location. Plus it has a genuinely tough course. Few Olympic-distance races can hold a candle to this one.'

▷ Australia's next generation of triathletes exit the waters of Byron Bay

▽ The Byron Bay Triathlon has been a fixture on the Aussie tri scene for nearly two decades

◁ The race regularly lures some of Australia's finest athletes to New South Wales

▽ Cape Byron Lighthouse provides the backdrop for the run laps

The Races
Challenge Bahrain

While December is usually a time for the world's finest athletes to recharge their batteries or catch up with the partner and kids, 2014 witnessed a mass pro pilgrimage to the Middle East for Challenge Bahrain. Although the chance for some winter race time and training load variety were lures for the pros, middle-distance triathlon's largest prize purse of $500,000 was the major draw to the Persian Gulf island.

Mirinda Carfrae, Jodie Swallow, Pete Jacobs, Tim Don and Sebastian Kienle were just a quintet of world champions on the start line, as the starting pontoon in Bahrain Bay warped under the weight of the best pro field this side of the lava fields of Ironman Hawaii or the Bavarian countryside of Challenge Roth.

The men's race witnessed Germany's double Ironman 70.3 world champ Michael Raelert exit the 1.9km swim ahead of 2012 Ironman world champion Pete Jacobs, and 2006 ITU world champ Tim Don. Raelert hit the highway at speed,

◁▽ Launched in 2014, Challenge Bahrain offers the biggest prize pot in all of middle-distance triathlon

▽ Athletes exit the 1.9km swim in Bahrain Bay with the Four Seasons hotel as the backdrop

◁ German superstar Michael Raelert won the inaugural men's event in 2014

◁◁ Denmark's Helle Frederiksen was the debut women's winner

averaging 44km/h on the first 30km and passing a stricken Kienle, who'd suffered a puncture a third of the way through.

In Kienle's absence, fellow German Andreas Dreitz destroyed the 90km bike leg on the Bahrain Formula One course to enter T2 with a few minutes lead over Raelert. Athletes were treated to a safari on the half-marathon run course as it weaved its way through the Al Areen Wildlife Park. 'I saw camels, gazelles and two ostriches ran in front of me!' laughed Don post-race.

Two-thirds of the way through the run, Raelert (brother of long-distance world record holder Andreas) passed a flagging Dreitz for the lead to take the title by virtue of a 1:10hr half-marathon split, recording a furiously fast 3:36hrs (the fastest time in Ironman 70.3 history is Raelert's 3:34:04 at Clearwater, Florida, in 2009) to take home the $100,000 first prize cheque.

The women's race saw Brit pro Jodie Swallow rocket out of the swim and occupy the lead throughout the majority of the 90km bike race, until Aussie athlete Annable Luxford pipped her into T2. Joining the leading duo were Denmark's Helle Frederiksen and Britain's Rachel Joyce. And it was to be Frederiksen's day on the run, as the young Dane's 1:17hr half-marathon saw her

establish a 2min advantage over the chasing pack to win in 4:49hrs.

While the game-changer term is consistently used to describe new triathlon events, Challenge Bahrain could be exactly that. The implementation of a 20m drafting zone – as opposed to 7m in Ironman – to encourage attacking racing was just one innovation positively received by the pro athletes.

The other major talking point is the $500,000 on offer, a record for a middle-distance race (and twice that given to the field at the Ironman 70.3 World Championships). Like the US Triathlon Series in the 1980s and the Hy-Vee Triathlon in the noughties, Bahrain has the potential to revolutionize the professional race scene at a time when the pros are becoming more vocal about the (lack of) prize money available to globe-trotting athletes.

Challenge Bahrain's future growth looks certain with the announcement of the Triple Crown for 2015, with Bahrain set to host the Grand Final of a Gulf-based mini-series including Challenge Oman and Challenge Dubai. The prize pot available for December's Bahrain Grand Final in 2015 will be a record-breaking US$1,000,000, which has the potential to alter and extend the pro racing season in 2015 and beyond.

Hamburg ITU

From Cape Town to Mooloolaba in Australia and Cozumel in Mexico, the International Triathlon Union's World Series and the federation's second-tier collection of World Cup races have plenty of jaw-dropping canvases for athletes to perform against. While it may lack the aforementioned trio's mountains, golden sands or azure waters, the ITU World Series regular race at Hamburg in northern Germany tops them all in the atmosphere stakes.

In a nation that also boasts Challenge Roth (220,000 spectators) and the Ironman European Championships (estimates vary from 100–500,000 on the sidelines), the ITU race in Hamburg completes the golden trio with a reported 300,000 competitors crammed into the old town of Germany's second-biggest city.

The race has been an ever-present entry on the ITU World Series since 2009 and has long hosted World Cup, World Championship, Mixed Relay and Paratriathlon events, with the ITU world champions Alistair and Jonny Brownlee, Gwen Jorgensen and Javier Gomez all breaking the tape to a crescendo of Germanic noise in recent times.

While some major city races stick around the outskirts with only brief forays into any central areas, part of the Hamburg race's appeal is how it takes over the heart of the city. The swim is positioned in the man-made Inner Alster Lake within the city limits, with the famous dark tunnel to be negotiated by both the elite athletes and 10,000 international age-group triathletes over the weekend.

▷ Three hundred thousand spectators cram themselves into Hamburg's Old Town for the annual ITU visit

▽ The elite race draws the finest ITU athletes to northern Germany, with Javier Gómez a two-time winner

▷ The Brownlee brothers boss the bike leg, with Javier Gomez in close pursuit

The bike course may be flat but it's one of the ITU's more technical routes, forcing athletes to weave around the streets of the old trading city and negotiate a number of switchbacks at the end of each of the multiple loops (the event offers both sprint and Olympic-distance races). The 5/10km run concludes at the Hamburg City Hall for one of triathlon's most epic finales.

The Races

Valencia Triathlon

Valencia is one of Spain's finest cities, a rewarding mix of classic Catalan *modernista* architecture and innovative contemporary design, with an upbeat atmosphere and a beautiful Mediterranean setting. The Valencia Triathlon captures its essence, taking in many of its most famous spots and offering a spectator-friendly major city-centre race experience for the hordes of age-groupers who sign up each year.

Launched in 2010, the instantly ambitious Valencia Triathlon sold out a month in advance of its debut race (a rarity for an event not from a major race organizer), with 1,200 athletes making the journey to eastern Spain in September that year. By 2014 that figure had risen to 3,500 triathletes from all over Europe for a weekend

of festivities, with the race format including paratriathlon events, women-only races and 'Best Buddies' waves (so friends can compete together) over super-sprint, sprint and Olympic distances.

The race kicks off in the waters adjacent to the award-winning America's Cup Building (the focal point of the Port of Valencia's regeneration), with spectators lining the dockside, before the bike leg of four 10km laps takes the athletes through the city. The route follows part of the former Formula 1 street circuit and passes over the city's famous swing bridge. The concluding run has the futuristic City of Arts and Sciences complex as its backdrop and takes the participants out to the Port Authority building, with its clock tower, and then back to the dockside finishing line.

◁ The Port of Valencia is the setting for the weekend of tri festivities in eastern Spain

▷ Both hardened racers and beginners fill the 3,500-strong field in Valencia

Ironman Frankfurt

S ince 2005, the World Triathlon Corporation has lured the world's finest long-course athletes to its Ironman European Championships in Frankfurt, with Chrissie Wellington, Sebastian Kienle and Andreas Raelert just a trio of long-distance legends to have won big in Wetterau. And like their Germanic event brethren in Hamburg and Roth, the race organizers sure know how to put on a show, with hundreds of thousands of spectators drawn annually to the race.

The race starts in two different waves, with the first wave consisting of 500 elite and top age-group athletes, with 2,000 more racers following soon after in the warm 22–24°C waters of the Langener Waldsee lake, 15km south of Frankfurt. After two laps totalling 3.8km, the 180km bike course takes athletes through central Frankfurt, the surrounding region of Wetterau and north to Bad Nauheim.

The 42km marathon run is a crowd-pleasing and fast four laps along the promenade next to the River Main in Frankfurt before finishing at the Römerberg Square in the historic Altstadt of Frankfurt. Those becoming Ironman Europe champions since 2005 (the race was the Opel Ironman Germany Triathlon from 2003–05) include Wellington, who broke the course record in 2008 with an 8:51:24 time. Men to have smashed the magic eight-hour barrier in Frankfurt include Germany's Timo Bracht (7:59:15) in 2009, Eneko Llanos (7:59:58) in 2013 and new course record holder Kienle (7:55:14) in 2014.

▽ The marathon run of Ironman Frankfurt finishes in the city's historic Römerberg Square

Jeju International

△ Hwasoon Beach is the setting for South Korea's only long-distance race

▷ The single-loop bike course mixes flat straights and rolling roads

South Korea's small, fledgling triathlon scene includes an Ironman 70.3 in Guyre and the Tongyeong ITU race on the mainland, with July's Jeju International the only long-distance event in the Republic. Jeju is both the nation's largest island, nearly 100km south of the mainland, and one of the country's provinces. The Jeju International takes place at Seogwipo City in the south of the volcanic island.

It begins with a mass swim start in the calm waters of Hwasoon Beach. After two 1.9km swim loops in the East China Sea, the triathletes enter T1 before a 180.2km one-loop bike course that takes in flat, coastal roads and traditional fishing villages for the first 70km. After that things get tougher, with rolling hills and small villages acting as a prelude to the foothills of South Korea's highest mountain, Hallasan, a massive extinct volcano that dominates the island. Sweeping panoramas and coastal views reward the athletes at this juncture, with a short, sharp 2km climb at 108km providing the trickiest test of the course. Soon afterwards the route heads back to Seogwipo City, allowing competitors the rare chance to race on a closed highway.

The 42.2km four-lap marathon run course starts and finishes at the Jeju World Cup Stadium (which hosted a trio of matches at the 2002 World Cup), taking in shoreline views and an aid station offering 'watermelon, bread, pies and red bean gels' – reason enough to sign up, some would say.

▽ Jeju hosted an Ironman-branded race until 2011, attracting athletes of the calibre of Chrissie Wellington

The Races
Challenge Penticton

Featuring Paula Newby-Fraser, Peter Reid, members of the Big Four and both Ironman and Challenge branding, long-course triathlon has a long and storied history in Penticton, Canada. The race began life in 1983 as the pet project of Canadian fitness guru Ron Zalko, who channelled his soul, energy and no doubt plenty of cash into establishing a long-course triathlon in British Columbia.

After its northern neighbour Kelowna turned down the offer to host the race, Penticton's local government stepped in on hosting duties and so began a decade-long relationship with 226km racing. Like Roth's fellow early eighties bow, the debut race in Penticton in 1983 attracted less than 100 competitors, with just one woman and 23 men entering the waters of Lake Okanagan on 20 August 1983 to compete in what was originally named the Ultra Triathlon.

The winners that day were Mike Wagstaff and Dyanne Lynch, the first names on a Penticton legends board that would include Peter Reid, Paula Newby-Fraser, Big Four duo Scott Tinley and Scott Molina, Erin Baker, Heather Fuhr, Lori Bowden, Thomas Hellriegel, Faris Al Sultan and more.

The race became mainland North America's only sanctioned Ironman event in 1986, acting as a qualifier alongside Ironman Japan and New Zealand for the Ironman World Championships in Hawaii (Penticton would hold the sole North American honour until 1998 when Lake Placid joined the 226km M-Dot party).

That 1986 event would also witness a pair of racers begin their journey to Ironman Hawaii-immortality. 'Everyone in Penticton was thoroughly touched as they watched a father tow, then cycle and push his physically challenged son over the course,' Shawn Skene writes in *Triathlon Magazine Canada*. 'Rick and Dick Hoyt's astonishing and emotional story is deeply entrenched in Ironman history and that history started at Ironman Canada.' The Hoyts would go on to complete Hawaii in 1989 and now have 1,000 races under their belts, being accepted into the Ironman Hall of Fame in 2008.

Ironman's relationship with Penticton would continue until 2014, when Challenge announced that they were taking over the race licence and adding Half and relay events to the Full distance race. The Full course would again feature the clear waters of Okanagan Lake before a single-loop 180km bike course takes in a quintet of lakes, the Richter Pass and plenty of pristine scenery. The run again features a single-loop course and heads along Skaha Lake and into Okanagan Falls before returning to the crowds of Penticton for one of triathlon's truly iconic finishes.

The race would also feature one of Canada's most revered triathletes as an event ambassador, with three-time Ironman World Champion Peter Reid welcoming the 1,100 finishing athletes home. Ironman, meanwhile, would soon announce their return to Canada with a new Ironman Canada in Whistler, 400km west of Penticton.

◁▽ The Okanagan Lake hosts the swim for this jewel in Challenge's American crown

▽ The single-loop bike leg has been tackled by the world's best long-course athletes

Cannes Triathlon

A month before the great and the good of the international movie world grace the Cannes International Film Festival, triathlon has its chance to enjoy its day in the sun on the city's famous Promenade de la Croisette. But in the place of sequins, satin and Sandra Bullock are sweat, suffering and slow-twitch fibres, for the Cannes Triathlon has one of the toughest bike courses that you could ever hope to find.

After the now-defunct TriStar events hosted a series of TriStar Cannes races up to 2013, the New Dream Cannes Association stepped up to organize the Cannes Triathlon in 2014. And what stepping up they did, with over 1,000 pro and age-group athletes lining up alongside the then Ironman World Champion Frederik Van Lierde in April 2014 for the revamped Long (2km swim/80km bike/16km run) and Middle (1km/50km/8km) events.

Like its French Riviera neighbour, Ironman France, the Cannes Triathlon begins with a swim in the turquoise Mediterranean waters before hitting the hills of southern France for a bike course that seems to lack a single section of flat road. Almost as painful as the 7km climb out of the city and the beating Cote d'Azur sun is the smell of the boulangeries en route, with the aroma of freshly baked bread and pastries filling the Sunday morning air.

After some hair-raising descents back into Cannes, the run refreshingly features just 2m of climbing, with a flat looped section along the Promenade de la Croisette's lavish hotels and cocktail-sipping tourists. With 50 slots for Escape from Alcatraz on offer for the top finishing age-groupers, there are far worse ways to kick off the European tri season …

▷ The Cannes Triathlon was revived in 2014 with Middle and Long distance races

▷△ Frederik Van Lierde is just one superstar of tri to be lured to southern France

The Races

The Ballbuster

For 25 years, the Ballbuster has occupied a major spot in the UK duathlon scene with a deviously simple concept: run, bike and run up Box Hill five times and see who's the winner.

Formed in 1990, just two years after the UK's first-ever run/bike/run event, the Classic Biathlon, in Chessington, the Ballbuster was created by Human Race founder John Lunt and his team. 'The 1990 race would draw nearly 20 competitors,' recalls 1990 entrant Mark Kleanthous, 'with entry consisting of athletes sending off two self-addressed envelopes for the race info and results, which were typed out and sent 10 days later. That race started at a different part of the hill with let's bust our balls shouted at the start!'

The Ballbuster would become a fixture of the UK race calendar for the next 25 race seasons, hosting a spring and winter edition for some periods. The race itself consists of a 12.8km run/38km bike/12.8km run around and up the cycling mecca of Surrey's Box Hill, home to the 2012 Olympic Road Race, with each lap ending with a physically and mentally exhausting 2km climb.

'But that's what entrants to the Ballbuster prepare themselves for,' says author and adventurer Danny Bent, a former top-five finisher. 'Pain and lots of pain. There's no pulling out. The crowds gather for the fun and games and gore and eat the homemade cakes sold from the café … torturing the injured and energy-depleted further. The final run leg is pure survival. To finish the race entitles you to hold your head high, to win it puts you amongst legends.'

△ The top of Surrey's Box Hill is the starting point of the Ballbuster duathlon

▽ The race forces duathletes to tackle Box Hill five times; three times on the bike and twice on the run

▷ Box Hill is one of the UK's most popular biking routes and was the setting for the 2012 Olympic cycling road race

The Races

Challenge Rimini

Despite the nation's cycling heritage and miles of coastline, major triathlon events in Italy are few and far between. Challenge are hoping to change all that with their middle-distance excursion in Rimini set to join the Elbaman as the nation's biggest multisport event.

Hosted on one of Europe's most famous stretches of coastline (and birthplace of influential film director Federico Fellini), the middle-distance Challenge Rimini starts with a 1.9km swim in the clear blue waters of the Adriatic before giving way to a 90km bike leg that heads high into the hills behind the city. The historic, incredibly Italian-sounding towns of Coriano, Montegrimano, Monte Cerignone and Montescudo are all visited before a return to

Rimini for a flat 21km beachfront run along the famous promenade and into the Parco Fellini.

Challenge launched the race in 2013 and clearly have high ambitions for the event, luring two-time Ironman Hawaii champion Chris McCormack and six-time Powerman Zofingen winner Erika Csomor to the event in its first year. The two would negotiate tough swim conditions to take the inaugural titles, with top Irish competitor Eimear Mullan and Italian athlete Domenico Passuello the victors in 2014. In 2015 Rimini hosted the ETU European Middle Distance Triathlon Championships, another major draw to lure athletes to the Emilia-Romagna region … if the 15km of Adriatic coastline weren't enough.

△ The beachfront of the famous Italian resort hosts the half-marathon run

◁ Athletes prepare to enter the Adriatic in one of Italy's major triathlons

The Races
Vineman

Vineman is the oldest independent long-course race in continental USA and one of the most cherished races on the American circuit. The 2015 season marked the 26th edition of the Full Vineman event, with the race luring both long-distance beginners and grizzled 226km veterans to California each summer for a blast from the past in a sport that's changed beyond recognition.

The race gets its name from its setting: Sonoma County's vineyards and wineries, a short hop north of San Francisco. The 3.8km swim takes

place at Johnson's Beach on the Russian River at Guerneville, what the organizers call 'one of the most rustic swim venues you'll see in the sport.' The 180km bike course travels through the Alexander Valley and Chalk Hill grape growing regions, with a taxing 1,200m of elevation gain for the entire bike course. The spectator-friendly marathon run is a three-loop, out-and-back affair based on Windsor High School, with aid stations every mile to counter the rolling hills.

With a field limited to 1,100 participants, the Full Vineman bucks the trend of overcrowded race days, giving athletes plenty of space on the swim, bike and run to concentrate on their race without bashing arms, wheels and toes with fellow competitors. The organizers and their band of 800 stewards label it 'the people's full-distance event', priding themselves on the personal experience offered by the event since 1990. An Ironman-branded Vineman 70.3 race takes place two weeks before the Full event in early July, with a women-only race and a rare aquabike race (just the swim and bike sections of the race) held on the same day as the original full Vineman.

△ Sonoma County is the setting for one of triathlon's most beautiful marathon runs

◁△▽ The much-cherished Vineman is the oldest independent long-course event in continental USA

Ironman 70.3 Pucón

Pucón in southern Chile has long been a South American mecca for adrenaline junkies, an international outdoor sports playground akin to Queenstown in New Zealand. Ample snowboarding, skiing, canoeing, horse-riding and hiking opportunities give hoards of backpackers their athletic fix each year, with endurance sport addicts firmly added to the list

in 2008 as the M-Dot juggernaut rolled in for the debut of Ironman 70.3 Pucón.

With a backdrop of the smouldering, snow-capped Villarrica volcano (one of South America's most restless), the race begins with a two-lap 1.9km swim in the calm waters of Lake Villarrica before athletes face a hilly, two-lap 90km bike into the hills around the lake, along the highway leading

▽ The snow-capped Villarrica volcano looms over the 90km bike course

to Argentina and up to the Palguín hot springs. The half-marathon run leg takes competitors through Pucón town on a crowd-pleasing three-lap tour, with a pair of tough ascents on each lap before a raucous finish-line experience.

A strong contender for the most beautiful 70.3 race on the worldwide circuit, Pucón has become a popular stop for athletes keen to start their race season every January, and the event regularly sells out months in advance. The tall Brazilian, Reinaldo Colucci, is the undisputed King of Pucón, with four wins and a couple of second-place finishes in his six appearances at the race. The original incarnation of the Pucón triathlon, offering a different set of distances, began life in 1984 and attracted triathletes of the calibre of Paula Newby-Fraser, Mark Allen, Lori Bowden, Chris McCormack, Peter Reid and Heather Fuhr.

△ Pucón has been hosting top-draw triathlons since 1984

◁ Pro athlete Felipe Barraza Rojas celebrates finishing 70.3 Pucón in 2004

The Races

Strongman Japan

Miyakojima, one of the Miyako Islands, lies some 1,880km south-west of Tokyo and just 400km east of Taiwan. The Strongman All Japan Triathlon Miyakojima (to give its full title) was established here in 1985, when the Japanese Government was aiming to establish the island as a sporting hotbed. Since then the event has become one of the most historic races on the eastern Asia multisport scene. Drawn to the limestone island's beauty and the race's unconventional distances and point-to-point course, the USA's Paul Huddle, Lothar Leder of Germany and Peter Kropko of Hungary are just three international athletes to taste success there.

The 3km Pacific swim takes place off Yonaha-Maehama Beach in the west of the island before the athletes head off on a 155km clockwise bike leg (25km less than the standard Ironman distance), that hugs the coastline of Miyakojima. At three points athletes head over long, exposed road bridges to the smaller islands of Irabu (from 2015), Ikema to the north and Kurima to the south-west. The Gusukube baseball stadium, the Cape Higashi lighthouse at the main island's south-eastern corner and a German Culture Village are ticked off along the route. Athletes finally reach T2 at the central Miyakojima City Track and Field stadium before the out-and-return marathon course heads down the spine of the island and back to the stadium.

With over 2,700 athletes regularly vying for the 1,500 slots at Strongman Japan every April, the popularity of the event shows no signs of abating. Off the track, the local dance known as 'Kuicha' along with lion dances are some of the side dishes that add to the event's unique charm.

▷ The Strongman bike route sends athletes over sweeping, long bridges to nearby islands

▷▽ The memorable finish line experience of the Strongman All Japan Triathlon Miyakojima

◁ Yonaha-Maehama Beach on Miyakojima's west coast hosts the 3km swim leg

Beijing International Triathlon

Riding high after the city had hosted the 2008 Olympics and the 2011 ITU World Championships Grand Final, the Fengtai Sports Bureau of Beijing teamed up with major race organizer IMG in 2012 to launch the Beijing International Triathlon to the Chinese capital's profile in the sport.

The end-of-season scheduling in September, rare qualifying slots for IMG's Escape from Alcatraz and $100,000 in prize money instantly ensured that the race became a major draw for the pro and top age-group fraternities alike, with a clutch of medal-laden Olympians and Ironman athletes on the start line since 2012.

Javier Gómez, Chris McCormack, Sarah Groff and Bevan Docherty are just four of many who have tested their mettle on the Olympic-distance course. One of the inaugural Beijing International winners in 2012 was Groff; the other was New Zealand's Docherty, who had taken bronze at the 2008 Beijing Olympics behind Jan Frodeno and Simon Whitfield. 'It was the perfect day in the Fengtai district of Beijing for a triathlon,' added Docherty post-race. 'The air was clean, the water temperature comfortable and the course smooth with flat roads, good climbs and picturesque scenery; it had everything.'

The setting for the 1.5km swim is the reservoir-turned-bathing-beach Qinglong Lake Park ('like a valuable sapphire embedded in the area, when a breeze blows the waves ripple as if a naughty girl winks,' gushes a poetic local tour operator). This lies in Beijing's vast Fengtai District, 37km south-west of Tiananmen Square in the centre of China's most beguiling city.

The challenging 40km bike race takes competitors through the traditional villages of Fengtai and up to Qian Ling Mountain, the highest peak in the area. The concluding 10km run returns to Qinglong Lake and features a variety of terrain, with stone paths, wooded trails and plenty of bridges around the park for racers to cross.

After Docherty's win in 2012, Javier Gómez has made the race his own by producing wins in 2013 and 2014, posting convincing end-of-season victories over the likes of veteran Greg Bennett, Mario Mola and Matty Reed. Gómez's fellow 2012 Olympic silver medallist Lisa Norden took the women's title in 2013 ahead of Sarah Groff, with Aussie Ashleigh Gentle the winner in 2014. Fifth in that 2014 showdown was British pro athlete Emma-Kate Lidbury, who enjoyed the Beijing International experience:

> *The Beijing International Triathlon is a truly unique race experience, which blends the crazy chaotic culture of Beijing with the fun and intensity of Olympic-distance racing. The Chinese have discovered triathlon with immense passion, and this is reflected in the energy of the race.*
>
> *As soon as you exit the one-loop swim and begin the bike course you realize just how much work has gone into making this race a success: many of the roads which racers ride along have been created purely for the event. The run is most definitely one of the most challenging you'll find, so save plenty of energy for this! This race is much more than a triathlon; it's a destination event, where competitors can enjoy racing hard while discovering and exploring a new city and culture.*

◁ Qinglong Lake Park has been the setting for the Beijing International since the race's dawn in 2012

△▷ Traditional villages and Chinese culture populate the 40km bike course

▷ The Beijing International also attracts a healthy number of age-group triathletes to the Chinese capital

Ironman 70.3 Bintan

With a name that translates as 'Beyond Man', the MetaMan triathlon began life in 2012 with the promise of a challenging long-distance course, beautiful scenery and a bumper $154,000 prize pot. That it delivered, and more, drawing the likes of Powerman legend Erika Csomor in its first year and premier Iron athletes Caroline Steffen, Cameron Brown and Gina Crawford in later editions. Such was the success that Ironman took over the race in 2015.

Taking place every August, the setting for the long- and middle-distance event is the tropical Indonesian island of Bintan, located in the Riau archipelago and a major tourist destination just a 45-minute catamaran trip from Singapore.

The swim is one of the race's calling cards, starting with a mass swim in the sheltered, calm South China Sea waters of Nirwana Garden Resort, before uniquely taking athletes around a headland to a neighbouring bay for the swim-to-bike transition. The bike leg is a 90km-lap affair that combines elements of the Tour de Bintan route, meandering past the forests and rivers of the island's unspoilt interior before hugging the western coastline for the return back to Nirwana Gardens.

The flat, seafront three-lap run is set entirely within the grounds of Nirwana Gardens, with each lap including a 3km section of run over the trails of the Wakatobi Jungle Track where jungle canopy provides a welcome umbrella from the sun for the early runners (the trail is illuminated for the back-of-the-pack athletes when the day turns into night).

△ Local supporters come out in force during the 90km bike course

▷ Both the half and full marathon runs venture along the Wakatobi Jungle Track

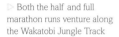

◁△ The Nirwana Garden Resort hosts the unique MetaMan swim every August

◁▽ Athletes exit the South China Sea ready to head into the island's interior on the bike leg

The Races
Celtman

If the thought of completing an Iron-distance race isn't enough, the organizers of the long-course Celtman have thrown in a deeply cold 3.8km swim in the 400m Loch Shieldaig, an extended 202km bike course before a marathon run over two Munros. Plus the Scottish weather. Calling it a Scottish Norseman wouldn't be wide of the mark.

Centred around the remote Torridon mountains (a five-hour drive north of Glasgow and Edinburgh), the Celtman was first run in 2012. 'The Norseman was a big influence – Dag Oliver and his team were the first people we spoke to as most of the Celtman team had either raced or supported in Norway,' says Celtman organizer Paul McGreal. 'We adopted many of the key features of Norseman – the ballot for entry, the need for a support crew, the small scale of the event and, of course, an extreme and testing route.'

The race would pick-up a British Triathlon Event of the Year award in its very first year, with the rare point-to-point course ('it's a journey right from the beginning,' adds McGreal), 4,000m of total ascent and the UK's most extreme run course finding favour with voters.

That run course is nearly all off-road, with McGreal filling in the grisly details. 'After an easy first half, the run course features a climb of over 1,000m to the first of the Munro hills. The exposed and spectacular ridge run to the second hill, which involves another 300m of climbing, is essentially over trackless and rocky terrain. Then the route follows an exceptionally steep descent down a rock-filled scree chute to the corrie of Loch Coire Mhic Fhearchair.'

◁ Only the brave take on the 248km Celtman experience

▷△ Athletes entre the wince-inducing waters of Loch Shieldag

▷ The 202km bike course is centred around the Torridon mountains in the Scottish Highlands

Mooloolaba
Triathlon Festival

Held in the triathlon heartland of Australia's Sunshine Coast, the Mooloolaba Triathlon Festival (MTF) has been a feature of the Antipodean race calendar since 1993 and is now the second largest triathlon in the southern hemisphere.

Run by USM Events, like the Noosa Triathlon 35km up the coast, the Mooloolaba race features a weekend of endurance activities for its 7,000 entrants and 30,000 spectators, including a twilight 5km run, a 1km sea swim, the Superkidz Triathlon and the Special Tri.

The focus of the weekend, though, is the Olympic-distance triathlon, which brings thousands of athletes to the golden sands of the Sunshine Coast suburb for one of the sport's most beautiful days in the sun. It starts with a 1.5km swim in the 18°C waters of the Pacific outside the Mooloolaba Surf Club before a fast and flat out-and-back closed-road 40km bike course and a two-loop beach-front run.

Since 2007 the event has also annually featured the pro-only Mooloolaba ITU Triathlon World Cup event, which usually kicks off the ITU World Cup season. This is held at the same time as the MTF, and the conjunction of the two allows age-groupers to share the water, roads and pavement with some of Olympic-distance triathlon's greatest names. Its past winners have included ITU World Champion athletes Javier Gómez, Emma Snowsill and Gwen Jorgensen, with Brad Kahlefeldt, Courtney Atkinson, Peter Kerr, Ashleigh Gentle and Sarah Deuble five of the Australian victors.

◁▽ Aussie hero Emma Moffatt (far left) leads the elite athletes to the Sunshine Coast waters

▽ The closed road out-and-back bike course crests a rare hill

Lavaman Waikoloa Triathlon

With a pro pedigree that includes Dave Scott, Simon Whitfield and Chris McCormack, the Lavaman Waikoloa Triathlon is proof that the Ironman World Championships don't have the monopoly on triathlon on the Big Island of Hawaii. But where the Ironman Worlds opt for one of the sport's toughest days of 226km racing, the Lavaman Waikoloa offers the more fun, yet still taxing,

option of an Olympic-distance race combined with one of the best after-parties in triathlon.

The 18th annual Lavaman Waikoloa was held in March 2015 at Waikoloa Beach Resort on the Kohala Coast, and was sold out months in advance. The 1.5km Pacific swim begins with a deep-water start at Anaehoomalu Bay in balmy waters of around 26°C (needless to say, wetsuits aren't mandatory) and with water visibility of 20m

▷ Held since the nineties, the run leg of the Lavaman features an energy-sapping run on beach trails

▽ The Pacific Ocean swim takes place in waters with 60m of visibility

or better. The out-and-back 40km bike route shares some of the same Queen Kaahumanu Highway routes as parts of the Ironman Hawaii course, before returning to the Waikoloa Beach Resort for a run that seemingly ticks off every known running surface to man.

The 10km begins with a lava field stretch before sending competitors over fast road sections, lawns and flagstone paths, concluding with an energy-sapping mile-long sandy run to the beachfront finish line/beach BBQ/after-party under the coconut groves of Waikoloa Beach.

Triathlon legends who have tamed the Lavaman include Whitfield and Macca, with Dave Scott placing 20th at the age of 57 and Formula 1 star Jenson Button sixth in 2012. A special mention also has to go to local pro Timothy Marr, who's made the top five in almost every edition.

▷ Tropical splendour and countless cocktails greet athletes at the Lavaman finish line

The Races
Vitruvian

△ Vitruvian racers are regularly greeted with a beautiful sunrise over Rutland Water

No advertising, little hype, minimal PR ... and still Pacesetter Event's Vitruvian sells out its 1,100 spots year after year within days, proof that a superbly organized race and word of mouth can overpower even the biggest of marketing budgets. But what makes the thousand plus numbers of triathletes each year want to become a Vitruvian man (or woman)?

Established in 2003 by UK triathlon veteran Mark Shaw at a time when middle-distance races were far from ubiquitous on the UK calendar, the Vitruvian began life with less than 250 starters in its first year. Since then the middle-distance event at Rutland Water in Leicestershire has grown into one of the most respected races on the UK calendar, voted by readers of *220 Triathlon* as its Race of the Year on three separate occasions. Entry is strictly capped at 1,100 per year – although numbers could be many times higher – to ensure athletes have space to race.

△ The event is one of the UK's essential middle-distance races

The race itself annually takes place in late August/early September, kicking off with a two-lap 1,900m swim in Rutland Water with the rising sun providing a bucolic backdrop. The pretty 85km bike course again features a two-lap, spectator-friendly format, ensuring that competitors have to take on the Rutland Ripple twice, a punishing three-hill test six miles into the first lap. While the rest of the course is largely gently undulating, competitors are at the will of the winds throughout.

The event finishes with 21km half marathon, two-loop run around Rutland Water, hugging the water's edge throughout and keeping in close proximity to the cheering crowds throughout. Accompanied by some of the best race music on the circuit, competitors are greeted at the line with the famous 'You are a Vitruvian' honour from the compere and plenty of supportive marshals.

Ironman Japan

△ The 180km bike course
is largely flat and heads
into lush countryside

◁ The 3.8km swim takes
place in Japan's cleanest lake

Its place on the worldwide circuit may be an irregular one, but Ironman Japan has produced enough landmark moments to last a lifetime. The 226km toughie was the first Ironman event in Asia and only the second international race in history (after New Zealand) to offer qualifying slots for Ironman Hawaii. Major landmarks in its initial 1985–2009 lifespan include Dave Scott's Ironman record breaking 8:01:59 time in 1989 and Paula Newby-Fraser's final long-course victory in 2002.

After a four-year hiatus from the Ironman circuit after 2009, M-Dot returned to Japan with a new location of Hokkaido in August 2013 for a sell-out event of 1,700 racers. Following Kona, Lanzarote and Pucón, the race continues the Ironman-theme of volcanic backdrops, with

the event taking place in the shadow of Mount Usu, reportedly one of the world's most active volcanoes.

The swim takes place in the drinkable waters of Lake Toya, officially Japan's cleanest lake, before a flat bike course past mountains and lush farmland, and a final marathon run alongside Lake Toya before a closing fireworks extravaganza closes the event.

While it might not offer much in the way of hills, Raymond Britt of the exhaustive statistics website, runtri.com, has revealed that the average finish time was a decidedly slow 13:39hrs, over an hour shy of the worldwide Ironman average of 12:35hrs. And at the finish line is the race director, hugging, bowing to or shaking the hand of every finisher.

Vancouver Triathlon

From the Winter Olympics to the Commonwealth Games and FIFA Women's World Cup, outdoor activities honeypot Vancouver is a city full of sporting heritage. Triathlon isn't exempt from the western Canada city's sporting prowess, with the nation's first-ever triathlon held in the city in 1981. Twenty-seven years later, the ITU would host its 2008 ITU World Championship final in the city, with Javier Gómez and Helen Jenkins taking the elite titles and a young Alistair Brownlee the U23 crown.

Away from the elite scene, the Vancouver Triathlon is one of Canada's premier multisport events for age-group athletes, with relays and sprint, Olympic and middle-distance events all offered. The race formed part of the Subaru Western Triathlon Series for eight editions from 2007 until 2014 alongside triathlons in Shawnigan Lake, Victoria and Sooke, before Ironman took over the running of the event from 2015 onwards.

The British Columbia city's Locarno Beach plays host to the chilly swim legs, with a Mass

▽ Canada's first-ever triathlon was held in Vancouver in 1981, with the city hosting the 2008 ITU Worlds

running start to reach the English Bay waters. The bike course mixes views of the downtown Vancouver city skyline to the south and the imposing North Shore Mountains northwards. Journeying west, the route takes in the nearby Spanish Banks Beaches area before subjecting competitors to the winds of the University of British Columbia Endowment Lands on the western edge of the city that nestle alongside the Strait of Georgia. The concluding run features a mixture of surfaces, again providing a rural/urban juxtaposition of city skyscrapers and towering mountains as the predominant views.

▽ British star Helen Tucker (soon to become Jenkins) wins the 2008 ITU Worlds on the Vancouver course

▷ The Vancouver bike course journeys west through western Canada's biggest city

New York City Triathlon

▷ Since 2001, the race has drawn the world's finest athletes to New York City

◁ Athletes dive into the Hudson River for a point-to-point swim leg of 20 Manhattan blocks

▽▷ Central Park is one of the most famous settings in all of triathlon

Since its launch in 2001, the New York City Triathlon has lured the great and the good of triathlon to the Big Apple. The roll-call of those who have graced the Central Park podium, especially in the race's early years, is immense, with Karen Smyers, Barb Lindquist, Emma Carney, Mirinda Carfrae, Loretta Harrop, Emma Snowsill and perennial winner Greg Bennett all dipping their talented tri toes into the Hudson River. The men's top three in 2003 alone featured world-beaters Simon Whitfield, Tim Don and Bevan Docherty.

The race has also played a role in American triathlon's recent history, being part of Bahram Akradi's groundbreaking, mega-money Life Time Fitness Series since 2002 (along with Minneapolis, Chicago, Los Angeles and Dallas), a forerunner of the ITU World Series with stacked pro fields racing on the same weekend as age-group athletes.

The Olympic-distance New York City Triathlon itself begins with a 1.5km point-to-point plunge into the Hudson River west of Manhattan's 99th Street, before exiting 20 blocks away on the 79th Street Boat Basin. Cyclists then head north on the Henry Hudson Highway out of Manhattan and over the Henry Hudson Bridge towards Mount Vernon and Yonkers. A U-turn in the Bronx signals the passage home, with the race concluding with a 10km clockwise-run leg through Central Park, arguably the most famous location of any triathlon leg in the world.

The Races

Challenge Denmark

Instead of embarking on a bout of soul-searching after the World Triathlon Corporation (owner of Ironman) acquired yet more of its races in Copenhagen and Aarhus in 2013, the Challenge Family were quick to announce their return to Denmark with both Full and Half distance races featuring a backdrop of, er, plastic bricks, bowl haircuts and a 13m long X-Wing Fighter.

Based in the country's western peninsula of Jutland, June 2015's Challenge Denmark took place in and around Billund, the home of Lego and the world's first Legoland resort. After a swim in Fuglsang Lake in Herning, the fast and flat bike routes take in some of the same roads as 2012's Giro d'Italia pilgrimage to Denmark. The run course is centred around Legoland Billund Resort and has a special inclusion of a lap around a horse racing track before finishing a short jump away in Lalandia, Denmark's largest water park.

Quite whether family members will be too busy playing with 4cm pirates to see their loved ones cross the finish is open to question, but Aussie tri legend Chris McCormack was just one athlete to sign up. "I'll be racing the Half event at Challenge Denmark. It's going to be an amazing race with both full distance, half distance and relay, and I'm so excited to come to Denmark. Billund is considered the children's capital of the country and I'll certainly be bringing my children with me. It can't get any better!" added Macca.

▷ Fuglsang Lake in Herning hosts Challenge Denmark each June, with the run taking in the unusual race sights of Legoland

Château de Chantilly

Held at the birthplace of Chantilly cream, a favourite spot of Teddy Roosevelt's and the home of Bond villain Zorin in the film *A View to a Kill*, the Château de Chantilly triathlon, like others in the Castle Triathlon Series, mixes both distant and contemporary history in its location.

Held annually in late August, the race is the French element of the five-date European series (see p. 152 for the flagship event at Hever). The event takes place at the town of Chantilly, 60km north of Paris, and, like the series races in Ireland, England and Italy, it boasts more race

△ The bike leg is largely flat and straight, and is hosted on closed roads

distances than you can poke a large baguette at; two thousand athletes, including children, adult beginners and grizzled middle-distance veterans rub shoulders on the Château's sizeable lawn over the weekend of action.

With the château as a backdrop (part of it mid-fourteenth-century and part rebuilt in the 1870s after being razed during the French Revolution), the swim takes place in the 2.5km-long Grand Canal before athletes transition on the Terrasse des Connétables and embark on a long, predominantly straight cycle circuit around the Forêt de Chantilly. After entering T2, competitors run on light off-road trails in the surrounding woodlands and gardens before finishing within sight of the Château.

Once the racing is over, athletes drag their weary limbs around the Château's Musée Condé, one of France's finest art museums. Or they can spot film locations used in James Bond's *A View to a Kill* and *The Pink Panther*, and see where footballer Ronaldo (the Brazilian one) hosted his lavish 2005 wedding.

The Gear

Quintana Roo

W hat Gary Fisher is to mountain biking or Adi Dassler to athletics on the track, Dan Empfield is to triathlon: the visionary who pioneered the design, development and distribution of multisport-specific gear. Others may have got there first (French brand Aquaman created a tri wetsuit in 1984), but it was Empfield who had the nous and business sense to take his pioneering ideas for wetsuits and bikes beyond prototypes and into the public sphere, revolutionizing the young sport of triathlon in the process.

Empfield, born in 1957, was no slouch on the race circuit, successfully completing the first-ever

Ironman Hawaii event to be held at Kailua-Kona in 1981. The hours spent submerged in the water, perched on a saddle or pacing on two feet gave Empfield key first-hand experience of the unique demands of multisport athletes, as opposed to their single-sport brethren. This accumulated knowledge found an outlet in 1987.

Back when Dave Scott was ruling the Ironman Hawaii race course and the world was dancing to

△ The Quintana Roo CD0.1 provides plenty of aerodynamic trickery and continues QR's history of melding innovation and aesthetics

▷ Quintana Roo founder and triathlon gear pioneer Dan Empfield at Ironman Hawaii in 1993

'La Bamba', Empfield was busy forming Quintana Roo (named after one of his favourite destinations in Mexico) to produce, market and sell triathlon-specific wetsuits customized to the needs of triathletes. Where triathletes previously swam in heavy, inflexible and ill-fitting surfing wetsuits (or, if the water was warm enough, attempted the first discipline in just a pair of Speedos or a cossie), Empfield's Quintana Roo designs offered movement around the shoulders, thanks to the thinner and more pliable rubber, and long zips on the back for a speedier swim-to-bike transition.

Forward-thinking pro athletes Brad Kearns and Andrew MacNaughton were two instant converts to the Quintana Roo suit, and by the end of the 1987 season half of the Pacific West's fervent triathlon community were wearing them. A tipping point had been reached; as Empfield himself has noted, 'Nobody wore wetsuits prior to 1987, and everybody wore wetsuits after 1987.'

Having become the Godfather of a multi-million dollar industry that now, in the second decade of the twenty-first century, features countless brands from around the globe, Empfield (re)turned his attentions to the road.

The widespread adoption of aerobars in triathlon in 1987 spurred Empfield and his collaborator Ralph Ray to look at building a bike specifically for triathlon, as opposed to a road bike with aerobars clamped on. Looking at female athletes especially, Empfield came to the realization that the triathlete's starting position on the bike needed to be moved further forward to avoid the discomfort of sitting on the nose of the saddle for prolonged stints. To do this he increased the seat angle to 80 degrees to move the saddle closer to the cockpit, which had the multiple aims of reducing the drag caused by the rider's body position, improving comfort, increasing the power output and keeping the legs fresh for the run leg. His other key innovation was to reduce the wheel size from 700c to 650c, again to improve comfort and power output: a tactic Mirinda Carfrae successfully adopted some 25 years later at the 2013 Ironman World Championships.

By 1989, the Quintana Roo Superform was ready for launch. Even in the forward-thinking

world of triathlon, free from the shackles of the UCI rulebook, the bike was greeted with scepticism. All that changed the moment Ray Browning (the second athlete to ride the Superform after John Gailson) smashed the Ironman New Zealand bike course record aboard the Superform, entering T2 with a 30-minute lead over pre-race favourite and Big Four legend Scott Tinley. The result saw a sharp spike in sales of the Superform.

Fom Ceepo to Cervélo, the influence of Empfield and the Superform is still being felt today – the *Velvet Underground & Nico* of the tri-bike world. But, since leaving Saucony, far from cashing his royalty cheques and becoming a recluse in his self-proclaimed endurance playground of Xantusia, north of Los Angeles, Empfield has gone on to launch the influential triathlon website, slowtwitch.com, and create the F.I.S.T bike-fitting system.

Quintana Roo, meanwhile, was sold and relocated to Tennessee in 2000 under the umbrella of the American Bicycle Group; it has continued to innovate with both its CD.01 and Illicito bikes, coming up with unique, award-winning ways of redirecting airflow from the drag-producing drivetrain side of the bike to the clean (non-drive) side.

△ The Quintana Roo Redstone, complete with bladed forks and a rear fairing to limit turbulence

▽ Present-day Empfield at his Xantusia multisport hive in California

The Gear
Felt Racing

Saturday, 12 October 2013. Rarely can a bike have made a more high-profile debut at the Ironman World Championships than the Felt IA. After months of bike expo showcases, frenzied forum chat and magazine teasers, Mirinda Carfrae was about to clip-in to triathlon's latest superbike in Transition One of triathlon's most famous race. Felt Racing's exhaustive wind-tunnel R&D had predicted that the company's premier triathlete would save more than 12 minutes over the 180km Ironman Hawaii course in typical conditions by switching from her old Felt DA to the new IA (Integrated Aero).

If the pressure on Carfrae to produce was immense, the diminutive Aussie didn't show it. By the late afternoon, she had broken the course record in 8:52:14 to regain the Ironman World Championship crown she'd first won in 2010. In the

process she'd cycled 13:58mins quicker than she did in 2012's defeat to Leanda Cave and run a 2:50:38hrs marathon that was faster than all but two men on the Big Island. While Carfrae's return to her coach Siri Lindley could undoubtedly have been a factor in her improved performance, as bike endorsements go, things couldn't have gone much better for the Felt IA.

Unusually for a time-trial/triathlon bike from a major brand, Jim Felt, working with the engineering expertise of Anton Petrov and Jeff Soucek, tore up the UCI handbook when it came to designing the IA (making it ineligible for the pro cycling circuit), an indication perhaps of triathlon's increased standing and marketability in the sporting world. Where UCI rules stipulate a maximum tube profile depth-to-width ratio of 3:1, that of the head tube area on the IA is an immense 11:1. Other UCI-bothering features include the low angle of the seat stays that reduces the frontal area by nearly 50% compared to conventional seat stays and is said to increase the lateral stiffness.

Make no mistake, this is a triathlon bike first and foremost, with the cockpit featuring an AeroPac cover for storing energy gels, bars and tools for extended sojourns in the saddle. Elsewhere, the adjustability on the seatpost, saddle and cockpit offer a huge range of options, maximizing the chance of achieving the perfect bike fit for triathletes. The bike also uses new carbon-fibre composites with a material called TeXtreme to reduce weight and improve frame stiffness, plus a 'workable' braking system designed alongside the frame that functions with all wheels and brake levers.

▽ Mirinda Carfrae aboard the Felt IA on her way to winning the 2013 Ironman World Championships

The Felt IA is also easy to dismantle and transport for globe-hopping racers. The result is arguably the most formidable triathlon bike ever released, a landmark in design that will make every bike designer on the planet sit up and take note. But how did Felt achieve this illustrious position? The tale starts back in the late eighties, with the unusual demands of a motocross star named Johnny O'Mara.

Around the time Dan Empfield was finalizing the designs on his Quintana Roo Superform, top motocross racer O'Mara, who was competing in triathlons as training for motocross, asked his motorbike mechanic and fellow pro rider Jim Felt to build him a time-trial bike. Felt, experienced in age-group triathlon, had clear ideas on how to improve on the designs of the time. Just as he did over 20 years later, with the hours spent optimizing Carfrae's position in the wind tunnel, he focused on optimizing the rider's position to increase aerodynamic benefits and improve comfort.

Almost instantly O'Mara started winning races, and Jim Felt soon found himself courted by the world's top triathletes. One was Zimbabwe's Paula Newby-Fraser, who won her fourth of eight titles at the 1991 Ironman World Championships on a Felt. A major name in bike design was born.

During the nineties Jim launched the component brand Answer Products, before refocusing on Felt at the end of the century. Industry veteran Bill Duehring and Michael Mullmann, a European distributor, joined the Felt fold, and the company ventured into road cycling (equipping the Garmin-Chipotle/Team Slipstream tour teams, featuring the likes of David Millar, Dave Zabriskie, Christian Vande Velde and Magnus Bäckstedt), mountain-biking and cyclo-cross with increasing success. All the while Felt Racing retained a personal touch, employing just 27 people across the globe ('Specialized probably have that [many] in their water-bottle department,' Felt told *BikeRadar* in 2008).

The triathlon world wouldn't be neglected, however. The Felt DA became one of the fastest tri-bikes on the planet, taking Andi Böcherer to glory at the Ironman 70.3 European Championships in 2011. (Aesthetically it's a corker, too, like the rest of Felt's tri-bike range, mirroring rock band the White Stripes' ethos of using only black, white and red.)

And 2011 was also the year Carfrae, who had won the 2010 Ironman World Championships on a Cannondale, joined the good ship Felt. Of her move, she said,

> Felt was just head and shoulders above [the rest] when it comes to their passion and what they're already doing with their bikes. They cater to the smaller athlete. We didn't even talk numbers. it was a case of which brand is going to make the most sense to me as an athlete.

Amongst other top pro triathletes to perch atop Felt's triathlon range was Daniella Ryf, the Swiss Olympian and crack biker, who stepped up to middle-distance racing with aplomb, winning the 2013 and 2014 Ironman 70.3 European Championships.

After the rapturous response that greeted the IA, the world's top athletes and bike designers will be closely watching to see where Felt Racing heads next. Its carbon-fibre frames will undoubtedly get lighter, the positioning of the components more wind-cheating, the fit options even more accommodating . . . and there will be a few surprises being toyed with in Jim Felt's Auburn, California, workshop.

△ The Felt IA is one of present-day triathlon's super-bikes, offering huge adjustability and groundbreaking seat stays

The Gear
Huub Design

'My head had gone, I was worrying about how I feed my four kids at Christmas, and I couldn't get any funding from the banks or investors.' It was September 2010, and Dean Jackson – a stalwart of the triathlon scene since the eighties – had hit a wall. Recently deemed surplus to requirements at blueseventy, he was looking for a personal project after a career working for Orca, Quintana Roo, Brooks and more.

Just two-and-a-half years later, the Brownlee brothers were wearing Huub when leading the ITU pack out of the blue stuff and Jackson was clutching a host of awards. But how did Huub reach this peak? It all started in a Derby running shop in 1989.

Born in 1970, Dean Jackson entered the world of triathlon in the mid-eighties after co-founding the Derby Triathlon Club and opening the Derby Runner shop. The nineties would see him work in marketing and product development for Brooks, ASICS, Orca, Quintana Roo and the American Bicycle Group, before establishing a UK office for blueseventy. When that venture ended it was time for Jackson to go it alone, calling in funding from a group of local Nottingham investors to the tune of £25,000 and riffling his Rolodex to make that dream a reality.

'I saw flaws in all triathlon wetsuits, as they didn't cater for the leg sinker, which is the majority of athletes,' says Jackson.

There had to be a marriage between what the swim coaching outfits were coaching and what the wetsuits were offering. So I met with Swim Smooth founder Paul Newsome when he was swimming the English Channel in 2011.

Up next was the acclaimed Dutch biomechanics and swimming scientist, Huub Toussaint. With the investors supplying another £100,000, Jackson converted his garage into an office. 'People who came to Huub headquarters had to push past wheel bins and over a washing basket.' By summer 2011 Archimedes wetsuit samples were being tested by Newsome in an Australian lab and by Harry Wiltshire, one of British triathlon's top swimmers.

Whereas triathletes could choose the geometry of a bike or the guidance of a running shoe, depending on their skill set and physiology, Jackson's cohorts (also including Swim Smooth's Adam Young) believed that weaker swimmers weren't being catered for in the triathlon-specific wetsuit industry. In a break from tradition, Huub's debut release of wetsuits all had the choice of differing neoprene thicknesses, with the flagship Archimedes letting athletes pick either 3:5 or 4:4 options. Aimed at newcomers to triathlon, the 3:5 suits have 3mm neoprene on the upper body to promote flexibility, with 5mm neoprene on the lower body aimed at preventing the legs from sinking. The 4:4 suits, meanwhile, were designed with 4mm neoprene throughout for experienced swimmers who need little help with their position in the water; while the thinner 3mm Aura 3:3 suit was designed specifically for female athletes after studies found that female bodies are naturally more buoyant.

The Huub range was released in record time to hit the 2012 triathlon season. The Brownlee brothers jumped aboard for the 2013 season, with Caroline Steffen and Helen Jenkins soon following, and Dave Scott working on their tri-suit range.

The Gear
Kestrel

Aerodynamics began creeping into bike design in the 1980s and has increasingly influenced the form of every type of high-performance road bike since then. That, plus the engineering possibilities of carbon fibre, has produced a plethora of bikes tailored to the specific demands of road racing, time trials and triathlon. But all of them owe a debt to the bikes built by Kestrel in the late 1980s.

Founded in 1986 by a mixed group of bike designers from Trek and engineers from the aerospace industry, Kestrel set out from the very beginning to do things differently. It demonstrated that in 1987 by becoming the first company to produce a full-carbon, bladder-moulded monocoque frame – the Kestrel 4000.

Carbon bikes had existed before this, but they had always been based on traditional frame designs that used lugged metal joints to marry round carbon tubes together. Kestrel took an entirely new approach for bike manufacturing and moulded the 4000's carbon-fibre construction in one piece. Doing so not only allowed them to ditch the metal lugs but also to shape the frame's tubes into more aerodynamic profiles.

In 1989, Kestrel unveiled the first full-carbon fork, the EMS, and the KM40 – the world's first full-carbon triathlon bike. The KM40 took the profiled tubes and internal cable routing of the 4000 and paired them to frame geometry optimized for riding long distances in the tuck position and smaller 650c wheels to give the rider a lower front end and better weight distribution.

Kestrel's different approach didn't end there, though. The next development was arguably

the one the company is most well known for. In 1992 it released the Kestrel 500SCi, a bike unlike any other up to that point. The lack of a seat tube provided aerodynamic benefits but also demonstrated just what possibilities a carbon-fibre construction allows. The 500SCi was able to provide a supremely comfortable ride while still being strong enough to handle the rider's weight and all the pedalling forces they could generate – despite missing what had been believed to be an integral part of its structure.

Although ostensibly a road bike, the 500SCi's design meant it was illegal for use in events sanctioned by the Union Cycliste Internationale, cycling's world governing body. But the bike carved a major niche for itself in triathlon, thanks to the sport's more open-minded approach to bike technology.

The 1990s saw Kestrel really make a name for itself. All the while new iterations of the 500SCi kept appearing; although renamed the Airfoil and redesigned to keep up with the latest developments, they retained the signature 'missing' seat tube. Then, in 2010, Kestrel reintroduced the bike that started everything off: the 4000.

The new design for the company's flagship bike was just as eye-catching as the original but its appearance, including its rear-wheel hugging seat tube, had been updated for the twenty-first century.

△ Chris McCormack enjoyed a productive partnership with Kestrel in his early Ironman years, taking numerous Ironman Australia titles on their tri-bikes

▽ Kestrel are one of the pioneers of carbon bike design

The Gear
Ceepo

The normal rules don't apply when it comes to Ceepo. It's one of the few companies that's a genuine product of triathlon rather than one of the many that were established in swimming, cycling or running before expanding into the sport. And, unlike the vast majority of bike companies, which use their bike-making expertise to produce bikes suitable for triathlon, Ceepo was established to use triathlon expertise to make triathlon bikes. It isn't simply a bike manufacturer; it's a triathlon bike manufacturer.

The seeds of Ceepo were sown in 1990 when Nobuyuki 'Joe' Tanaka began competing in triathlons in his native Japan. The more races he did, the more he became aware of the limitations of the road bikes he was using, which had been developed for road racing and time-trialling. Tanaka's frustration built up and finally came to a head in 1992, when he addressed the problem by having a bike custom-made to cope with the specific demands of triathlon racing. The result of his work – an aluminium-framed racing machine – saw the light of day in 1993 and, legend has it, helped Tanaka shave 90 minutes off his personal best on its maiden 180km long-distance outing.

Although much refined since then, the triathlon-specific principles behind that successful design remain fundamental to the bikes Tanaka continues to make. He wanted a machine that enabled him to hold an aerodynamic position and allowed him to optimize his pedalling power without unnecessarily fatiguing his legs before the

run. And, crucially, the bike also had to remain stable and easy to control despite the rider being pitched forward and tucked low over the handlebars.

To achieve these goals, Tanaka made a more steeply angled seat tube (77–78°, as opposed to the usual 73–74° seen on road bikes) that brought his hips further forward, positioning them almost directly over the bottom bracket. Not only did this allow him to get his upper body lower over the aerobars more comfortably, but it also increased the angle between his hips and knees. This position reduced the stress on his thigh muscles and lower back while pedalling, so that he could start the run with less of the lower body soreness that cycling long distances often causes. Tanaka also wanted to improve stability, as he'd noticed that bikes often became harder to control when the rider is hunched over the front end. To manage that, the bottom bracket was lowered and the bike's wheelbase lengthened, primarily by increasing the distance between bottom bracket and front axle.

△ With its 'bat wings' protruding out of the seat tube, the Viper is Ceepo's most distinctive bike

In the years following that initial success with aluminium, however, carbon fibre became the material of choice for performance bikes, and Tanaka was not going to let his bikes get left behind. In 2002 he joined forces with a Taiwanese manufacturer to produce carbon-fibre versions of his tri-specific frames on a larger scale. It was then that Ceepo began to blossom and grow.

By 2007 it had launched onto the world stage with a name inspired by a legendary samurai and a range of bikes that looked as if they belonged in the Batcave. And by 2009 Ceepo had become the official bike partner of Ironman.

Besides their triathlon-specific nature, the other characteristic that sets Ceepo bikes apart is their distinctive looks. As with most high-performance bikes, aerodynamic concerns shaped the design of the company's early carbon-fibre frames. But, while other manufacturers tinkered with teardrop-profiled tubes, Ceepo's Viper frame was a collection of curves and spurs. The somewhat webbed appearance of its tubes that wrapped themselves around the front and rear wheels gave Ceepo's flagship Viper its distinctive love-'em or hate-'em looks.

However you felt about it, the Viper was unmistakable, especially its distinctive wheel-hugging seat and down tubes with jagged edges resembling the wings of bats. And to those who chose to ride it, its appearance was as important as its performance, as founder Joe Tanaka explains, 'I ride the Viper. It's the perfect bike for long-distance triathlon – very stable and comfortable, which helps me save more effort for running.'

Those 'bat-wing' features have been gradually dialled back in recent years, but still basic to every Ceepo bike are the sport-specific fundamentals, which now include integrated mounts for Bento boxes and CO2 canisters. And those fundamentals are continuing to produce results on the race course, with the likes of New Zealand's Gina Crawford occupying Ironman podiums across the world aboard her Ceepo.

▽ The Katana is another eye-popping tri-bike from the Ceepo stable

Cervélo

△▷ The P3 helped cement Cervélo's status as a serious force in tri-bikes

▽ The P5 is the brand's top-end steed and was ridden to Kona glory in 2013

I f there's one company that can justifiably lay claim to bringing aero-optimized bikes into the mainstream, it's Cervélo. The Canadian company wasn't the first to create drag-reducing frames but it has done more than any other manufacturer to show the importance of airflow when it comes to designing high-performance bikes.

The Cervélo story began in 1994 when Dutchman Gerard Vroomen met Canada's Phil White while both were working on designs for human-powered vehicles (essentially various

forms of bike that deviate from the traditional upright configuration to prioritize aerodynamic performance). Soon after, they joined forces, and the results brought them to the attention of Italy's world road race champion Gianni Bugno. Bugno wanted the pair to design the fastest-possible time-trial bike for him.

They duly set to work creating a machine with unbeatable aerodynamics, and what they came up with – the Baracchi – was unlike anything anyone had seen before. Despite the conventional

positioning of its wheels, saddle and drivetrain, almost nothing else about this bright green machine was like a bike in the traditional sense. Replacing the typical diamond-shaped frame of metal tubes was a carbon wishbone that wrapped one 'arm' around the front wheel and reached up to the saddle with the other. In front of the bike's body was a 'prow' that integrated the narrow, near-vertical forks and low-profile, bladed tri-bars into a single unit.

Bugno was reputedly infatuated with it, not least because of the way it performed in timed tests. His sponsors, however, refused to allow him to use the Baracchi in competition. But the interest in the bike from other road racers and triathletes convinced Vroomen and White that there was a market for their radical approach to bike design. And in 1995 Cervélo was born.

As they showed with the Baracchi, Vroomen and White were never afraid of disregarding conventional wisdom and going back to the drawing board. They did it again in 1996, when developing the company's first two consumer models, and they followed the five core principles that have been used to create every Cervélo bike since: aerodynamics, stiffness, weight, comfort and simplicity.

In 2000 the first of Cervélo's benchmark-setting P-Series triathlon bikes made an almost immediate impact on the multisport scene. The arrival of the P3, with its rear-wheel-hugging seat tube and hourglass head tube, cemented the company's status. The next few years saw Cervélo's transformation from just another manufacturer into the most popular bike brand used by athletes at the 2005 Ironman World Championships in Hawaii: an accolade it has held for ten consecutive years.

Over that period Cervélo has partnered an enviable succession of champion triathletes, most notably Chrissie Wellington. The British athlete turned up at the 2007 Ironman Hawaii as a virtual unknown and, with the help of her Cervélo P2C, raced to the first of her four victories on the Big Island.

In 2012 Cervélo unveiled the P5, perhaps its biggest step forward yet. Not only did this integrate a purpose-built 3T aerobar and Magura hydraulic brakes, it also had a completely redesigned frame that reassessed the conventional wisdom on aerodynamic bikes.

This back-to-basics approach spawned a machine with a dropped downtube, to smooth the airflow off the fork crown, and even the surfaces onto which hydration and storage packs could be mounted had been carefully shaped to ensure they disturbed as little air as possible.

The P5 quickly began racking up impressive results, and in 2013 claimed triathlon's biggest title when Belgium's Frederik Van Lierde rode it to victory at Ironman Hawaii. 'It's not only the fastest bike, it also gives me great comfort,' the new world champion said afterwards. 'It's the best bike and an honour to ride that machine.'

But the company's success isn't limited to long-distance triathlon; its S-series aero road bikes have also carved an impressive niche on the high-speed, draft-legal Olympic-distance circuit. The S5 has contributed to many outstanding performances, and in the hands of Britain's Jodie Stimpson has triumphed in a number of ITU World Triathlon Series races and at the 2014 Commonwealth Games.

△ The P2 was Chrissie Wellington's bike of choice at Hawaii in 2007

The Gear
blueseventy

Blueseventy may have officially begun in 2005 but the brand specializing in all things aquatic have been a presence in triathlon for a considerably longer time, starting out as Direct Innovations in Napier, New Zealand, in 1993 with neoprene bike seat covers. That same year also saw the fellow triathlon wetsuit giants, Orca, launched by triathlete Scott Unsworth in Auckland, and the two Kiwi brands would soon become major players in the burgeoning triathlon wetsuit market.

Direct Innovation's debut triathlon-specific wetsuit followed later that year, leading to the brand becoming the official wetsuit of Ironman and a name change to Ironman Wetsuits.

By the end of the decade, Ironman Wetsuits' sales had doubled year-on-year and the brand were also pioneering their VO2 Stealth wetsuits, which were developed using clinical studies to improve respiratory performance. The cost of the Ironman licence and the fact that Ironman were only promoted in the name restricted further growth, however, and in 2005, with Brit entrepreneur and Ironman Tim Moxey at the helm, the brand severed their M-Dot contract and changed their name to blueseventy, coming from the fact that 70% of the world is covered in water.

The results were almost instant, with the brand's signature Helix wetsuit first released to instant acclaim in 2005. The suit pioneered the use of ultra-thin neoprene under the arms for increased arm mobility and a split chest panel to again aid respiration, with the distinctive arm design swiftly becoming a recognizable sight throughout the sport's pro and age-grouper swim legs.

Elsewhere, blueseventy's revolutionary Pointzero3 swimskin was worn by Normann Stadler to victory at the Ironman Worlds in 2006 and 75% of swimskin-wearing athletes would choose blueseventy at Kona in 2007. The next year would be even better for the Napier outfit, seeing Chrissie Wellington wear the Pointzero3 on her way to Ironman Hawaii glory.

The Helix wetsuit remained all-conquering in the open-water, worn during his 2009 ITU World Championship-winning season by Alistair Brownlee. The Helix would also exit the water first at the London Olympics, worn by Britain's Lucy Hall and the Slovakian swim specialist Richard Varga.

▽ Blueseventy are a major and innovative force in triathlon wetsuits, with their Helix one of the sport's most famous suits

The Gear
Storck

△ The ultra-light Aero II is one of the most advanced tri-bikes in history

Markus Storck began his company with one simple aim: to make the best-quality bikes in the world. It started in Germany in 1995 and in the twenty years since has resulted in a procession of award-winning machines that have set new standards for performance.

It's fair to say that cycling is in Markus Storck's blood. His great grandfather was a keen cyclist, and of his grandfather's nine brothers and sisters, five of them rode professionally. His father also raced as a youngster before opening a bike shop in Rodelheim, Frankfurt, in which Markus would work while he was growing up.

It was there that he gained valuable experience not only as a salesman but also as a bike-builder helping local riders construct custom machines. During the mountain bike boom of the late 1980s Markus became the German distributor for a number of American brands, most notably Klein. But after Trek bought Klein in 1995 it terminated its contract with him, and he decided it was time to stop selling other people's bikes and start making his own.

With the release of his very first bikes – the innovative Scenario and Scenario Pro road bikes and the Legend for triathlon – Markus Storck started as he meant to go on. More milestone designs were to follow, including the full-carbon Stiletto Light fork in 1999. Developed for the Scenario road bike, the Stiletto Light set new benchmarks for stiffness and, weighing just 280g, provided further evidence of a determination to make components of unparalleled quality.

Storck's ability to reduce weight without sacrificing rigidity had already won it many industry awards and fans, but it was the unveiling of the Storck Aero 2 in 2009 that really caught triathletes' attention. Aside from the front- and rear-wheel-hugging, aerodynamically profiled tubes and integrated brakes, the bare Aero 2 frameset alone boasted a bank-breaking price tag of almost £7,000.

Whichever way you looked at it, the Aero 2 was phenomenally expensive but it was in keeping with Markus Storck's uncompromising pursuit of performance. Your money was buying what was possibly the most efficient, lightest and stiffest race machine around.

A fully built-up size 55cm Aero 2 could tip the scales at an amazing 7kg. That weight's very good for a road bike, but it's exceptional for a triathlon bike, with all its extra bars and frame material. Former Ironman Hawaii champion Faris Al-Sultan quickly began collecting wins aboard Storck's flagship triathlon machine. To further prove his point, Storck published Al-Sultan's ride data from his 2012 Ironman Hawaii performance, which showed that, despite his fifth-place overall, he'd expended the least energy of the top finishers while racing around the 180km Hawaii bike course.

The Gear
Wheels

Bike wheels are still round; that's one thing that hasn't changed. But almost everything else about them – the material they're made from, their size, the spokes and nipples used to build them, the rim profile – has been altered, adjusted and adapted numerous times.

Even in triathlon's relatively short history the variety of wheels that have come into fashion and fallen out again is remarkable. In the early days of Ironman racing during the late 1970s and throughout the 1980s, standard aluminium road wheels proliferated. But, needless to say, there were plenty of innovators willing to experiment with set-ups that deviated from the typical box-section 700c wheels.

Size was the first thing to come under scrutiny, with some athletes opting for 650c wheels. The smaller-diameter wheels were a lighter option, and this prompted some racers to use them at the front and rear of their bikes. But more maverick competitors realized that they could get the best of both worlds by using a 700c wheel on the back and a 650c wheel on the front, which would allow them to ride in a lower, more aerodynamically efficient position. This led to the hot-rod-esque bikes that were briefly in vogue in the mid- to late 1980s.

Weight was always a concern, but the lack of climbing compared to road racing meant aerodynamics soon came to play a major role in shaping wheel designs for triathlon. Disc wheels offered significant aerodynamic advantages and were available during the 1980s, but, due to their instability in crosswinds, they were impractical. Fortunately, a number of people were working on alternatives, including one of the men whose work with composite materials and aerodynamics had helped popularize disc wheels in the first place: Steve Hed.

The American came up with the Hed 3 wheel – more commonly known as the Trispoke – in the late 1980s. Its three broad, teardrop-profile spokes sliced through the air far better than the numerous round spokes on traditional wheels but, unlike a disc, allowed air to pass through it, preventing it from being snatched away in crosswinds. The wheel was so effective that, aside from an overhaul to the hub, its design remained almost entirely unchanged until 2014. Since its introduction, the Trispoke has found its way on

▽ Many triathletes opt for tubular over clincher wheelsets, like these from Easton, for their lighter weight and lower rolling resistance

to the bikes of numerous Ironman and Tour de France winners. Hed also had a hand in another area that has shaped the development of aero wheels: rim width.

Deep-section rims were already well established by 2006 but what was holding them back was the fact that a tyre had to be mounted onto them. Regardless of the depth of their profile, most rims were 19mm wide. But the tyres they were paired with were typically 21–23mm wide, which, when inflated, gave the wheels a profile more like a light-bulb than the intended teardrop.

Hed's bright idea was to broaden the rims to 23mm, to match the width of the tyres they would most likely be used with. This development, christened C2 technology and integrated into Hed's wheels in 2006, allowed a tyre's sidewalls to sit flush with the sides of the rim and form an almost continuous and more streamlined surface that allowed the air to flow smoothly onto the rim's trailing edge.

Before the introduction of wider rims, though, the must-have wheel technology for triathletes was deep-section rims. Like the Trispoke, these function as a halfway house between the aero benefits of a disc wheel and the stability offered by a traditional wheel.

Traditional round or flattened spokes are used to make deep-section wheels, but they're laced to a rim taller than that of a standard 'box-section' wheel, and also tapered. The rim's extra height and shaping allow it to work as a fairing to streamline the airflow over it.

Many fairings were based on a flat-sided, V-shape of various depths but Zipp, an American company based in Indianapolis, not far from the famous 'Brickyard' oval used for the Indy 500, found that other shapes provided bigger benefits.

The first breakthrough came in 1998 when Zipp's engineers discovered the effects an ovalized fairing had on a wheel. This new 'Hybrid-Toroidal' shape had a bulge that was wider than the rim the fairing sat on and allowed the air to flow over it more easily than it did over a V-shaped fairing. But, perhaps more

△ French-brand Mavic are one of the world's race wheel pioneers

importantly, the new profile could be made to work with a wider variety of tyre widths.

What Zipp and many manufacturers failed to appreciate for a long time, though, was the fact that wheels are round and a profile that works well at the front of the wheel doesn't necessarily work as well when it's reversed during the wheel's rotation.

This realization prompted Zipp to begin working with profiles that had blunter trailing edges, so they could perform equally well whether they were facing forwards or backwards. During the new rim profile's development, each of the prototypes was assigned the name of a different bird, and it was the one named after the tiny firecrest that proved most effective. It was faster, but the new shape also altered the way crosswinds acted on the wheel. The Firecrest pulled the centre of pressure back, so that the wind's effects were felt just behind

the hub, instead of in front of it, meaning the wheel would self-correct in crosswinds by counter-steering into them.

Many people were sceptical about the new shape when it was introduced in 2010, including the 2007 Ironman Hawaii champion Chris McCormack. The Australian was sponsored by Zipp but wanted to use the company's Super 9 disc wheel instead of the new Firecrest wheels for his crack at the 2010 Ironman World Championship. Zipp's personnel worked hard to convince him that running a disc would be unwise, given crosswinds on the Hawaii bike course and the greater efficiency of their new Firecrest wheels.

McCormack reluctantly took their advice, and it was a good thing he did. The Australian covered the 112-mile bike leg in 4:31:51 – the fourth quickest bike split of the day – and came off it

▽ The Vision seen here is influenced by Hed's three-spoke wheels from the late 1980s

▷ Led by aerodynamic whizz Paul Lew, Reynolds are pushing the boundaries of wheel design

▽ Zipp are regularly the most popular brand with athletes at the Ironman World Championships

fresh enough to post 2:43:31 for the marathon, to seal his second Ironman Hawaii victory.

The vast majority of innovations have come about through people trying to make wheels go faster. But progress has been made in stopping them more effectively too. While athletes have welcomed the reduced weight and improved aerodynamic performance offered by wheels made of carbon fibre, they've also complained about the material's poor braking, especially in the wet.

Since 2010 French company Mavic has added a special 'Exalith' coating to its carbon wheels to provide extra stopping power, but the next big step in bringing triathlon bikes to a stop is likely to be disc brakes.

These may provide more braking power and modulation, but many manufacturers, athletes and consumers have yet to be persuaded that they are necessary on road and triathlon bikes. They make sense on mountain bikes, where the style of riding demands frequent, hard stops, but for the sort of braking most often required on road or triathlon courses there are still strong arguments in favour of rim brakes. Nevertheless, it seems disc brakes are coming, and their arrival is certain to bring about even more changes to the ways bike wheels are designed and made.

Heart rate monitors

While training with heart rate monitors and power meters is common in the present data-crunching days of triathlon, endurance athletes haven't always had the luxury of analyzing their performance in the sort of fine detail such instruments now provide.

Polar will forever be synonymous with changing the way elite and recreational athletes train. Where once athletes relied only on feel and intuition, Polar's creation of the first-ever heart rate monitor, way back in the 1970s, provided the basis of an instrument that would enable athletes to accurately hit training zones and enjoy the performance benefits, whether in speed, stamina or strength.

Polar Electro was formed by Seppo Säynäjäkangas in central Finland in 1977, soon after the idea of a wireless, portable heart rate

△ Garmin are the current kings of the heart rate monitor and GPS watch market

◁ Sigma are also a major player in the HRM/GPS run watch market

▽ The Polar V800 marked the Finnish brand's return to the upper echelons of top-end performance watches

monitor was conceived on a cross-country skiing track. The firm's first product, the Tunturi Pulser finger-tip heart rate monitor, was launched in 1978, and its first patent for wireless heart rate measurement followed three years later. In 1982 it launched the first-ever wearable wire-free heart rate monitor, and triathletes soon started to reap the benefits.

Although not the first athlete to use one, Finnish athlete Pauli Kiuru nonetheless pioneered use of the Polar heart rate monitor in triathlon's elite circles. As fellow pro Mark Montgomery observed on Slowtwitch.com,

He wouldn't go out the door without his monitor, and everything he did was dictated by it. There was no pace with this training scheme – no interval, no time – just heart rate. I considered Pauli the most boring guy to train with on the pro circuit. Was he successful? In a word, yes. He probably turned in more low-eight-hour Ironman times than anyone to date. So aligned with Polar was Pauli that he became part of the global sales team from 1998 to 2000, as his career wound down.

Yet the dangers of racing purely on data and disregarding intuition were famously exemplified in 1993. In front of watching spectators the methodical Finn threw his instrument to the ground, abandoning its promptings, while (unsuccessfully) attempting to chase down Mark Allen at Hawaii. Allen, too, was an advocate of training by heart rate, though he used it alongside his more spiritual approach to training and racing:

During my fifteen years of racing in the sport of triathlon, I searched for those few golden tools that would allow me to maximize my training time and come up with the race results I envisioned. At the top of that list was heart rate training.

All the same, the debate over intuition versus data has continued to rage ever since Kiuru's technological tantrum, with some hugely successful athletes using data (2013 Hawaii champ Frederik Van Lierde is Polar's current poster boy), while others, like Chrissie Wellington, advocate training and racing more on feel. She adds,

You can race without technology; you can't race without intuition.' That's not to say technology is bad. But people need to trust their bodies more, recognize the signals and respond to them. Over-emphasis on gadgetry detracts from that. That said, I used a Garmin to hone my swim and run pace. After a while, if you asked me what pace I was running at I wouldn't have to look at my clock – I knew instinctively what pace I could sustain.

Heart rate training finally reached the masses with the arrival Polar's Windows-based analysis software in 1991. In the twenty-first century, though, certainly in the multisport world, Polar's mantle as the leader in sports technology was wrested away largely by Garmin (other major HRM brands include Timex, Sigma, Suunto, TomTom and Mio).

With their Forerunner range Garmin latched onto the sporting benefits of GPS – especially when integrated into one unit – while Polar lagged behind.

The Forerunner 910XT was launched in October 2011, and a new multisport world was born. Here was a training tool that delivered a triathlete's dream – metrics across three disciplines. That, aligned with Garmin's ability to create gadgets that are easy to use, elevated the 910XT to an almost mandatory purchase for number-crunching triathletes.

Polar finally joined the integrated-GPS-data party when they released the RCX5 – which was an impressive first all-in-one stab. The brand then made another giant leap in 2014 with the V800, which offered customizable profiles for each discipline, countless route, distance and speed features, and an insight into an athlete's recovery status.

Garmin's updated Forerunner 920XT followed later in the year to further acclaim. With brands such as Mio pioneering the use of HRMs without a chest strap, plus the increasing number of affordable power meters on the market (usually mounted on the crank arm of the bike to record the power output of the rider in watts), the upshot is that triathletes have never had it so good when training with data.

The Gear
Tri nutrition

△ The development of endurance sports nutrition has accelerated in recent times

▷ Recovery powders are an essential nutrition aid for many triathletes

From Dave Scott's rinsing of cottage cheese in the late seventies to Pauli Kiuru's poorly mixed carbohydrate drink at Hawaii in 1993 and a dehydrated Ali Brownlee at Hyde Park in 2011, the key role nutrition plays in fuelling endurance sport has long been clear to see. Yet until recent times awareness of functional sports nutrition, as well as its availability and taste, have long lagged behind triathletes' specific needs, especially when racing up to seventeen hours in the heat and hills of Hawaii, Lanzarote and Nice.

The first energy bar in the American marketplace was Space Food Sticks, created by the Pillsbury Company in the late 1960s to capitalize on the popularity of the space programme. The first carbohydrate drinks arrived during the same period – most famously Gatorade – and moved the game on by offering the key nutrients for endurance (carbohydrate and fluid) in a convenient form, which was rapidly absorbed and far less likely to cause nausea or stomach cramps.

Popular as carbohydrate drinks were, however, they didn't tick all the boxes all the time. To begin with, liquid is heavy, and lugging enough carbohydrate drink to fuel a long event is no fun if the race feeding stations only offer water. A lot of athletes also discovered that there's only so much fluid you can drink for energy without craving something a bit more concentrated – especially in cooler conditions. But an answer was at hand, as sports nutritionist Andrew Hamilton points out:

Enter the energy gel, which addressed both of these issues at a stroke. Like carbohydrate

drinks, gels provide readily and easily absorbed carbohydrate, often with electrolytes too.

The first gels appeared on the market in the late 1980s, but in the years after their introduction gels were still something of a cult product, because of their unique taste and texture.

Gels are now becoming increasingly ubiquitous on the multisport and single-sport circuits. Notable gel brands including PowerBar, SiS, High5, Clif, Torq, Hammer and Mule, make use of natural ingredients and offer flavours like banoffee pie and raspberry ripple ice cream, and brands like Huma and 33

Shake are experimenting with ingredients such as chia seeds. Ever the pioneers, Gu are also exploring more savoury flavours like salted caramel.

So what does the future hold for sports nutrition? Six-time Hawaii champ Mark Allen is confident things will continue to evolve:

Nutrition science is just acknowledging that the digestive system doesn't work the same in labs compared to the real world. They're trying to close the gap between what an athlete burns and what they can absorb in an extreme environment like Hawaii. I think you'll see big jumps in functional sports nutrition over the next couple of years, which will lead to a big drop in times.

△ Energy bars have become an essential way to fuel during long training rides and races

◁ Race day fuelling is often supplied by aid stations throughout the bike and run courses

▽ From berries to salted caramel and chia, the choice of energy gel is now exhaustive

The Gear
Tri-suits

While they may lack the wow factor of a pair of deep-rim wheels, the thrill of a new wetsuit or the feeling of slipping on a new pair of run shoes, the humble tri-suit remains the most underrated piece of triathlon gear, the only item that will be with athletes from the starting horn to the finishing tape. An ill-fitting, slow-drying and poorly-constructed tri-suit can leave you feeling slow, cold and sore, and witness your personal best performance pretensions demoted to DNF proportions.

Unlike tri-specific wetsuits and bikes, the evolution of tri-suits doesn't have a fabled backstory. It's thought that early pro triathlete

Mark Montgomery (who collaborated with Dan Empfield on Quintana Roo's ground-breaking tri wetsuits and bikes) asked his sponsors, Forte clothing, to make the athlete a cycling-type skinsuit without arms and including a lightweight cloth chamois. They duly obliged, and in 1982 one of the first tri-suits was created (an athlete and future race director called Dave Horning also sported a tri-suit at this time, so there's not a single founding father).

A key advantage of wearing a tri-suit for the whole race is that athletes saved plenty of time: instead of changing from swim to bike, and bike to run clothing, they could breeze through T1 and T2, saving valuable seconds that – especially in short-

▽▷ The Speedo Aquablade came out in 1996 and reinvigorated the tri-suit market

course racing —could make all the difference at the elite end.

Zoot, a brand now synonymous with triathlon, were created in 1983 by a woman named Christal Nylin. She lived in Kona and spotted that the athletes competing in the annual Ironman Hawaii event needed something more functional to race in. After sewing pads into run shorts, experimenting with swim fabrics and attaching run singlets to bike shorts, she soon created the Zoot Racesuit – one of the earliest suits for triathletes racing at the sport's pinnacle in Hawaii.

A number of brands on both sides of the Atlantic experimented with tri-suits, but they didn't become mandatory race wear for another decade. They often became heavy after the swim, with athletes preferring to race in a run singlet and shorts, or just a pair of tiny Speedos in the case of duathlon star Kenny Souza.

Then Speedo came out with the Aquablade suit in 1996, which managed to prove both hydrodynamic and quick-drying, changing of the course of tri-suit history in the process. Today, triathletes are spoilt for choice with these Lycra creations, with pockets for nutrition, leg grippers, chamois suitable for both short- and long-course racing, and the choice of front or back zips. Many contain a hydro-phobic coating for increased speed in the water, some are even made of wool (Endurance Junkie) and contain carbon (Arena), with plenty also purporting to offer compression benefits.

Sleeved tri-suits look set to be the next big thing (two-piece suits are also making a comeback), with Louis Garneau, Huub, Castelli and Fusion already releasing suits with short sleeves to increase aerodynamics, comfort and protection from the sun. And what does the future look like for tri-suits? 'It's going to get even more technical,' says Huub's Dean Jackson, 'and is going to go beyond the typical needs of breathability and lightweight fabrics to combine the benefits of swim skins and tri-suits to deliver the fastest swim suit that'll still perform on the bike and the run.'

▷ Sleeved suits are becoming more common on the long-distance race circuit especially

▷▷ American superstar Gwen Jorgensen rocks a Roka tri-suit in 2014

The Gear
Aerobars

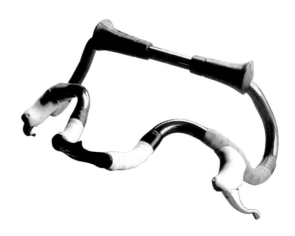

△▷ The Scott DH aerobars were made famous by Greg LeMond in the 1989 Tour de France

Nothing says triathlon bike more than a set of aerobars. Even to the untrained eye, a pair of parallel bars extending forwards over the front wheel immediately identifies the bike they're attached to as one tailored towards speed and efficiency.

Triathletes opt for this seemingly odd cockpit arrangement for the simple reason that aerobars do more than any other single piece of equipment to take time off your bike split. And they do it by enabling you to ride in a more aerodynamic 'tuck' position.

Aerodynamic drag is a rider's worst enemy because the faster you go, the more energy it takes to push the air in front of you out of the way. The problem is, however, that due to the shape and size of the typical human, it's the rider

that generates most of the drag. The solution is to make the rider as small as possible so the air doesn't have to travel as far to pass over them – which is exactly what aerobars do. They allow you to reduce your frontal area, by getting your head lower and your back flatter and by bringing arms and elbows in underneath your shoulders.

The bike leg is by far the longest of any triathlon, so aerobars have the potential to make the biggest improvement in your overall performance. This is why they have become as ubiquitous in triathlon as telephones are in everyday life. And, just like telephones, a number of people claim to have invented them.

America's Greg LeMond, who used a set of Scott aerobars to help him win the 1989

▽ A contemporary integrated set of aerobars from Vision

Tour de France, probably did more than anyone else to bring them into the mainstream, and so the Scott brand got the credit for introducing them to the world. But by then aerobars were already widely used in triathlon and were believed to have originated in 1987, having been developed and patented by US ski coach Boone Lennon and Scott engineer Charley French. The generally accepted story was that the pair realized performance gains might be had by enabling cyclists to adopt a position similar to the tuck used by downhill skiers.

The trouble was a similar design not only already existed but had been used by Pete Penseyres to win the non-stop ultramarathon bicycle Race Across America (RAAM) in 1986. Complicating matters further was the fact that

Penseyres may have taken inspiration for his design from the bars made by Richard Byrne for Jim Elliot's bid to win the 1984 RAAM. Scott Tinley believes Brad Kearns and Andrew McNaughton were the first multisport athletes to use the bars at the Desert Princess Duathlon in 1987.

However, it was Scott who held the patent, so he was able to reap the rewards of licencing the design until the patent expired in 2006.

Today, hundreds of aerobars are available (from Zipp, Profile Design, 3T, Vision and many more). They come in a range of configurations and are made from either aluminium or carbon fibre, but they all share the same goal: to make you a faster, more efficient rider.

△ All-in-one aerobars like this are illegal in draft-legal racing but are a regular sight in Ironman racing

▽ Clip-on bars are a cheaper and more versatile alternative to integrated bars

Triathlon run shoes

Featuring aerobars, an aggressive geometry and all sorts of UCI-busting design to boot, triathlon/time-trial bikes are noticeably different from their road bike counterparts in aesthetics and performance. And the benefits of triathlon wetsuits over their surfing equivalents are also clearly evident to anyone who's tried swimming in both – the flexibility and buoyancy provided are far superior in the tri-specific models.

Between triathlon-specific run shoes and traditional road racing shoes the performance and aesthetic differences are subtler and less celebrated, however, for footwear development has lagged years behind the advances Dan Empfield and others made in the triathlon wetsuit and bike market in the 1980s. Now, though, major running-shoe manufacturers are becoming increasingly aware of the lucrative sport of triathlon, and the transition-friendly features that triathletes crave – heel loops, quick-tie laces and ratchet systems – are all increasingly evident on shoe racks worldwide.

In the running-shoe industry triathlon credentials don't come much bigger than those of Zoot, a company born in Hawaii and now based in San

▽ Pearl Izumi are just one brand to release tri-specific run shoes

Diego County. We have already documented the brand's innovations in the tri-suit industry, but in 2007 Zoot was also one of the first brands to make serious inroads into the tri-specific running-shoe market with its Ultra line. Other brands had conducted fleeting flirtations with tri-specific models, but Zoot was now going the whole hog and devoting a whole footwear line to triathlon.

After years working on triathlon-specific apparel ranges, Zoot had identified four particular footwear problems specific to triathletes:

- Speed of Entry: The need to get in and out of T2 as quickly as possible;

- Sockless Wear: Triathletes don't want to take the time to put socks on;

- Water Retention: Studies have shown that traditional running shoes can gain an extra 30 per cent of their weight during a race;

- Biomechanics: Athletes run differently after racing on a bike.

The four-strong range included the Ultra TT and the Ultra Race (updated versions of which are still being used today), with easy-to-grab heel loops and large tongues – just two features aimed at speeding the bike-to-run transition. Today the brand is said to have been worn to more triathlon victories than any other brand in history (they once graced the Galician feet of Javier Gómez, after all).

An increasing number of major shoe manufacturers (including K-Swiss and Asics), as well as smaller companies like Inov-8, On and Pearl Izumi, successfully began to focus on creating triathlon-specific shoes after Zoot, offering internal liners to aid sockless running, plus heel loops and elastic laces for a speedy T2.

The annual shoe count at the 2014 Ironman Hawaii performed by *Lava* magazine, however, still showed that athletes are torn between tri-specific and classic running shoes, with Newton and

△ Zoot are pioneers of the triathlon run shoe, with ratchet dials included for a speedy T2

▽ Heel loops and quick-tie laces are features of Inov-8's tri range

Brooks (increasingly synonymous with the sport) riding high in the rankings despite not producing triathlon-specific shoes. Topping the list were Asics with 17.7%, Saucony 14.5%, Newton 10.7%, Brooks 10.3%, Adidas 6.9%, Hoka 6.0%, Mizuno 5.9% and Zoot with 5.9%.

The Gear
Eurobike/Interbike

△ The cavernous Messe Friedrichshafen showcases the latest bikes (and plenty of German pilsner) every August

We've provided an insight into some of triathlon's leading brands and essential pieces of kit on these pages. But these are only the tip of the iceberg in the ever-expanding world of multisport gear. So how does one get to see it all? The two big and bold answers are the bicycle industry's two big annual trade fairs: southern Germany's Eurobike and Interbike in Las Vegas, held in August and

September, respectively. Both show's initial days are for distributors and press only, but on the final day the doors are flung open to the public for a day of 'kid in a sweet shop' excitement.

Taking over the German town of Friedrichshafen, on the northern shore of Lake Constance, for five days in late August, Eurobike is the world's biggest bike show. It began in 1991, has rapidly expanded, and now fills the 14 halls/aircraft hangars of the Messe Friedrichshafen exhibition centre on the town's north-eastern fringe.

The present-day numbers are staggering: 2014's show attracted 60,000 visitors, 300 new bike launches and 1,280 exhibitors from 54 countries, and a reported 253,000 sausages were consumed. In addition to the vast numbers of shiny bikes, pumps, pedals, wheels, clothes, helmets, eyewear and more on show, Eurobike also has a healthy star presence, with top cyclists Alberto Contador and Marcel Kittel, and even German Chancellor Angela Merkel paying recent visits to the show.

Held three weeks after Eurobike – and with the small matter of the ITU World Championships sandwiched in-between – Interbike is North America's largest bike show. Since 2013 it's been held at the cavernous Mandalay Bay Convention Center, at the southern tip of the neon lights on Las Vegas' (in)famous Strip.

So, apart from sharing a predilection for all things bike, bread, meat, absolutely no greens and plenty of beer, how do the German and American mega-shows differ? 'I do 80% of my business at Eurobike,' says Quintana Roo's Steve Dunn, 'Interbike is where the industry comes to have some fun.'

Good times are indeed the order of the day at Interbike, acting like a smaller, cooler cousin to its European big brother, with a boisterous atmosphere featuring DJs and lifestyle brands rubbing shoulders with the carbon-bike big boys to provide plenty of gear and clothing in Las Vegas. Interbike's triathlon presence has increased in recent times, too, with 2XU, Louis Garneau and Quintana Roo all present and correct, and a designated 'Tri Pavilion' housing Huub, blueseventy, Zone3, pro Ironman TJ Tollakson's own bike brand, Dimond, and many more.

Given that it's Vegas, there are plenty of shining lights of the endurance sport industry chatting away to punters, and in recent times Olympic champs Simon Whitfield and Chris Boardman have been visitors, Greg LeMond has occupied the LeMond bikes stand himself, and tri gear pioneer Dan Empfield has given

talks. Coinciding with Interbike each year is USA Triathlon's Elite Sprint National Championships race in Vegas's mid-town, which has recently attracted some of the world's finest ITU athletes – including Gwen Jorgensen, Paula Findlay, Erin Densham and Sarah Groff.

Other major bike and tri shows worldwide include the Taipei International Cycle Show and the Toronto International, with the UK providing the Bike and Triathlon Show in Manchester and the long-running 220 Triathlon Show near London amongst others. What they lack in natural daylight, they all more than make up for in everything carbon- and Lycra-related.

△ The twice-daily Eurobike fashion show complete with European techno and a whole lot of Lycra

▽ Gear and clothing in Las Vegas at the annual Interbike show

The Gear
Concept bikes

△ Always seeking innovative ways to shave his splits, Mark Allen sits atop his Hufty Triton

There's a reason why so many odd-looking bikes have been racked in triathlon transition zones over the years. Triathlon doesn't fall into the jurisdiction of the Union Cycliste Internationale (UCI), and, unrestricted by its rigid design guidelines, the engineers who build triathlon bikes are free to let their ingenuity run wild.

Were it not for triathlon, the radical 'concept bike' designs, such as the Canyon MRSC, with its active suspension system, and BMC's mono-forked prototype with a single chain stay and no seat stay (seen at 2014's Eurobike) would rarely, if ever, make it off the display stands.

The once ultra-conservative world of road racing is slowly waking up to the possibilities of breaking with the established traditions and using quantifiable results to challenge conventional wisdom. But triathlon has from the outset been open-minded and willing to at least experiment with, if not whole-heartedly embrace, extraordinary new technologies.

One of the first concept bikes to make a big splash in triathlon was the Huffy Triton. Ridden by America's Mark Allen to his third consecutive Ironman Hawaii victory in 1991, this aluminium-framed machine was based on a design Chester Kyle came up with for the 1984 US Olympic track cycling team.

Like many other athletes' bikes the Triton had aerobars and bar-end gear-shifters but it also paired a 700c three-spoke rear wheel to a smaller 650c front wheel to get Allen into a lower, more streamlined riding position. Accommodating the lower front end also meant the bike had a sloping top tube that curved down towards the head tube and a subtly dog-legged seat tube that brought the rear wheel in underneath Allen to improve handling.

The next outlandish machine to grab triathletes' attention was a bike that looked as though it had jettisoned half of its tubes. The Softride Powerwing had no seat tube or seat stays, and in place of a top tube had a beam made of a visco-elastic carbon-fibre sandwich that kinked up to the saddle.

The missing tubes provided some aero benefit but the innovation at the heart of the Powerwing was that it had suspension. The 'carbon-fibre sandwich' was made up of layers that were able to slide back and forth over each other. This action enabled the beam to flex underneath the rider and soak up the bumps from the road. The extra comfort helped the rider to stay fresher, but there was a price to pay – the bikes were appreciably heavier than their more conventional counterparts. But that didn't deter Greg Welch when the Australian won the 1994 Ironman Hawaii title with the help of a Powerwing.

Perhaps the most effective concept bike is the Cat Cheetah, ridden to eight consecutive Ironman Hawaii victories between 1998 and 2005: six by

Switzerland's Natascha Badmann and two by Lori Bowden of Canada. This full-carbon monocoque machine resembles the Lotus superbike bike that Chris Boardman rode to victory in the 1992 Barcelona Olympics, but it differs at the front end. Where Boardman's bike had a 'monoblade' one-sided fork, the Cheetah uses an X-fork that integrates the aerobars directly into the fork crown, and does away with both the stem and base bar.

The other obvious visual clue that the Cheetah is an extraordinary bike is that it seems to lack brake levers. It does have brakes – hydraulic ones, in fact – but, instead of pulling levers, the rider operates them by twisting the aerobar extensions. Aside from the frame and the absence of brake levers, the lack of a base bar also signifies just how aggressively the Cat Cheetah has been aerodynamically optimized. Other bikes not only expect but also enable the rider to come out of the tuck position once in a while. The Cheetah does not – and with those eight Ironman world championship titles to its name, it makes a strong case for the exclusively aero approach.

△ The Softride may have lacked most of its tubes, but it was ridden to Ironman Hawaii glory by Greg Welch in 1994

Acknowledgements

Thanks to Karry and our beautiful boys Alfie and Elliott, Mum and Dad, Nat, Tom and Enid, the Eatocks and Testers. Thanks to the tireless and talented team of Jennifer, Lucy, Rich, Daniela and Charlotte at Aurum Press and copy editor John Wheelwright; the *220 Triathlon* team; Rob Banino, Mark Kleanthous, James Witts, and Tom Ballard for your words; all of the athletes – especially Spencer Smith, Mark Allen and Craig Alexander – for your input; Vics Murray and the Challenge Family; Erin Green and the ITU; Waveney at Ironman; Raphi at Powerman, Trey at Xterra, Dean Jackson at Huub; the Legends of Triathlon podcasts, Tri247, Slowtwitch, Trihistory and Xtri; all of the hugely talented photographers – including Rich Cruse, Delly Carr and Timothy Carlson – who capture this amazing sport in all its glory. And thanks to the sport itself for being so exciting, enticing and addictive.

Text credits

Tom Ballard: Norseman
Rob Banino: Kestrel, Ceepo, Cervelo, Storck, wheels, aerobars, concept bikes
Text for all other entries by Matthew Baird.

First published in Great Britain
2015 by Aurum Press Ltd
74–77 White Lion Street
Islington
London N1 9PF
www.aurumpress.co.uk

Copyright © Aurum Press 2015

A catalogue record for this book is available from the British Library.

ISBN 978 1 78131 439 5

2015 2017 2019 2018 2016

1 3 5 7 9 10 8 6 4 2

Designed by Carrdesignstudio.com
Printed in China by C&C Offset Printing

Picture credits

p2-3 © Jason Newsome; p4 © Storck; p6 © Thomas Barwick / Getty Images; p8 © Walter Iooss Jr./ Sports Illustrated/Getty Images; p9 © Walter Iooss Jr./Sports Illustrated/Getty Images; p11 © Sampo Lenzi; p12 © David Aliaga/Cordon Press/Corbis; p14-15 © Janos Schmidt/ITU via Getty Images; 16 left, 17 © Rich Cruse; 16 right © Press Association; 18 left © Jero Honda; 18 right © Jero Honda; 19 © Jero Honda; 20-21 © Rich Cruse; 22-23 © Rich Cruse; 24 © Lutz Bongarts/Bongarts/Getty Images; 25 © ITU; 25 right © ITU; 26-27 © Rich Cruse; 29 bottom © Barry Bland/EMPICS Sport; 28 bottom © Getty Images; 28 top © Rich Cruse; 29 top © Rich Cruse; 30 top © Phil Walter/Getty Images; 30 bottom © Jens Wolf/epa/Corbis; 31 left © ITU; 32 © Adam Pretty/ALLSPORT; 33 bottom ©EMPICS Ot; 34 top © ITU; 34 bottom © ITU; 35 bottom © Chris Stewart/AP/Press Association Images; 36 left top © ITU; 37 top © ITU; 37 bottom © PHILIPPE DESMAZES/AFP/Getty Images; 38 top left © Adam Pretty / Allsport; 38 bottom © Delly Carr / ITU; 39 right © ITU; 40 top © ITU; 40bottom © ITU; 41 © ITU; 42 top © ITU; 43 top © ITU; 43 bottom © ITU; 44 © Richard Lam/ITU; 45 top © ITU; 45 bottom © ITU; 46 © John Prieto/The Denver Post via Getty Images; 47 top © Rich Cruse; 47 bottom © Rich Cruse; 48 top © Quinn Rooney/Getty Images; 48 bottom © Quinn Rooney/ Getty Images; 49 left © ITU; 49 right © Quinn Rooney/Getty Images; 50 © Gary Newkirk /Allsport; 51 © Gary Newkirk /Allsport; 52 © Darren England/ALLSPORT; 53 © Brian Bahr/ALLSPORT; 54 © Gary Newkirk /Allsport; 55 top © Gary Newkirk /Allsport; 55 bottom © Mike Powell / Staff; 56 © Alexander Hassenstein/Getty Images for Challenge Roth; 57 top © Alvis Upitis/Getty Images; 57 bottom © Getty Images. for Lion Nathan; 58 © ITU; 59 top © ITU; 59 bottom © ITU; 60 © Charlie Crowhurst/Getty Images; 61 top © Rich Lam/Getty Images; 61 bottom © Charlie Crowhurst/Getty Images; 62 © Alvis Upitis/Getty Images; 63 © Quinn Rooney/Getty Images); 64 © Mike Powell / Allsport; 65 top © Rich Cruse; 65 bottom © Rich Cruse; 66 © Rich Cruse; 67 top © Mike Powell / Staff; 67 bottom © Rich Cruse; 68 © Sandra Mu/Getty Images; 69 top © Alvis Upitis/Getty Images; 69 bottom © Alex Grimm/Getty Images; 70 © ITU; 71 top © ITU; 71 bottom © ITU; 72 left © Holde Schneider/Bongarts/Getty Images; 72 right © Donald Miralle /Allsport; 73 left © Wilfried Witters/ Witters/Press Association Images; 73 right © Christof Koepsel/Bongarts/Getty Images; 74 © Christof Koepsel/Bongarts/Getty Images; 75 top © Elizabeth Kreutz/Corbis; 75 bottom right © Alexander Heimann/Bongarts/Getty Images; 76 right © TrimaxHebdo.com; 76 left © TrimaxHebdo.com; 77 top © Darren England/ALLSPORT; 77bottom © WILLIAM WEST/AFP/Getty Images; 78 © Rich Cruse; 79 left © Frank Peters/Bongarts/Getty Images; 79 right © Marco Garcia/Getty Images; 80 top © Kevin C. Cox/Getty Images for ITU); 80 bottom © Kevin C. Cox/Getty Images for ITU; 81 top © Joern Pollex/ Getty Images for Ironman; 81 bottom © Clifford White/Corbis; 82 left © Adam Pretty/Getty Images; 82 right © Cathrin Mueller/Bongarts/Getty Images; 83 © Rich Cruse; 84 left © Alvis Upitis/Getty Images; 84 right © Simon Hofmann/Getty Images for Ironman; 85 © Nick Wilson/ALLSPORT; 86 © Jamie Squire /Allsport; 87 left © Jon Buckle/EMPICS Sport; 87 right © Jonathan Ferrey/ALLSPORT; 88left © BRUCE OMORI/epa/Corbis; 88 right © Simon Hofmann/Getty Images for Ironman; 89 left © ITU; 89 right © Janos Schmidt ITU; 90 top © actionplus sports images; 90 bottom © PA Photos / TopFoto; 91; 92 left © ITU; © ITU; 92 right © Rich Cruse; 93 top © Al Bello/Getty Images; 93 bottom OLIVIER MORIN/AFP/Getty Images); 94 top © Imago/Actionplus; 94 bottom © John Walton/EMPICS Sport; 95 left © Arnd Hemmersbach/NordicFocus/Getty Images; 95 right © Michael Sheehan/Gallo Images/Getty Images; 96 left © Aurora Photos / Alamy; 96 right © dpa picture alliance / Alamy; 97 © ITU; 98 top © Boris Spremo/Toronto Star via Getty Images; 98 bottom © Boris Spremo/Toronto Star via Getty Images; 99 top © ITU; 99 bottom © ITU; 100 © LUX* Sports – Jean Jacques Fabien Photographer; 102-107 © TEAMCHALLENGE GmbH; 108-111 © Rich Cruse; 118-125 © Rocky Arroyo; 122 © JAKUB MOSUR/Press Association Images; 122-123 © Brightroom Photography; 125 © Kurt Hoy; 126 © jonatha borzicchi editorial / Alamy; 127-131 © Getty Images; 132-137 © Romilly Lockyer; 138-143 © Laguna Phuket; 144-149 © Henry Iddon; 152-157 © Castle Triathlon Series / Colin Baldwin; 158-159 © Christ Hitchcock / © Craig Muller / © Richard Melik; 159 © Outlaw Triathlon / David Pearce; 160-161 © FinisherPix.com; 162-163 © Timothy Carlson; 164-165 © Blair Glencourse; 166-167 © Outlaw Triathlon / Dave Tyrell; 166-167 © LUX* Sports – Jean Jacques Fabien Photographer; 168-169 No credit; 170-171 © Delly Carr; 172-173 © Alvis Upitis/Getty Images; 174-175 © Robert Beck/Sports Illustrated/Getty Images; 176-177 © Marco Garcia/Getty Images; 184-189 © Barry Alsop | IRONMAN Asia-Pacific; 190-195 © NILS NILSEN/XTERRA; 196-201 © José Luis Hourcade / nxtri.com; 202-205 © Phil Walter/Getty Images; 206 © Simon Watts/Getty Images; 207 © Phil Walter/Getty Images; 208-213 © LAURENT SALINO / ALPE D'HUEZ TOURISME; 220-225 no credit; 226-231 © TRIMAXHEBDO.COM; 232 © Diego Santamaria; 233 and 237 © Bob Foy; 234-235 © Getty Images; 238-241 © SavageMan Triathlon; 242-243 © Elbaman Triathlon / photo by Marathon Photos; 246-249 © Jason Newsome; 250-251 © Jakob Edholm/ÖTILLÖ2014; 251-253 © NadjaOdenhage/ÖTILLÖ2014; 254-257 © London Triathlon - WME IMG; 258-261 © Charlie Neibergall/Press Association Images; 262-265 © Simon Hofmann/Getty Images; 266-269 © Byron Bay Triathlon; 270-273 © Stephen Pond/Getty Images for Challenge Triathlon; 274 © Dennis Grombkowski/Getty Images; 275 © Andreas Rentz/Getty Images for Dextro Energy; 276-277 © Janos Schmidt/ITU via Getty Images; 278 © MANUEL BRUQUE/epa/Corbis; 279 © Francisco de Casa / Demotix/Demotix/Press Association Images; 280-281 © Simon Hofmann/Getty Images for Ironman; 282-283 No credit; 284-285 © Rich Lam/Getty Images; 286-287 © THIERRY DEKETELAERE/Belga/ Press Association Images; 290-291 (L) © DIEGO DE GIORGI (R) © PIERO INCALZA; 292-293 © Jeff Kapic; 294-295 © Club Deportivo Universidad Católica; 296-297 © Jero Honda; 298-299 © Rocky Arroyo; 300-301 © Larry Rosa and MetaSport; 302-303 © Sampo Lenzi; 304-305 © Barry Alsop | IRONMAN Asia-Pacific; 306-307 © David O. Baldwin; 308-309 © www.pacesetterevents.com; 310-311 © FinisherPix.com; 312 © Darryl Dyck/The Canadian Press/Press Association Images; 313 top © ZUMA Press, Inc. / Alamy; 313 bottom © Lyle Stafford/Reuters/Corbis; 314 © Matt Peyton/Invision/ Press Association Images; 315 © Dario Cantatore/Getty Images; 316-317 © Rasmus Kortegaard; 318-319 © Castle Triathlon Series; 322-323 © Quintana Roo/Steve Sayers; 324 © Felt; 325 © Romilly Lockyer; 326 © Huub Design; 327 © Kestrel; 328-329 © Ceepo; 330-331 © Cervelo; 332 © blueseventy/Brendon O'Hagan; 333 © Storck; 334-337 © www.thesecretstudio.net; 338-339 © www.thesecretstudio.net; 338 © Polar; 340-341 © www.thesecretstudio.net; 342 © Speedo; 343 © www.thesecretstudio.net; 343 © Asics; 344-347 © www.thesecretstudio.net; 350 © Rich Cruse; 351 © Softride